FLYING SOLO

Single Women in Midlife

D0251926

FLYING SOLO

Single Women in Midlife

Carol M. Anderson

Susan Stewart

with Sona Dimidjian

W. W. Norton & Company · New York · London

Copyright © 1994 by Carol Anderson, Susan Stewart, and Sona Dimidjian
All rights reserved
Printed in the United States of America

First published as a Norton paperback 1995

"Can't Help Lovin' Dat Man": Written by Jerome Kern and Oscar Hammerstein II. Copyright ©
1927 PolyGram International Publishing, Inc. Copyright renewed. Used by permission. All rights
reserved.

The lines from "Song" are reprinted from *Diving into the Wreck, Poems 1971–1972*, by Adrienne
Rich, by permission of the author and W. W. Norton & Company, Inc. Copyright © 1973 by
W. W. Norton & Company, Inc.

"Indian Summer" by Dorothy Parker, copyright 1926, renewed © 1954 by Dorothy Parker, from
The Portable Dorothy Parker, Introduction by Brendan Gill. Used by permission of Viking Penguin,
division of Penguin Books USA Inc.

The text of this book is composed in Bembo,
with display set in Footlight.
Composition and manufacturing by the Haddon Craftsmen, Inc.
Book design by Justine B. Trubey.

ISBN 0-393-31347-6

W. W. Norton & Company, Inc., 500 Fifth Avenue, New York, N.Y. 10110
W. W. Norton & Company Ltd., 10 Coptic Street, London WC1A 1PU

3 4 5 6 7 8 9 0

To my daughter Maria, with the wish that she and all the other girls of her generation will be more free to dream all kinds of dreams and fly wherever, whenever, and with whomever they choose.

Carol M. Anderson

To my mother, and all the other women of her generation, who might have chosen to fly solo had they seen a choice, and for my friends and family, whose love keeps me aloft.

Susan Stewart

To Chuck, for his enthusiasm and willingness to fly with me into uncharted territories, and to my family, whose love has given me the courage to dream of new destinations.

Sona A. Dimidjian

Acknowledgments

This project could not have been completed without the support of the leadership of the University of Pittsburgh Medical Center. We appreciate the support of David Kupfer, Chairman of the Department of Psychiatry and the Executive Committee of Western Psychiatric Institute and Clinic. We are grateful to Thomas P. Detre, Senior Vice Chancellor for Health Sciences, a long-time mentor and friend, who provided general encouragement for the idea, took the time to read drafts of several chapters and encouraged us when we worried if we were ever going to finish it. We are also grateful to Jeffrey Romoff, President of the Medical Center, who provided financial support for conducting and transcribing the interviews and the travel to distant cities to meet with women to hear their stories.

Thanks also go to Julie Scrima, Melinda Schreib, and Joyce Homa in Pittsburgh and Bennie Hearne, Linda Davis, Helen Yoder, and Susan Vinson in North Carolina for their patience and supportive services.

Special thanks go to our editor at Norton, Susan Munro, who was enthusiastic about the project from the outset and has continued that enthusiasm throughout the prolonged process of multiple drafts and revisions. We are grateful to our copyeditor, Margaret O. Ryan, for her careful attention to detail and sensitivity to the message of the book. Also, we would like to thank Patricia Deitz, whose "flying solo" workshops for men and women on their own gave us the idea for the title.

We also thank our families and friends who tolerated our increasing preoccupation with the topic and sacrificed their time with us so that our book could be finished in only twice as long as we had projected and promised.

Finally, and perhaps most importantly, we thank the many women who gave generously of their time to tell us their stories and to share the experiences that make up this book. They have been an inspiration to us, as we are certain they will be to other women who are flying solo or even considering such a flight as an option. They are truly pioneers charting new maps of unfamiliar territories for us all.

Contents

SECTION THREE: MIDLIFE: CHARTING A NEW
COURSE

SECTION FOUR: THE PROBLEM OF MEN

SECTION FIVE: THE QUESTION OF CHILDREN

SECTION SIX: CHALLENGES AND TRIUMPHS OF
FLYING SOLO

FLYING SOLO

Single Women in Midlife

Introduction

A woman without a man is like a fish without a bicycle.
—Gloria Steinem

Whether you're married or not, whether you have a boyfriend or not, there is no real security except for whatever you build inside yourself.
—Gilda Radner

E va, a woman we know, recently moved from a small town to a very big city. She is a forty-five-year-old successful professional with a rich network of friends and a loving family. She has a wide variety of interests and frequently travels to exciting places. When we asked her why she was willing to expose herself to the hassles of urban life and crime, Eva didn't talk about the pace and excitement of a large metropolitan area, the cultural diversity, or even the good restaurants. She said simply, "I'm single." The unspoken assumption, the assumption Eva was sure we shared, was that since she was single, her top priority was finding a man.

Flying Solo is for all the Evas who can't quite shake the feeling that because they are single, they are somehow failures, who look in their mirrors and say, "If *only*. . . . " It is also for all the Evas who are not unhappy but think they ought to be, believing that there must be something wrong with them because they feel content without a husband by their side. It is for all those single women who feel as if they are breaking a law or violating a taboo when they try to describe their life satisfaction only to have married listeners nod their heads slowly, brows knitted together in thinly veiled disbelief. Finally, it is for all of Eva's married sisters who feel trapped in unhappy or lifeless marriages, because they are afraid that if they leave they won't find another man and will be sentenced to a single life which is, *by definition,* lonely and miserable.

In recent years, movies, television shows, and magazine articles have perpetuated these fears by describing the depression and desperation of single women, particularly those in or approaching midlife. News programs have featured stories about women flocking to health clubs, plastic surgeons, and dating services in record numbers, in hopes of increasing their chances of finding their prince (or some prince) and living "happily ever after." Movies and television programs have depicted single women alternatively as pathetic leftovers from the marriage market—hovering depressively in the background, trying to hide their unhappiness and desperation—or as power-obsessed barracudas bent only on greedily acquiring the empty rewards of money and fame. In fact, almost every media and literary source has characterized single women as deficient, depressed, lonely, and desperately unfulfilled.

During the late 1980s, we began comparing all these negative images of single women to the many single women we actually knew, and to our own experiences as single women. The picture just didn't ring true. We weren't depressed and neither were most of the other single women we knew. None of our lives bore any resemblance to the frantic and miserable portrayals so commonly depicted in the media. We were active, productive, and for the most part, satisfied. Midlife was not a period of diminishing opportunity, but rather a time of expanding possibilities. When we reviewed the psychiatric and sociological literature, we kept coming to the same conclusion: being single was seldom a negative experience for women and definitely not one that was harmful to their physical or mental health. Many studies, in fact, demonstrated that being single, in many ways, seemed to be quite advantageous. The results of these studies and statistics were compelling in and of themselves; more importantly, however, they confirmed our experience of our own lives and the lives of the single women with whom we came into contact every day.

We grew increasingly interested in examining the discrepancy between the images of single women presented in the popular culture and our observations of the single women we knew, so we initiated a series of informal contacts with single friends and colleagues who were successful, upbeat, and making it on their own. From the outset, the women we approached responded to our requests for interviews with enthusiasm and excitement. They gave generously of their time, meeting with us over lunch, on the weekend, in early morning hours before the beginning of the workday, and late in the evening after putting their children to bed. These women volunteered to contact their friends and colleagues, inviting them to participate in our project. Through those conversations, we began to believe that the cultural images of single women were in fact *cultural myths*.

Although most women at some point during their lives had experienced feelings of depression, misery, or desperation, these feelings did not dominate their life stories. While most had not set out to live on their own, they had all used their resources to create rewarding and meaningful lives. They told us stories about overcoming adversity, stories of self-reliance and perseverance, tales of adventure and even joy. With great courage, they had turned away from the roles society had prescribed for them to define what *they* wanted and what *they* could create for themselves. They had made peace with their old dreams and illusions and had let go of the ones that had not fulfilled their promises. Rather than spending their time bemoaning their fate or searching for husbands, they were busy leading interesting lives. Their excitement about a book that would finally document their successes and satisfactions, rather than their alleged depressions and pathologies, encouraged us and provided us with the diverse stories that are the foundation of this book.

When we began working on this project, we had no intention of challenging our culture's most widely accepted and deeply cherished beliefs about women and families:

- The family, as it has been traditionally defined, is the only healthy, satisfying, and ideal state in which a woman can live.
- Marriage is and should be *every* woman's dream.
- Bearing children is *every* woman's highest calling, her most sacred duty and most rewarding accomplishment.
- A good woman is a selfless woman who does not put her own needs first in any situation at any time.

Frankly, as family therapists, we had spent our professional lives working to uphold the integrity of marriages and families, sometimes against overwhelming odds, so we weren't particularly interested in questioning these basic assumptions. However, as we continued interviewing women, we became increasingly convinced that the stereotyped portrayals of single women in midlife were grossly exaggerated and often largely fictitious. Certainly, some single women are unhappy, but so are some married women.

Perhaps, we wondered, becoming single isn't such a catastrophic event, perhaps *staying* single has previously unrecognized benefits, and maybe it isn't such a great idea for all women to put so many of their "eggs" in the marriage "basket." We asked ourselves: Could the widely held belief that single women are inevitably unhappy be the biggest lie since "one size fits all"?

The women whose stories we tell on these pages challenge the belief that in order to be happy, to feel secure and successful, all women must be married or at least living with a man. Their stories do not glorify singlehood at the expense of marriage, but rather show that being single can be a legitimate and positive alternative for women, whether for portions or for all of their adult lives. They are women who have learned to feel comfortable swimming upstream against the current of popular opinion, which dictates, as surely as if there were an eleventh commandment, "Thou shalt not be single, over thirty, and happy." On their own, these women have taken their lives into their own hands, and in so doing, have opened themselves to a wide range of opportunities and experiences. They have created lives that "fit" their own personalities and goals. They believe strongly that being single has provided them with choices they would not have had the freedom to make if they were married. Their stories encourage all women to make *choices* about their beliefs, their hopes, their dreams, their lives.

In these ways, the women in this book are truly qualified to serve as models for other single and even married women—both of whom desperately need such models today. Current statistics suggest that most women will spend substantial portions of their lives on their own. Women today are marrying later, divorcing more often, and outliving their husbands by years, if not decades. Since being single is such a commonly experienced state, it makes no sense to continue to shroud the single life in myths that expound disadvantages while denying potential advantages. Models of single women who have successfully negotiated a place for themselves in this new world, who have learned how to fly solo, are essential for all women struggling to make it on their own.

Positive models of single women could also have a profound impact on women who may never be single. Women are more likely to find satisfaction in their intimate relationships if they do not feel desperate about them. Knowing that other women are creating happy lives on their own can give their married sisters the courage to negotiate relationships in which their opinions, wishes, and needs for intimacy are taken more seriously, and in which there is a more equal division of daily responsibilities. Knowing that *single* does not mean *miserable* puts women in relationships in a better position to discuss everything from a lifetime commitment to who takes out the garbage.

THE WOMEN IN OUR PROJECT

Between 1990 and 1992, we talked to approximately ninety women, never married, divorced, and widowed, whose stories form the basis of this book. For the most part, these women were between the ages of forty and fifty-five, which was the range we defined as midlife. We did interview a few younger and a few older women to gain a perspective on how women anticipated and looked back on the midlife years. All of these women have lived on their own a few years, a few decades, or all of their lives. Many of them are involved in committed, monogamous relationships with men; however, if they maintain separate and independent households, we have included them as women flying solo. Although each of the women we interviewed contributed to our understanding of being single and at midlife, we have chosen to focus on certain of their stories in greater detail because their experiences were so typical or because they were extraordinarily articulate about issues of concern to all.

We began this project looking for "successful" midlife single women, a term we originally assumed would be associated with women who had high salaries, impressive offices, and fine homes, as well as advanced degrees, prestigious positions, and busy schedules. When we began asking for the names of women whom people regarded as successful and single, however, we found ourselves directed to some women who did not necessarily match our definition; although upbeat, positive, and satisfied with life on their own, they were not necessarily prosperous. Sound finances and prestigious positions were not prerequisites for women to feel successful. These women were successful in the most profound sense of the word: that is, *they felt good about themselves and their lives.* Jean, 45 and divorced, captured the essence of our revised definition of successful:

I was surprised you wanted to interview me at first because I don't think I'm very successful financially. I rent somebody's third-floor attic. I was equating success with a woman who's an attorney or a woman who is a researcher. At first, that's what I thought it was about.

But I'm getting to the point now where I realize you're just talking about people who feel good about their lives.

In the beginning of our project, this element of satisfaction was an elusive quality to define. While we could have used various research tools and questionnaires to measure women's feelings about their lives, we ultimately decided that we were most interested in their subjective assessments. We did not require that they meet an external definition of satisfaction, nor did we ask them to complete formal surveys or questionnaires. Instead, we relied on their statements about their lives and our personal impressions of them from the time we spent together. We did ask them to rate their life satisfaction informally on a scale of one to ten, but we did not provide any criteria, again feeling their subjective answers would be more meaningful. Like Jean, the women we interviewed for this book felt good about their lives, even though some of them were still struggling with how to be single.

We talked with women from cities on the East Coast, the South, the Midwest, and the West Coast who represented a variety of education and income levels, occupations, life styles, and family situations. Some worked in traditional women's professions and some in fields that, until recently, were dominated by men; some were administrators and supervisors, some were secretaries. While they were predominantly white, several were women of color. We did not include midlife single lesbian women in our study because we felt that, while some of the issues lesbian women face are the same, their experiences are also qualitatively different. Certainly one significant difference is that, in addition to the stigma of being single and in midlife, lesbian women bear the additional burden of society's homophobia. But perhaps even more significant for our purposes is the fact that much of *Flying Solo* focuses on the ways in which traditional gender roles make it difficult for women to prosper emotionally and psychologically in the context of marriage and intimate relationships with men. While lesbian women are undoubtedly influenced by these traditional roles and expectations, the impact on their efforts to form successful relationships is significantly different. Although discussing these differences is beyond the scope of this book, we would hope that our project might motivate others to study the unique experiences of singlehood among this specific group of women.

THE EXPERIENCES OF THE AUTHORS

Carol's Story   I had been a marital and family therapist for well over a decade when I went back to graduate school at the age of thirty-six. I barely noticed turning forty because I was busy finishing my doctoral degree and wrapping up a ten-year research project on families of patients with schizophrenia. I was working night and day, and loving it. Perhaps I had initially thrown myself into my career to avoid my personal life, but it had become incredibly gratifying on its own merits. By midlife, none of the dates I found myself going on were as exciting as the therapy, writing, and research I was doing. So I can't say that I mourned the passing of my youth or my child-bearing years. I was just too busy. If an interesting man dropped into my life, I was usually receptive to a relationship. Otherwise, being both overcommitted and shy, I did not spend much time looking for one. In my spare time (what there was of it), I was overwhelmed by all the interesting things on my relentless "to do" list. I built friendships, wrote books, and traveled. Even as a little girl I remember always wanting to "see the world." By the time I was forty-five, I had traveled all over Europe, Asia, South America, and just about every island in the Caribbean. I had hiked the mountains of Peru and cruised in the Mediterranean.

Since I wasn't unhappy, I had no plans to do anything drastic about my life. Then events took over and changed my world. The seeds of midlife change were planted with my aging mother's decline, which accelerated during her late eighties, leaving my sisters and me to watch her crumble both physically and psychologically. Already suffering from Alzheimer's disease, she was discovered to have cancer. Until that time she had lived alone, fiercely clinging to her independence. Suddenly she seemed to be drying up and withering away, to be operating without a compass. There were middle-of-the-night scares about gas stoves left burning, falls, possible broken hips, and other crises that sent family members scurrying to help. Suddenly I became aware of my own aging, something I had never thought much about; I had always acted as if my time were limitless.

It was a year before she died, but this brush with the reality of aging and the threat of death sent me into an examination of my goals and my commitments, awakening me to a new way of looking at life and its meaning. I became acutely aware that life is too short for all the unimportant things that too easily became a focus of my time and energy. I also became aware of the ease with which we all can be hurt, impaired, our lives even snuffed out altogether. Witnessing my mother's death made me think about how little I really could control. I thought about Lily Tomlin saying, "Life is what happens to you while you are making other plans." My life had gone on making its own plans, producing troubles and joys. While time now seemed short, but there *was* time left, and I had the freedom to choose what I would do with it.

Then came a turning point. One day, shortly after my mother died, a man planning to write a book on aspects of the mental health care of children interviewed me about the hospital system in which I work. At the end of the interview, he asked casually if I minded not having a family. When I admitted regretting only that I had no children, he told me it wasn't too late, that he himself was in the process of investigating international adoption, and that applications were accepted from prospective parents up to the age of fifty-nine. I knew immediately that this was what I wanted to do with the next part of my life. I had spent twenty-five years working twelve to fourteen hours a day and not minding. I had had more adventures than you might find in the average paperback novel. I knew that the experience I was most sorry I had missed, and now most wanted, was that of being a mother. With absolutely no further deliberation, I immediately applied to adopt a child from South America. Three years ago I flew to the southern tip of Chile to pick up a wonderful seven-year-old little girl, my daughter Maria. She came not knowing a word of English and took over my life in the most profound way imaginable. While almost everyone else I know has been busy launching their children into colleges and inflicting pictures of their new grandchildren on their friends, I have been learning how to be a mother for the very first time. It is an adventure right up there with sailing in the Galapagos or trekking through the Andes. I never dreamed how much I could love a child, how much undiluted joy I could feel. Maria is funny, pretty, and incredibly wise. Of course, I am not one bit prejudiced!

Some people believe that the happiest and most carefree time of life is during high school and college. Perhaps because my father died when I was thirteen, or perhaps just because my memories of adolescence are always inextricably intertwined with anxiety, I do not remember these years as carefree. In fact, I found my high school years to be filled with insecurity and misery. In those days, I was totally traditional and had no vision of a life that did not include marriage and motherhood. I was more than willing to play Cinderella, but my problem was that the story never told us what qualities to look for in a prince! Think about it. What do we know about the prince, beyond the fact that he could dance and may have had some sort of foot fetish? Still, I spent years consumed with auditioning potential princes. I always had a "steady," and spent countless hours with my girlfriends during which we planned our weddings and wrote our names as they would look if we married the boys we were currently dating. Maybe it should have been a clue to me that, while I loved the thought of being a bride, I never spent much time fantasizing what life would be like after the wedding. The detailed part of the script always ended with the kiss at the altar. We all knew we would be wives and mothers, but thinking about that part of our futures was not the stuff of which our dreams were made.

Neither were careers. I always had planned to go to college, but I saw college less as a place to begin a career and more as a place to learn interesting things, have fun, and meet that someone special. I had no specific dreams or plans about what I would be. When I was a sophomore, I quite accidentally got a part-time job on a child psychiatry unit at the university hospital. I had worked since I was fifteen, but for the first time in my life I found work and school exciting. I quickly changed my major from English to child development and psychology, and took a job in a children's residential treatment center upon graduation. I had never thought about going on for an advanced degree, but the frustration of this job sent me back to school after just one year in the real world. I graduated with a master's in social work in the mid sixties, committed to doing something about the ills of society, and took a job in the inner city of Detroit working with troubled adolescents and multiproblem families. After three years of very hard work and the 1967 riots, it still wasn't professional ambition that propelled me to take a job at Yale, but rather the desire to stop working with street gangs, and probably even more importantly, to meet more interesting men.

It was sometime during those early years at Yale that I finally got really turned on to work as an end in itself. Working with families made sense and I was good at it. Still, it wasn't until much later, probably not until after forty, that it dawned on me that I might never get married. Over the years of immersion in my work, I had put less and less time into finding Mr. Right. Besides, being intensely committed to your career is a little like being in a prison for workaholics; the number and type of men I met were seriously restricted. Those who were interesting were at least as driven as I was, and prone to seeking gratification through the mission or dream that guided their career. It was easy to get involved, but these relationships never seemed to be good bets for solving the problem of my anemic social life. Those men who were available expected me to make my life revolve around them and, as the years went by, an ever growing proportion of the men I met were married.

That never stopped them from making propositions, but they certainly didn't seem able to provide any solution. When they occurred, heated romances were wonderful at first, but there inevitably came a time when I was somewhat relieved to see that phase of the relationship fade because it took so much time away from my career and my friends. I just wasn't good at being "all things to all people." So, gradually my semi-active search for a man dissolved and work became the most important thing in my life. Starting to make really good money certainly contributed to this evolution. A high salary allowed me to do lots of fun things, giving me both the life style I wanted and a legitimate adult identity.

Here I am, a single mother at fifty-four, and not the least unhappy about it. I have a wonderful life. I have my daughter, a successful career, a good income, and really terrific friends. There have been interesting men in my life who have been important to me. In fact, a few of these relationships have lasted longer than the marriages of many of my friends. In recent years, the guest appearances men have made in my life have been less frequent, and my "refractory time" between relationships has grown longer. All things being equal, I would still prefer to be in a relationship. But these days, while it's nice when there is a man around, it is also okay when there isn't. My life works either way. What's particularly good about midlife is not feeling pressured to live up to anyone's expectations but my own, to be able to chase my own dreams without feeling guilty, to be who I am. To me, it's exciting to be living during a time when women seem to be coming into their own.

Susan's Story   As a child I was a great reader and a great dreamer. I always identified with the heroes, oblivious to the fact that they were male and I was not. In neighborhood theatrical productions I always claimed the role of the hero—be it Robin Hood, King Arthur, or even the beast in "Beauty and the Beast." I didn't want to be a man, but I did want to be the hero, the swashbuckler, not the one who applauded from the sidelines.

When I reached adolescence, I almost stopped dreaming altogether. Unlike many young women, I rarely rehearsed the role of being Mrs. So-and-So, and I never remember fantasizing about my wedding. What fantasies I had were of romantic encounters with men that had no "happily ever after" endings; they just faded out after a passionate embrace. My mother appeared to be depressed and angry much of the time, so that when I looked at her, being Mrs. Anybody was not a very attractive option. The problem was, in my very limited suburban experience, the only role other than wife and mother I saw available to me was that of old-maid school teacher. I remember admiring the wit and intelligence of my high-school English teacher who was unmarried and in her fifties, but I could not imagine her having a life outside the classroom.

Once I actually started dating, trying to get along with males in the traditional female manner, it became clear to me that this was not going to be my forte anyway. I wasn't very pretty, I wasn't very good at flirting, and I thought I was smarter than most of the boys I met. (Actually, in those days, I thought I was smarter than most of the people I met.) Consequently, I didn't date often and spent a lot of time feeling like a failure. All through high school I lurked on the fringes of the in-crowd, reading books and feeling miserable about myself. Feeling like a failure was bad enough, but being without a dream was worse.

The whole business of becoming a woman seemed confusing and depressing. If you didn't fit in, you were totally lost. If you couldn't dream the universal dream, you had no dream; and if you had no dream, you had no hope. I carried my unhappiness and resentment inside me like a secret scar. My mother couldn't help me. With an air of resignation, all she could say was, "It's a man's world." It never occurred to me that the problem might *not* be me, nor could I conceive the idea that there ought to be more options than being Mrs. Somebody or being nothing. My favorite fantasy was to run away and join Castro's revolution, probably becoming Che Guevera's mistress. I knew nothing of the politics involved, but this plan sounded a whole lot more inviting than anything "typical" I could imagine. Looking back, I can see that I must have been moving toward a traditional feminine identity, since I no longer wanted to *be* Che Guevera!

In college, I continued to do well academically but felt awkward and profoundly bored on the dates that were arranged for me. I retreated into books again, but this time there was a payoff: I was able to build an identity for myself as an intellectual on the campus of the small woman's college I attended. I was a woman who had more serious things on her mind than getting pinned or engaged. My depression went underground as I discovered the captivating worlds of literature and philosophy, mythology and history. I made a lot of friends who seemed to admire my academic talent. But aside from becoming a college professor, which involved more school than I could imagine at the time, I still didn't feel as if I fit in anywhere. All my friends were planning weddings after graduation. Four days before graduation, I decided to leave New Jersey and cross the continent to California with a classmate I barely knew, who was going to join her fiancé there, because I didn't know what else to do, and because I believed I somehow might find some sort of future.

Shortly after arriving, I got a job as a public assistance worker in southwest Los Angeles. I didn't think of it as a career, just a job until someone decided he wanted to marry me. I was more resigned to that idea than happy about it—like someone on parole who knows she is going to be caught in violation sooner or later because she doesn't know how to stay free. When Betty Friedan's *The Feminine Mystique* was published, I felt incredible relief. I inhaled that book. I revelled in the idea that there were other women who felt out of place in the roles that had been reserved for them, other women who didn't dream of husbands and children, other women who, like me, could hardly dream at all. The jumble of feelings that had plagued me since I could remember suddenly fell into place and made sense. I immediately decided that I could do something with my life without getting married (at least immediately), and I signed up for graduate school. My "parole" had been extended. Although I chose a traditionally female profession, it was still a huge step for me. Southwest Los Angeles had changed my politics forever and going into social work helped me to feel I was working toward a worthwhile goal. The depression that had hovered around me since adolescence faded again, at least for a while.

I was in graduate school in the late sixties, a time when the whole world, as I had known it, started to fall apart. I was frightened and delighted. Part of me wanted to march in the streets; part of me wanted to find a man to keep me safe. I ended up doing a little of both. I was too timid to be much of a revolutionary and I never believed in violence, but I loved the idea of bringing down all the old rules that I found so constricting, and I loved the easy comraderie of the anti-war, anti-almost everything movement that gripped the city where I lived. If there ever was a terrific time to be single, it was the late sixties. But despite the excitement of the times, my depression returned. I could not shake the feeling that I was a "freak" because I was not married. I felt a penetrating loneliness, a hole in my soul, that I thought getting married would surely fill.

By this time, the acne that scarred my adolescence had cleared and I had become reasonably attractive. I started meeting men who were bright, knowledgeable and even caring, men who were far more attractive to me than those I had met in college. But I always seemed to pick the "wrong" man and the relationship would end disastrously for me. With the help of a therapist, I finally decided that, if the only way I was going to feel good about myself was to get married, I consciously ought to look for someone who was both available and acceptable. Once I decided to marry, it wasn't very hard to find such a man, even though by that time I was twenty-eight and presumably all the good guys had been taken. I found a man who, far from being intimidated by my wit and intelligence, was actually attracted to me because of these traits. Of course, he was also just as phobic about marriage as I was. Had I possessed the self-confidence and self-definition I have now, we would have had a great affair and gone on to be friends. But I *had* to prove I wasn't a freak. I insisted on marriage and, rather than lose me, he agreed, but for me, our relationship was always an uneasy compromise between trying to avoid becoming my mother and feeling legitimate in my community. I didn't have to give up much in the way of freedom and autonomy, as he was a born feminist without knowing it. In the spirit of the times, we were both committed to trying to have a non-traditional marriage without having any clear idea as to what that might mean. I was free to pursue my career and other interests as I saw fit and often vacationed without him when he was busy. However, I confess that in trying to be free we both sometimes mistook autonomy for a license to abuse and neglect our relationship. Nevertheless, the marriage lasted twelve years and it felt like death when it ended.

Once I got over the pervasive depression of the divorce, which took a long time, I was astounded at how free I felt—not of the bonds of matrimony, because I had never felt burdened by my marriage—but of the feeling that *I had to be married to be happy.* By this time, I was in midlife and no longer felt I had to satisfy somebody else's definition of what it meant to be a woman. I had been married, BEEN CHOSEN, and I didn't have to prove anything anymore. I remember calling up my husband several years after we had separated and telling him I was finally ready for our divorce; I no longer needed to hang onto the idea of being married. We worked out the legalities amiably, having always been friends.

I would not say that my life now is better than it was in my twenties and thirties, because those years were certainly interesting and necessary for me to have achieved, in midlife, more self-sufficiency, self-confidence, and competence than I had ever hoped to have. But I must say I was not prepared for how good midlife would feel, how relaxed and yet exciting. I have a multitude of options open to me primarily because I am single and don't have to negotiate where or how I'm going to live with anyone. I feel comfortable knowing that I have very little left to prove. The hole in my soul is gone.

Sona's Story   I was twenty-two years old when I began working on this project. Recently graduated from college, I interviewed with Carol for a job as a research associate. She was creating a position for someone who could help her carry out a project on single women at midlife. The details seemed a little vague, but I liked Carol during our meeting and respected the work she had done, and since my own goals were also a little vague at the time, I decided to take the job. At least, I figured it would be interesting and good research experience and would give me a chance to determine where I wanted to go next. I went back home to Chicago, talked things over with Chuck, the man with whom I was living, and together we packed up a U-Haul truck and moved to Pittsburgh. I began working on this project a couple weeks later.

Almost three and a half years have passed, and what I thought was going to be a relatively short-term job has turned into a significant life experience. It may seem odd that a project on midlife single women could hold such interest for a woman in her early twenties, particularly someone involved in a committed relationship. Could the issues be relevant, meaningful? Didn't the lives and struggles of midlife women seem a bit outdated, remote, even boring? I soon discovered, however, that working on this project was not only interesting and relevant but in some ways transformative.

The greatest gift of working on this project came from the experience of interviewing the women whose stories we tell in this book. I learned a tremendous amount from them. Most importantly, they taught me that I had many choices and encouraged me to figure out what I wanted in my own life. Moreover, they also helped me to recognize that I had a heritage of strength in my own family from which I could draw as I began this process.

My mother raised my younger sister and me after she and my father divorced when I was six years old. Although we remained close to our father and saw him regularly, my mother had the day-to-day responsibility of raising us, and she faced many struggles as a single mother. Before I began working on this project, I often found myself focusing on the negatives when I thought about my childhood. A sense of difficulty and difference colored many of my memories. As I met the women in this book, however, my focus on my own past shifted, as I began to recognize that I had also learned a great deal from my mother and in particular from her experience as a single woman.

From the age of twenty-eight, my mother worked full-time, went to graduate school, and raised my sister and me. She taught us that it is possible to accomplish much with few resources. She taught us to be responsible for ourselves and gave us opportunities to develop confidence in our abilities to take care of ourselves. Her commitment to and love for us instilled within us the belief that we were special and important. Because of her, I have never doubted that I would want and would deserve to have a meaningful and rewarding work life; nor have I ever imagined that I would be dependent on someone else for my livelihood or well-being.

Now, as she approaches her fiftieth birthday, my mother continues to be a role model of courage and independence. Three years ago, she began a midlife renaissance much like that of many of the women in this book. Deciding she wanted a new job and a change in her life style, she moved from Pennsylvania to Miami, where she didn't know a soul. She bought a house on the beach, secured a new job with a good salary, and is now happier than I have ever seen her. She has made new friends, swims in the ocean every day, travels around the world on her own, and pampers herself with the little luxuries she could never afford before—new clothes, concert tickets, weekly massages.

I am grateful for the ways in which this project has changed my attitude and my life, but this is not to say that the experience has been an easy one. Recognizing the positive lessons I could take from my family eased but did not resolve the many challanges. A generation younger than the women we interviewed, I never believed that there was only one way for women to live happy lives, to have successful careers, to be involved with men, to raise children—and yet meeting so many women who were happy with such a wide range of life styles was overwhelming. The sheer magnitude of their diversity made me realize that I was the only one who could make choices about my future—not an easy task for someone who wanted to live on her own, get married, go to medical school, get a Ph.D., live in another country, work as a park ranger, work in a bakery, and run a bed-and-breakfast, all at the same time. Realizing I had so many choices—and not being sure which to pursue—felt tantamount to having none at all. At times, I envied the women I met who had been raised as though their destinies as wives and mothers were etched in stone.

In addition, working on this project initially stressed my relationship with Chuck. Having become acutely aware of the price of overaccommodating and the power of tradition, I vigilantly scrutinized our relationship for such patterns. I had to be sure that I was not unwittingly accommodating myself out of existence, as many of the women I interviewed had done in early adulthood. For a while, it seemed like Chuck and I were arguing about *everything*—and I was very uncomfortable with this level of conflict. I had become more aware of my own needs and preferences and the importance of voicing them, but I was still alarmed when we argued. It didn't seem like my friends argued so much with their boyfriends or husbands. I feared it was a sign that we were incompatible, a "bad match."

Over time, however, my life has reached a more comfortable equilibrium. I realized I could pursue my varied dreams sequentially and decided to apply to graduate school. Chuck and I have also become more practiced in resolving our disagreements, and I have come to see the value of disagreeing. We still have more stormy times than many other couples I know, but I have come to cherish these times and to appreciate the fact that, as Carolyn Heilbrun has said, ". . . the sign of a good marriage is that everything is debatable and challenged; nothing is turned into law or policy."

I suppose I am less of a romantic than I used to be. I don't believe in easy answers or "happily ever after." Sometimes I feel a little regretful about this, but I wouldn't trade what I have learned from the experience of working on this project for the world. I feel more secure in myself, my choices, and my relationships and am excited about what the future holds.

Taking Off:
The Dilemma of
Automatic Pilot and
Excess Baggage

Chapter 1

The Unexpected Joys of Flying Solo

One can never consent to creep when one feels an impulse to soar.
                                                                                        —*Helen Keller*

A woman sits in her living room, all but immobilized by a broken leg. She is forty-six, single, and a little overweight. Our culture dictates that she is a woman who has lost her chance at happiness, since she has failed to catch and hold the golden ring of marriage. Having lost her youth, she has also lost her hope. On interviewing her, one might expect to hear a string of complaints about the sorry state of her life. It is easy to imagine her as unhappy and unfulfilled. Instead, over the sound of the telephone ringing as yet one more friend calls to see if she needs anything, she tells us that, on a scale of one to ten, her life is a nine-and-three-quarters. "What would make it a ten?" we asked. With a droll laugh, she quipped, "I think if I were thinner."

Meet Grace, a woman who has soared past our culture's dual prejudices against women being *single* and in *midlife*. Grace is making her own choices and enjoying her power; she is active in her career and family, and she thrives on friendship as well as solitude. Divorced eighteen years ago, she has raised two children on her own and has forged a successful career in a traditionally male-dominated field, all the while a steady support for friends and an inspiration for her community. How did she manage to accomplish so much?

Grace was raised by her grandparents after losing her mother when she was only five. Despite this loss, she felt nurtured by her family. Together, her grandparents and her father, who lived in a nearby city and visited often, taught her that she was special and that, because she was African-American, she would have to work harder in life. Grace says this early training in pursuing excellence despite the odds "stood her in good stead" later in life when she had to fight not only racial but gender discrimination:

> I've always had high self-esteem. I've always felt that I could do whatever I set out to do. I know a lot of women will say, "Well, I could never do that." If there was a dilemma, I only thought about *how* to solve it, not that I couldn't.

Grace excelled academically throughout high school, but when she graduated she unexpectedly encountered a brick wall. No adequate scholarships for promising young black women were available and her family could not afford to send her to college. A school counselor suggested she enter the military as a way of obtaining specialized training and education. Despite family objections because "that wasn't considered an honorable profession," Grace joined the Air Force. While in the service, she married and had two children:

> The first part of our marriage was very sharing and giving. Then it got to the point where I was expected to do certain things because I was a woman. Then there was an episode where my husband was physically abusive. The day he became abusive was the day I decided I wanted *out*. I wasn't going to tolerate physical abuse. And I got out.

Looking back, Grace feels fortunate that she was able to get out of a bad situation as quickly as she did. Since that time, she has come to know many women, both professionally and personally, who have felt trapped in abusive relationships. She explains that she was able to leave her marriage, in large part, because she was economically independent. No doubt, the high self-esteem her family had nurtured in her helped as well.

Shortly after Grace left her husband, her grandmother died and she returned to the city of her birth to settle her grandmother's affairs. Realizing that her hometown offered her a much stronger support system of family and friends, Grace decided to make the move permanent. She left active duty, which meant she had to seek not only a new job, but a new profession. Her description of how she found what was to become her life's work is typical of the "accidental" way many women now in midlife developed their careers:

> I filled out applications for the post office and then somebody gave me an application for the police department. They said, "You certainly

have all the qualifications and they're going to hire women." It was a man and he thought it was a big joke.

Grace submitted her application that summer and has been on the police force for the past seventeen years. At first, working shifts while raising two small children was difficult and would have been impossible without the help of her family and friends. Nevertheless, Grace persevered and eventually became the city's first female police commander. She is as modest about that achievement as she is about her many other successes:

I think that I just came through an era, the sixties and seventies, when there was a lot of change for women in the workplace. So I got to be the first in a lot of things. I figure that it wasn't primarily me, but it was just the era I came through.

Grace has done much more than achieve the highest rank any woman has achieved in the city's police force. She has been a foster mother and has volunteered her time and abilities to numerous agencies and organizations that promote social change. She has helped children get a better start in life, has worked to promote women's rights, and has provided protection and support to women and children who are abused. Grace has received many awards and much community recognition. Recently she had the honor of being made a Distinguished Daughter of Pennsylvania.

Grace's ability to make these inspiring contributions in part has depended on her freedom to pick and choose what she does with her time. This freedom is one of the advantages of flying solo that Grace most values:

I think my life is great. I work with a lot of different groups and I know if I were in a relationship, I probably would have to give up some of that just for time reasons. I have some long days and I don't worry about cleaning the house or cooking and that sort of thing. I could go for days and days and days without making my bed and nobody would know about it.

Far from feeling deprived, Grace feels immensely fulfilled. She sums up her experience as a single woman:

I never feel lonely. In fact, I don't think I have enough hours in a day. I mean, I certainly miss the part of life where you're intimate with another person and that sort of thing. But on the whole, I think I'm okay. I really don't feel that there is anything missing. When I go to bed at night, I go right to sleep because I've had a full day. I feel that my life is full.

A MATTER OF CHOICE: THE IMPORTANCE OF AUTONOMY TO WOMEN

Although midlife single women like Grace want us to know they are satisfied, they are hardly revolutionaries intent on overthrowing the institution of marriage. They are well aware of the many joys and satisfactions that good relationships with men can provide. In fact, all things being equal, most would welcome forming a union with a man they could love and respect. But, having worked hard to establish lives on their own, these women have also come to value the many unexpected joys of flying solo.

The women we interviewed discussed the benefits of being single in unique ways. Some, like Grace, emphasized the direct connection between being single and their ability to succeed professionally. Although few actually made a conscious choice early in life to stay single in order to pursue professional goals, looking back over their lives these women were clear that success meant a great deal to them and that they could not have been as successful or as satisfied in their work if they had also had family responsibilities.

Somewhat surprisingly, some of the women who raised children on their own discussed a similar connection between being single and their ability to make parenting a priority in their lives. Apparently seeing a spouse as one more demand on their time rather than as a source of help, some women said that being single allowed them to focus a limited supply of energy on taking care of their children. While those who once had been married acknowledged the advantages (particularly the financial ones) that remarrying could offer, they were also aware of the possible emotional costs of dividing their attention. Audrey explains:

Because my children's father was completely out of the picture, it was of paramount importance to me that whomever I dated liked my children. I was a package deal—as is anyone who is divorced and has children. Even when I liked a man and enjoyed his company—this happened in three instances—I called a halt to the relationship because I knew he didn't care about my children. He just didn't fit what I thought my package deal required.

Other women discussed the benefits of their years on their own, not in terms of major priorities such as work or parenting, but in terms of seemingly minor aspects of their lives such as being able to play tennis or go fishing on a whim, eat potato chips in bed, or have nothing but cookies for dinner. These small liberties may seem trivial when compared to the warmth and security of the Norman Rockwell portrait of family life we all carry within us; however, they reveal the universal qualities of the single life that some women find extraordinarily valuable: freedom, independence, and most of all, *self-determination*. Heidi is explicit about enjoying the autonomy she now feels as a widow, despite her long and happy marriage:

> I like being my own boss, doing my own thing. I like determining if I want to buy this, if I want to buy that. I like being in charge, paying my own bills, being responsible for my own livelihood. It's a good feeling to sit back and say "this is mine."

The freedom to make the many small, daily choices, taken together, renders a much larger gift: a sense of control and mastery. This is the gift of being single women most cherish.

Women, like men, exist along a continuum, with some wanting a lot of independence and control and others being content to defer and support. Most women's needs for autonomy also evolve over the course of their lives. By midlife, many find that, while they enjoy being in relationships and collaborations with others, they want to be the driving force in their own lives. Hannah, who is successful, economically secure, and upwardly mobile, talks about how therapy helped uncover her need to have some sense of control over her life:

> My therapist asked me to recall a time when I was with a man. She said, "Put yourself in that situation. Imagine even a good time." So, I was thinking about a man I lived with in New York, and I was remembering a time when we had bought the Sunday *Times* and were driving across town to go to breakfast at some chic restaurant. My therapist said, "Now, think what you want to say to him." I couldn't think of a damn thing. Literally, my pondering went on for so long she

left the room and made a telephone call. When she came back, I said, "I finally thought of what I wanted to say." "What is it?" I said, "It's *my* car. I want to drive."

Most of the women we interviewed felt that they would have to give up the chance to remain in the driver's seat of their lives if they were to marry or remarry. Time and again, they expressed their concern that entering intimate relationships, particularly formal marriages, might threaten the hard-won sense of autonomy they had gained through life on their own. Jamie explained:

I guess it's the freedom. It's having to give up the ability to choose for myself. It's that matter of choice again. In a relationship, you have to make compromises. For much of my life, I saw women making the choice to be married and that took away all other choices, because then you had to do what the other person wanted; you had to live *his* life, or at least give up a whole lot of your own.

Terry spoke of similar feelings:

On my own, I am responsible for my own choices, both good and bad. I am no longer really directed by anyone other than myself. And in some ways, I think I've made the most of it. I've really done things and made choices in my life that I could not have made if I were married or in a more traditional relationship.

Being on their own has allowed these women to experience a freedom most believe would be incompatible with the traditional structure of marriage. This freedom has given them the opportunity to think clearly about what they really want and need and to build their lives based on their own individual desires and goals rather than the opinion of others. Jessie, an artist who has never married, is aware of what she does not have, but she also knows that the choices she has made work *for her*. She explains that she needs something different in her life than the portraits she once saw on the cover of the *Saturday Evening Post*:

I'm aware that some people looking at my life from the outside would probably think that it was a disaster. I don't have much money, I don't have a mate, I don't have a child. You know, it looks pretty sparse, but I don't need money, a mate, or a child to make my life complete.

Ria, a woman who never married the father of her youngest two children and who abandoned her career as a college professor to stay home and raise them, states unequivocally, "I have finally learned to listen to myself well enough that I did something that I really wanted. I think I'm happy because I was able to say, 'This is what I really want.' " Jean effectively summarized these women's feelings on the joys of flying solo, "The point of all this—the reason you take the tougher route of being a single woman—is that you want to live your own life and not somebody else's. Knowing that your life is in your own hands, that you can make your life what you want it to be—I think *that* is worth something."

FINDING THE FREEDOM TO FLY SOLO

The ability to feel good about the positive aspects of being single and in midlife is not always developed quickly or easily. Women's feelings about themselves and their lives have been contaminated by cultural values that romanticize and idealize youth, beauty, and marriage. However, through our interviews, it became clear to us that women could overcome the obstacles posed by traditional expectations, even though it was sometimes an arduous and painful process. Once they did, they could embrace the idea of living on their own and move on to "custom tailor" their lives to bring enormous rewards and satisfaction. In so doing, they demonstrated that being single and being in midlife was not the two-headed dreadful dragon implied in the cultural myths. Indeed, women reported that, once they looked the frightful beast directly in the eyes, it turned out to be surprisingly tame.

How do women flying solo free themselves from the down drafts and wind shears of our culture's negative messages about being on one's own at midlife? How do they develop the ability to appreciate and even celebrate their lives? The women we interviewed told us that being in midlife actually makes flying solo easier, not more difficult. Midlife encourages women to evaluate the assumptions, expectations, and attitudes that have guided their lives thus far. Our interviewees told us that, in essence, women need to examine their own attitudes for signs of unconscious prejudice against themselves. Chances are high that they have internalized the myths of our culture at face value, and in so doing, have left themselves vulnerable to self-denigration simply because their lifestyles do not emulate the cultural ideal.

Although many of the women we interviewed underwent traumatic divorces or other ordeals that had the effect of "jump-starting" them in a new direction, others made the transition slowly and gently. Most women certainly did not feel they needed to acquire a "yuppie" job or a whole new set of friends to accommodate their midlife status. Nor did they find themselves compelled to purchase a sports car, a stylish condo, or an Elizabeth Arden makeover. They did not even feel they had to give up intimate relationships with men, as if men were the problem in and of themselves. Instead, women told us that the key to their satisfaction was in *giving up certain ideas*. One idea was that only a man, marriage, and motherhood together could make a woman happy; another was that youth and beauty determined the quality of a woman's life. They explained that, while the ability to find satisfaction in life on one's own may not develop easily, it begins with an internal shift, a change of perspective and a change of attitude. The crucial factor was the realization that *they* were the best judge of what was meaningful for them, and that they had the power to determine how they would feel about their lives, particularly about being in midlife and being single.

The importance of this shift in attitude cannot be overstated. Jean explains, "I had to start thinking about my life in a different way. It was not about learning sky diving or seducing a seventeen-year-old guy." Sandi agrees:

> I can moan and groan about the situation just as easy as the next person, saying, "This is not what I want." And maybe we all have to do that sometimes—for a while. But then, it's not fun anymore. This isn't a dress rehearsal, so I'd rather choose the upward path. It takes you to more interesting places.

Dramatic changes can occur once women begin this process of choosing how they will feel about their lives. The women we met spoke with energy and excitement about learning to fly solo. Jessie, who explained earlier that her life looked a little bleak from the outside, told us that she had experienced a genuine transformation:

> I was always feeling like, well, maybe next year I'll be married. That has really shifted in the last couple of years and everything is finally falling into place. I understand why I made the choices I've made. I feel a celebration of my spirit at this point—which was not so much my experience in the past.

Shannon reiterates the sense of celebration:

> I never set out to be single at the age of forty-two. It was a complete surprise to me! But I think it's just fabulous that I'm happy, single. The joy of the last couple years has been the joy of feeling, "Wow, it is really okay this way. My life is rich and full."

Sandi was as surprised as Shannon to find her life "rich and full":

> After my divorce, I thought, "I have nothing to look forward to in life. I just have hardship and aloneness ahead of me." And now, it feels like a field of clover! I'm just coming into my own!

Because these women are no longer bound by societal prescriptions of how their lives should be lived, they are finally free to write their own stories. Because they are no longer so vulnerable to the opinions and expectations of others, they can create rewarding lives in a variety of ways, weaving together different threads into rich and sometimes quite unique patterns. As a result, they experience an enormous diversity of options opening before them. As Morgan, a forty-eight-year-old divorced woman, exclaimed, "Wow, the whole world is open to me. I don't have to be encumbered." Terry similarly remarked, "The world is like this great big candy store and I can't get enough of it. I want to see everything I can see and do everything I can do."

Chapter 2

"Fish Got to Swim and Birds Got to Fly"

Fish got to swim
and birds got to fly,
I got to love
one man till I die.
Can't help lovin' dat man
of mine . . .

Tell me he's lazy
tell me he's slow.
Tell me I'm crazy,
maybe I know.
Can't help lovin' dat man
of mine . . .

He kin come home
as late as kin be,
Home widout him
ain't no home to me!
Can't help lovin' dat man
of mine!
—"Can't Help Lovin' Dat Man" from *Show Boat*

The single idea that most interferes with single women's chances of feeling happy on their own is "Fish got to swim and birds got to fly." While recent social changes have made it acceptable to love more than one man (as long as women do so sequentially), the underlying belief on everyone's part is that, instinctually, a woman has "got to" have a man to have any chance of being happy and fulfilled in life. To deny this instinctual need is to go against nature. This idea, passed from generation to generation, has achieved the status of myth in our society. It is the myth that drives teenage girls into a deep depression when they don't have a date for the prom; it is the myth that makes mothers feel they have failed when their daughters have not married by the age of thirty; and it is the myth that Eva assumed we shared when she explained her move to the city by simply saying, "I'm single." It's a depressing myth that is guaranteed to keep women mired in the mud of self-pity, self-doubt, and self-criticism.

To fly solo and enjoy it, women must first free themselves from the twin beliefs that "real" women always want to be married and, therefore, that only women with personal problems and hang-ups want to be single. This is not an easy task in a society that cherishes the "fish got to swim" myth. The women we interviewed told us that, when they venture to talk about their lives, their statements about how much they value and enjoy the independence of their single lives are often categorized as "sour grapes" or the defensive rhetoric of women whose early family relationships were pathologically confining or involved devastating losses that left them unable to commit themselves to a man. As they grow older, their comments are more frequently dismissed as unconscious rationalizations constructed to "save face" in light of their poor chances for marriage or remarriage. Very few people seem willing to accept their statements about valuing autonomy at face value. Popular opinion would have us believe either that autonomy is not important for women, or that any well-adjusted woman should be able to experience all the independence she needs within the structure of marriage. The women we interviewed felt this task, if feasible at all, took a lot of effort. In their experience, the structure of marriage often felt incompatible with the independence and freedom they had come to value. Examining the history and current structure of marriage in our society, and its impact on women's lives, reveals that these women have very valid reasons for viewing marriage cautiously.

WHY WOMEN FIND IT SO HARD TO FLY
WHILE MARRIED

Our culture has long revolved around traditional values which dictate that married women must accommodate themselves to the needs of their husbands and children. Although the women's movement has championed the idea that women should be allowed to have full-time careers as well, beliefs persist that women should somehow manage these careers without disrupting the structure of traditional marriage. Most women find, however, that the saucy little woman who sings, "I can bring home the bacon and fry it up in the pan and never let him forget he's a man," while she dances around the stove in a business suit, apron, and five-inch heels—implying that she is a real woman in control of "the situation"—is not remotely related to "the situation" that they encounter as they struggle to juggle career and family.

The history of women's roles in the institution of marriage illustrates that, for centuries, marriage has precluded the possibility of leading a self-directed life. Until relatively recently, women were virtually invisible except as daughters, wives, and mothers. They had no legal rights because they were the possessions of husbands and fathers. In fact, once married, a woman became a non-person, defined only by her relationship to her husband. In 1854 Barbara Leigh Smith Bodichon summarized the legal rights of married women in a pamphlet entitled, "Married Women and the Law":

> A man and wife are one person in law; the wife loses all her rights as a single woman, and her existence is entirely absorbed in that of her husband. He is civilly responsible for her acts; she lives under his protection or cover, and her condition is called coverture.
>
> A woman's body belongs to her husband; she is in his custody, and he can enforce his right by a writ of *habeas corpus*. What was her personal property before marriage, such as money in hand, money at the bank, jewels, household goods, clothes, etc., becomes absolutely her husband's, and he may assign or dispose of them at his pleasure whether he and his wife live together or not.
>
> The legal custody of children belongs to the father. During the life-time of a sane father, the mother has no rights over her children, except a limited power over infants, and the father may take and dispose of them as he sees fit. . . .
>
> A husband and wife cannot be found guilty of conspiracy, as *that offense cannot be committed unless there are two persons*.

Married women lacked authority over their belongings, finances, children, and even their own bodies and minds. They were considered property to be disposed of according to their husbands' whims. There was no legal recourse for a woman who was beaten by her husband, much less one who simply disagreed with him. As one nineteenth-century woman summarized, "[Married women are] so completely merged in the existence of another that the law takes no cognizance of us."

The story of Elizabeth Parson Ware Packard, the wife of a nineteenth-century Presbyterian minister in Illinois, illustrates this oppressive and frightening reality. In the following passages, Elizabeth describes the events that occurred after she expressed religious views conflicting with the creed of her husband's church:

Early on the morning of the 18th of June, 1860, as I arose from my bed, preparing to take my morning bath, I saw my husband approaching the door with two physicians, both members of his church and of our bible-class—and a stranger gentleman, sheriff Burgess. Fearing exposure I hastily locked my door and proceeded with the greatest dispatch to dress myself. But before I had hardly commenced, my husband forced an entrance into my room through the window with an ax! And I, for shelter and protection against an exposure in a state of almost entire nudity, sprang into bed, just in time to receive my unexpected guests. The trio approached my bed, and each doctor felt my pulse, and without asking a single question pronounced me insane. . . .

My husband then informed me that the "forms of law" were all complied with, and he therefore requested me to dress myself for a ride to Jacksonville to enter the Insane Asylum as an inmate. I objected, and protested against being imprisoned without any trial. But to no purpose. My husband insisted upon it that I had no protection in the law, but himself, and that he was doing by me just as the laws of the State allowed him to do. . . .

When once in the Asylum I was beyond the reach of all human aid, except what could come through my husband, since the law allows no one to take them out, except the one who put them in, or by his consent; and my husband determined never to take me out.

This glance backwards in time helps to explain why women today have difficulty achieving and maintaining a sense of self within marriage. Only a few generations ago, wives were not considered to be separate people from their husbands! Still, today, there are many deeds and mortgages that list only a man's name, with *et aux* signifying the wife. Although women today do not suffer under the same legal yoke that oppressed them in the 1800s, *the values and assumptions underlying such laws have been passed down as unconscious expectations that continue to influence the actions and attitudes of both men and women.*

Women today are entering the labor force in increasing numbers, breaking into traditionally male-dominated professions, and receiving some cultural support for including careers in their life plans. Yet, despite the radical changes in the past thirty years, much remains the same. Women's employment opportunities remain relatively low status with low pay. Since money is power, the disparity between men's and women's wages has ramifications that extend far beyond their weekly paychecks. Not only does earning less keep women in disempowered positions in the world at large, making marriage a financial necessity for many, but it also reduces their bargaining power at home. As Maxine, a fifty-three-year-old divorceé recalls:

My husband was very demanding, very critical. I remember once saying to him, "How come you always criticize me when things go wrong but you never say anything when I do something right?" He said, in a sharp tone, "Because that's the way it's supposed to be!" And I accepted that, because I believed he knew better than me. After all, he went out into the world and earned hundreds of thousands of dollars.

Because women continue to earn less, it continues to make "sense" for the survival of the family unit that they make more personal and career sacrifices than their partners. Women may be encouraged to pursue careers, but only so long as their work does not interfere with their family responsibilities or their husband's plans. A great disparity emerges between spouses in terms of how much each sacrifices for the marriage—a disparity that is usually exacerbated when questions about children and child-care enter the scene. Women are expected to reduce their work commitments in order to manage child-care responsibilities, not only because they bear and nurse children, but also because they are paid less.

The same reasoning is applied to questions about relocating. It is "reasonable" for women, even those who are fully employed, to accept the need to relocate for their husbands' jobs, because their husbands generally hold higher-status, higher-paying positions. Furthermore, professional success is considered to be more important for a man. The assumption that women should adjust and accommodate is not limited to married relationships. For example, Jamie recently became involved with a physician from another state. As a lifelong resident of California, her life is organized around a rewarding and flexible job and a wide circle of friends. When the need to commute between states began to make it difficult to pursue this relationship, Jamie received pressure from family and friends to accommodate her partner's needs, to let him be the center of both of their lives:

> People around me started saying, "You're free, you could go to Maine. You could do that." The expectation is still there that, as the woman, I will just give up my life here, my friends, and everything that is important to me, and go off with this person.

Fish got to swim, birds got to fly. Women got to bend or relationships got to die.

During our parents' generation, whatever women lost in terms of career achievements or an independent sense of self was compensated to some degree by the security of "until death do us part" and the promise that a bargain made was a bargain kept. Women did not need job skills or a respectable employment record when they had this lifetime promise. But a funny thing happened on the way to the nineties. Our expectations of eternal union stayed the same, but our behaviors changed dramatically. Consider Michele, now a forty-two-year-old divorced obstetrician. From a strict religious background in a small town in North Dakota, Michele expected to graduate from college and find a husband who would "take care of me and make sure everything went smoothly." Although Michele did take the science courses in college necessary to apply to medical school, the decision to give up this goal in order to marry "the perfect guy" in her senior year of college was not a difficult one. It was, after all, her destiny.

Michele then spent many years following her husband (and his destiny) wherever his educational plans took her, finding temporary jobs to help support them while he went to school. She worked as an assistant in a physician's office, as a secretary in a bank, as a typist for a scientist, and as a real estate agent; she even worked for an insect exterminating company. In all the time she supported her husband's development, she never seriously considered her own:

My experience in my marriage was that I did everything—I mean, to
the point where it was ridiculous. I did all the housework, made sure
the car was okay. My husband was in graduate school; he was never
very good in languages, but I was, so I would translate his work for
him. I also used to do his statistics homework for him. There was this
unspoken perception of what marriage was supposed to be like. I was
supposed to be the nurturing caretaker who took care of all these
things. My sole job was to somehow keep him going, promote his
career, make sure he was fine. I don't think I ever even questioned my
assignment. I mean, it didn't seem strange to me at the time.

Michelle kept bending to accommodate her husband's needs, giving
ninety-plus percent of herself to the marriage, until one day her husband
disappeared, leaving her with thousands of dollars in outstanding gambling
debts. Michele was devastated. She had never lived by herself and had never
thought about defining her own plans for the future. Although she had a
college degree, she was now thirty-one and had a ten-year employment
history peppered with short-term, unrelated, unsatisfying "little" jobs. The
accommodation that had served her marriage so well, or so she had believed,
left her unprepared and unqualified in the job market. Shocked by her
husband's abandonment and unsure of how to support herself, much less pay
off his debts, Michele finally began to question the choices she had made.
Marriage had offered her a sense of security and direction, however illusory,
that she would never have questioned, much less *chosen* to relinquish. Only
now, alone and terrified, could she see the high price she had paid for all
those "secure" years in which she had focused on her husband's needs and
dreams. She quickly discovered that, along the way, she had lost her own
dreams, as well as the sense that she could and should have a life with a
direction of her own choosing.

The pattern Michele's story so vividly demonstrates has not changed
nearly as much as all of us would like to believe. Many of the women we
interviewed were shocked by the "adjustments" they had made in past
relationships in order to meet the needs of their partners, bending so much
that they became, not oaks or even willows, but mere caricatures of individuals, undefined lumps fashioned out of silly putty. On their own, they
did not mourn the loss of these past relationships so much as they mourned
what *they* had lost during those years. While marriage may provide sexual
and emotional intimacy, as well as economic and social advantages, these and

thousands of other women's stories suggest that it is still a risky institution for women who value their own autonomy.

LIVING SINGLY: VALID CHOICE OR UNHEALTHY DEFENSE MECHANISM?

The popular press dismisses the lessons inherent in stories such as Michele's as tales propagated by feminist malcontents or by hysterical women who are too easily victimized in their relationships with men. Arguing that most women do not have problems preserving and acting on their own goals, dreams, and identities in their marital or intimate relationships, they contend that women like Michele are "co-dependent," "undifferentiated," "enmeshed," or have other emotional problems with names like "dependent personality disorder."

Such "explanations" are tolerated and even welcomed today because they protect the familiar and seemingly safe traditional order in times of tumultuous and unsettling change. For centuries, women have been assigned, and have accepted, responsibility for nurturing and maintaining the entire range of family relationships. The apparent plague of co-dependent behavior assailing modern relationships provides a convenient explanation for the discontent women are expressing; it also conveniently continues the tradition of placing the responsibility for the well-being of relationships— and therefore the blame for their deterioration—squarely on the shoulders of women. Blaming women for the predicament of the family today is not only inaccurate and unfair, but leaves them in a no-win situation. They are at fault when they do not stand up for themselves in their marriages, when they stay with remote, abusive, or alcoholic men, earning such labels as co-dependent and women who love too much; but they are also at fault for shattering the social fabric if they leave these inadequate, depressing, and even dangerous unions. Women are led to believe that their inability to alter relationship patterns that have existed for hundreds of years, without upsetting anyone, is the result of some defect, deficiency, or diagnosable psychological disorder *in them.* When women, the architects of family relationships, cannot hold marriages together under such insurmountable pressures, the problem is *theirs,* not the institution's. It has little to do with antiquated cultural values or even the behavior of the men to whom they are married. The problem is that *they* make foolish choices, love too much, and can't say no. The problem is that *they* are angry or *they* are ambivalent. Pop psychology, in its attempts to help women mired in unrewarding relationships without disturbing the institution of marriage itself, has obscured the probability that the basic difficulty for Michele and women like her lies in the structure of the foundation on which their marriages were built. Thus, becoming or staying single is never a valid solution for a woman. Instead, it remains a badge of failure.

Sadly, the books that describe how women's personality problems are to blame for the social upheavals of our time have been commercially successful because women, always willing to accept responsibility for maintaining family ties, have been the ones buying them. These books may blame them unfairly, but they also seem to offer "solutions." We can scarcely blame women for grabbing at anything that claims to solve the complex and often mystifying problem of how to maintain a secure and satisfying relationship in a decidedly insecure social climate—even if the "solution" involves accepting more than their share of responsibility for the problem.

Once again, women are being placed in a situation which obscures individual differences as well as the real reasons so many women are unhappy. The crucial difference between a marriage that supports and fosters a woman's self-identity and one that does not is never exclusively the personality of the woman involved. Together, a man and a woman create the structure of their marriage, the unwritten and sometimes unconscious role expectations that dictate what attitudes and behaviors are acceptable for whom. In an ideal world, marriages would be based on a foundation of true compromise, so that women would not have to forfeit their sense of self in order to enjoy the benefits of intimacy, companionship, and security. The decisive factor in determining whether a marriage does or does not support *both* partners is how a couple contends with the influence of deeply entrenched cultural values that designate rigid and inequitable roles for men and women.

Maintaining "freedom and equality for all" within a marriage today remains a difficult task, one which some couples can manage but many cannot. While many women don't mind accommodating themselves to their partners and thus enjoy being part of a traditional marriage—finding it a relief to eschew decision-making, money management, and car repairs—other women desire and require more space, control, and freedom than traditional marriages can provide. The problem with the *fish got to swim and birds got to fly* mentality is that it assumes all women are the same and that a need for independence is unnatural, effectively eliminating the possibility of true choice.

Chapter 3

The Marriage and Motherhood Mandate

. . . all that [a woman] may wish to have, all that she may wish to do, must come through a single channel and a single choice. Wealth, power, social distinction, fame—not only these, but home and happiness, reputation, ease and pleasure, her bread and butter,—all, must come to her through a small gold ring.

—*Charlotte Perkins Gilman*

In those days, it didn't matter: you could be a Wimbledon champion, Phi Beta Kappa, Miss America, Nobel Peace Prize winner, but if they asked you about marriage and you didn't at least have a hot prospect ready to get down on one knee, you knew you were considered to be no more than half a woman.

—*Billie Jean King*

A logical outcome of the *fish got to swim and birds got to fly* assumption, one that women now in midlife were taught early, was that they had only one real choice in life; that there was only one way they could achieve happiness. They were inculcated throughout their childhoods with the mandate that would rule their lives: *Marry and have children.* Before they could walk and talk, the process of indoctrination had begun. They learned to be ready to sacrifice personal dreams for marriage and motherhood, and they learned to do so willingly. This indoctrination continued throughout childhood and adolescence, gaining such strength that its power lingers today, even influencing the lives of women who adamantly state they want no part of "traditional" dreams. This strong value placed on marriage and motherhood did not begin, however, during the childhoods of today's midlife women. It has gained force and momentum over centuries.

THE UNHOLY STIGMATA

Single women have faced immense pressure to marry for hundreds of years. In fact, during some time periods, single women were viewed as so evil and subversive that they faced not only stigma but overt violence. During the 1600s and 1700s in New England, single women (and especially those over the age of forty) were particularly vulnerable to being convicted of witchcraft—and some were even put to death! By the mid 1800s the status of single women in England, while not grounds for execution, was only slightly better. When England's 1851 census revealed that as many as thirty percent of all English women between the ages of twenty and forty were unmarried, W.R. Gregg, an influential journalist and essayist, without pause or shame, proposed that these "redundant" women be forcibly exported to the colonies, where they could mate with available men and cease to be a threat and a burden to polite society. Attitudes of the early 1900s were no less disturbing. In a 1911 article entitled "The Spinster," unmarried women were described, in a disturbingly paranoid voice, as a serious threat to society:

> [The Spinster], unobtrusive, meek, soft-footed, silent, shamefaced, bloodless and boneless, thinned to spirit, enters the secret recesses of the mind, sits at the secret springs of action, and moulds and fashions our emasculate society. She is our social nemesis.

Obviously, much had changed by the time today's midlife single women were being raised. Single women in the fifties and sixties were not burned at the stake or banished from our shores. But such extreme hostile and even paranoid attitudes do not vanish in a century. The single women who were a part of most women's extended families or social networks ("maiden aunts," nuns, widowed and occasionally divorced mothers and grandmothers) were still frequently seen as defective, as somehow "less than" married women. Theirs were cautionary tales, told by those who knew them in tones conveying underlying disapproval and condescension. Judith, for example, recalled only one single woman from her childhood:

I had an aunt who was not married. She lived with her sister and her sister's husband. Sometimes she would go off to Spain and live inexpensively in an artist's community. She was also an alcoholic. She wasn't a woman I recall having particular appeal. Her lifestyle, though exciting, was also deficient, inadequate in some way.

Despite their achievements, these single women served mostly as strong reminders of the price paid for following alternative paths—paths not endorsed as ones young girls should follow. At best, these single women were seen as eccentric; most, however, like Judith's aunt, were viewed as odd and abnormal, on the edge of family life.

MARRIAGE AS THE HOLY GRAIL

In the fifties and sixties, getting married represented a woman's principal rite of passage into adulthood, the pinnacle of her development. A woman's wedding day was seen as the most important day of her life. Aleta, now divorced, told us:

I was an adolescent in the fifties and I absolutely believed that my whole world revolved around getting married, having kids, and living happily ever after. That was the end of development. That was the end of life. I wouldn't have felt complete if I had not gotten married.

Becoming a bride, a wife, and later a mother confirmed a woman's worth and defined her status, her limits, her life style, her very identity. According to Mrs. Thomas Edison, who said "the woman who doesn't want to make a home is undermining our nation," marriage even defined her patriotism.

Women who did not want to marry, or who were less than thrilled with their roles as full-time homemakers, learned that, according to the experts, they were "biologically and temperamentally" *abnormal*. When Benjamin Spock, a leading authority on family psychology, stated categorically, "Biologically and temperamentally . . . women were made to be concerned first and foremost with child-care, husband care, and home care," women got the picture. And the picture displayed as the ideal involved the same sequence of life events for all: an insignificant and undemanding job, followed by marriage, motherhood, and living happily ever after. Or, if they happened to be from upper middle-class families, the picture allowed a few extra flourishes: a good education, a minor career easily relinquished, then marriage, motherhood, and happily ever after. Marriage and motherhood was every girl's dream; it was the "Holy Grail" of female development. Any other achievements were considered secondary to this goal; in no way should they interfere with it. Women's individual talents, interests, and ambitions were evaluated in terms of their marriageability quotient: they either helped or hindered women in achieving the primary goal.

Kelly, for example, was "assertive" even as a young girl, a characteristic her mother did not view as an asset in the marriage market. Kelly remembers her mother telling her, "Keep your mouth shut until you're married. Don't let people know how opinionated you are." Sandi tells a story from her childhood that captures this same view of women as fit only for marriage. She remembers talking with her mother, mapping out the futures of her three younger brothers:

> As we were growing up, my mother was always wondering, "What will they be?" I remember her saying that one son loves to work with his hands, so he ought to be an engineer, or since he loves to build things, he ought to be an architect. And this son is so orderly, he could be in banking or accounting or law. And this other son loves to write, so he'd be a good journalist.

Their conversation never got around to creating a custom-tailored plan for Sandi. Her individual skills and talents did not guide her parents' plans for her future; her *gender* did. Sandi says, "My mother always assumed that I would marry and have children and that would be my path. And I just accepted her view."

Women's chances of marrying, and their ability to approximate the ideal of the "good wife," depended on their ability to become and remain selfless—that is, to put the needs of their husbands, children, and other family members before their own, drawing their sustenance from the satisfaction and happiness of others. In the process of developing this highly valued quality of selflessness, women learned two essential lessons: to wait and to accommodate.

LIVES ON HOLD:
WAITING BUT NOT WONDERING

Because a woman's future was determined primarily by the needs and desires of her husband, it was important that she not focus too much energy, time, and attention on defining her own needs and desires. To do so would reinforce all the wrong behaviors and might impede her ability to sense *his* needs. An attractive woman was a waiting woman. Like Sleeping Beauty, she was to remain in a state of suspension until her Prince finally arrived to sweep her off her feet and whisk her into the land of "happily ever after." Women were not even encouraged to be assertive in their search for this all-important facet of their futures—their Prince Charming. In fact, they were cautioned *against* overtly pursuing men. ("Nobody likes a woman who is aggressive, and remember, when you dance, *the man leads*.") Simultaneously, however, they were told to use every wile they could muster to "catch" a husband. *Wait*, but be ready to take advantage of the opportunity, when it presents itself.

This emphasis on waiting to be chosen permeated most aspects of women's lives. Sandi's mother did not even want her to talk to a woman who had decided to pursue her own goals while delaying marriage until the advanced age of twenty-eight. Sandi explains:

> I remember having a conversation with a friend of the family. She was saying to me, "I was a chemist. I didn't get married until my late twenties, and those were the best years. Then I had these children— five, one after the other. But I was so glad I had those years." My mother came bustling up and said to the friend, "Stop talking to my daughter that way." In other words, my mother's message was, "Don't you dare have a career—I want you to get married!"

Women were not supposed to define career goals, think about establishing a permanent home of their own, or plan adventurous vacations (unless these vacations were in the service of finding a man). They were not even supposed to buy monogrammed stationary or towels, since at any minute, their initials could (and should) change. Until a woman was married, a sense of impermanence and unreality dominated her life. She was not quite an adult, not quite mature, not quite real, not quite yet.

Many women were actively dissuaded from pursuing professional goals because these goals would demand long-term investments and commitments that might conflict with the "prime directive" to follow their men . . . whenever, wherever they might go. Instead of careers, women were supposed to have "little jobs"—something they could do after marching down the aisle at high school or college commencements and before marching down the aisle at their weddings. Jean, now an admissions officer at a small college, had remarkably clear ideas about what she wanted to be when she grew up. But even at the age of twelve, she was directly discouraged from even entertaining such dreams:

> I wanted to be a doctor from the time I was a little girl. I would operate on earthworms with my mother's grapefruit knife out on the front stoop. We had a next-door neighbor who was a bone surgeon. I would go over as a little kid, not even knowing what I was looking at, and borrow his American Medical Association journals to do my science projects. When I was about twelve, he talked to my dad and said, "You've got to start discouraging her because she is serious. Women can't be doctors."

Julia, now a successful executive, also encountered opposition when she sought to design her own life. The process of selecting colleges was particularly significant for her:

> I remember going into this interview with the guidance counselor, Mr. Palmer. I still remember his short-sleeved shirt and ugly red tie. He said, "Well, do you want to be a secretary, a nurse, or a teacher?" And I said, "Well, actually, I was planning on the idea of art history." And he said, "On what?" Then he said, "Look, let's go back to the beginning. You didn't take secretarial courses, so you can't be a secretary. You're no good in science, so you probably can't study nursing. Here is a list of teachers colleges. If you are interested in art, try this one. That's where all the art teachers come from." I sat there and said, "I thought I'd like to go to Barnard." And he said, "Where? Never heard of it." So I sent for all the catalogues and he said, "You don't want to go there. It's in New York City. What are you going to do if you go there and major in archaeology or art history or something? You'll never have a career. You'll probably just want to teach and have something to fall back on *in case you need it later.*"

The Mr. Palmers of the world delivered many of the formative messages that today's midlife women received. The attitudes of such guidance counselors were not unusually conservative—merely a reflection of mainstream society. To most people, a woman's education was not a serious commitment, not a foundation for a career, but an insurance policy to be used only if her husband died or deserted her. Josie recalls being told by her mother: "You ought to have something you can do in case your husband dies." This work was not supposed to add pleasure and meaning to her life. "It was more like whenever you go swimming, you should have a life jacket nearby," Josie explains. If women went to college, they were sent off with the motto "In Case You Need It Later" etched into their minds. Since divorce rates were low in those days, even this insurance policy wasn't viewed as particularly crucial. Valerie summarizes this era's priority: "The old tape that played continually in the back of my head was, you study, you do well, and get your M.R.S. degree."

Since their lives would ultimately be shaped by those of their husbands, many women naturally questioned the point of having careers, defining a strong sense of self, or having a clear idea of what they as individuals wanted from life. At best, such activities represented a waste of a woman's time and energy; at worst, they diminished her chances of being chosen at all. Women thus tended to adopt an attitude of passivity toward their own lives—an attitude which made it difficult for them to realize even that they *could* take charge and make decisions.

"CHESHIRE CAT" WOMEN: THE IMPORTANCE OF ACCOMMODATION

Women learned not only to put their lives on hold, but also to accommodate themselves to the attitudes and opinions of those around them, particularly the men in their lives. Most women were taught to accommodate rather than to initiate, to accept and tolerate rather than challenge or oppose. As children, today's midlife women saw their mothers and female teachers deferring to male authority figures as a matter of course. They noticed, without even knowing they noticed, that presidents of countries and corporations were almost always male and that acquiescing to men seemed the natural thing for women to do.

The women admired in the culture were not those who fought for themselves, but those who were quiet, affectionate, accepting, demure. Consider the movie heroines of the fifties and even the sixties. Women like Doris Day, Debbie Reynolds, and Maureen O'Hara could be "feisty" for a while, but we all knew they would be tamed soon by a strong man. Consider also one of our timeless childhood heroines, Cinderella. The opening lines of Walt Disney's film version of this story explain that, "Cinderella was abused, humiliated, and finally forced to become a servant in her own house. *And yet, through it all, Cinderella remained ever gentle and kind.*" Most women grew up yearning to be like Cinderella. As children, they were not aware of the meaning of this identification, but the values of what it meant to be a "good" woman were inculcated nonetheless. They hoped to learn to be able to endure and accept without complaint or criticism, being "ever gentle and kind." Clearly, no one admired the angry, demanding, noisy, and argumentative stepsisters. After all, it was Cinderella who got to marry the Prince.

Hannah told us a story that stood out distinctly in her memory as an example of how women were expected to mold themselves to their husbands' desires. Her mother had gone shopping at a fancy dress shop. Purchasing a dress, she had rushed home with great excitement to try it on for her husband and Hannah. Hannah still recalls the pride she felt looking at her mother in that dress:

> My mother was a beautiful woman. She really was quite stunning. The dress was metallic, paisley, sheaf, orangey. It was stunning. She returned it the next day because my father didn't like it. I don't remember saying anything to her about it, but I will never forget it.

Putting aside their own tastes in clothing to accept those of their husbands' was only one of many behaviors women learned were necessary in order to be good wives. Women also learned to give up their ideas, beliefs, interests, and even their friends, if they were not in accord with their husband's wishes. The ideal wife and mother was always gentle and encouraging of her husband and children. She did not have (much less express) her own needs, desires, or dreams. Emma, fifty-one and divorced, told us:

> The way I was raised, you did what your husband wanted. You had dinner on the table, you washed, lightly starched, and ironed his shirts. If he wanted to go see Dick Tracy movies, that's what you went to see. You sat and watched football games on television. It was all what *he* wanted.

Women learned that preparation for marriage meant preparation to live in a world in which almost everything would be negotiable. Jean recalls:

> We were raised to believe that our "job" was the marriage and so, yes, we would sacrifice anything for that. We were taught that the "name of the game" is compromise. Actually, we were expected to be chameleons, able to change our entire perspective in mid-sentence in order to be in agreement with our husbands.

The mandate demanded an ability and a willingness to accommodate that was total. Accommodation became "second nature" to most women—something they did not think about, question, or sometimes even notice. Cocoa Day, of Gloria Naylor's *Mama Day,* describes the experience well, as she admits shortly after her marriage:

> I wanted us to work so badly that I would be tempted to try and squeeze myself up into whatever shape you had calculated would fit into your plans. How long could I do it? The answer scared the hell out of me: I could have done it forever. You start out feeling a little uncomfortable, but then when you look around that's the shape you've grown into.

Women now in midlife have ingrained habitual responses of accommodation that are very difficult to alter even when they are inappropriate and even destructive. Many have accommodated to such a degree that, whenever they enter intimate relationships, they automatically defer to their partner's needs and opinions. Jean vividly described this phenomenon as one in which women begin to "disappear around the edges," like the Cheshire Cat in *Alice in Wonderland.* One minute they are there—bright, assertive, psyches intact; the next minute they begin to fade, their sharp images becoming fuzzy, and before long, only their haunting smiles remain.

The role of accommodation in women's lives is a complex issue to discuss. Some theories of female psychology suggest that a woman's sense of self is relationship-based and that the ability to accommodate is thus a natural and important female strength. While this may well be true, it is also true that these potentially useful qualities can be exploited within families, work environments, and society to the detriment of women and the relationships they nurture. Obviously all relationships require some compromise and negotiation. For most women, however, the problem has been that *they* have been expected to do the bulk of it. Rather than serving as a tool for building equal and satisfying relationships, accommodation has been a tool for cultivating women's selflessness. And yet, this ideal of selflessness expected by the mandate was so unattainable that guilt and fear of disapproval and rejection became a basic staple of most women's daily diets. As writer and feminist Erica Jong has observed, "Show me a woman who doesn't feel guilty, and I'll show you a man." Michele clearly recalls the messages from her youth that left her vulnerable to this chronic guilt:

> You always think of the other person first, you try never to hurt anyone's feelings, and you do whatever you have to do so that the other person is happy. There was the expectation that you sacrificed yourself, and if you didn't do that, there were consequences. I remember feeling guilty if I said, "Well, I don't want to do that." "Well," came the instant remonstration, "what kind of a daughter are you anyway! What kind of a person?!"

When women did not live up to the expectations of the mandate, they also found themselves subject to threats that men would not choose them. Men, they learned, did not select women who were "assertive" and did not stay with those who were "difficult." As Jean says:

> To disagree, to create conflict, meant that he would say, "I'm not interested then. There's somebody else who will not be as difficult as you are." So you compromise to keep him happy, to keep him there, to keep him from leaving.

Maxine describes a similar reality:

> If I had spoken up in the beginning, there would have been no marriage. He simply wouldn't have tolerated me. The attitude was, aren't you lucky to get a husband?

In these ways, women's abilities to accommodate and compromise were reinforced by an ironclad prohibition against expressing anger and creating conflict. As Carolyn Heilbrun writes, "Above all other prohibitions, what has been forbidden to women is anger, together with the open admission of the desire for power and control over one's life." The consequences for expressing anger, particularly against men, were extreme. In her best-selling book, *The Dance of Anger,* Harriet Goldhor Lerner states:

Women who openly express anger at men are especially suspect. Even when society is sympathetic to our goals of equality, we all know that "those angry women" turn everybody off. Unlike our male heroes, who fight and even die for what they believe in, women may be condemned for waging a bloodless and humane revolution for their own rights. The direct expression of anger, especially at men, makes us unladylike, unfeminine, unmaternal, sexually unattractive, or, more recently, "strident." Even our language condemns such women as "shrews," "witches," "bitches," "hags," "nags," "man-haters," and "castrators." They are unloving and unlovable. They are devoid of femininity. Certainly, you do not wish to become one of them.

IN THE SHADOW OF THE MANDATE

Although the marriage and motherhood mandate dominated the era in which today's midlife women were raised, the messages that women received during their early years were seldom monolithic. Many women reported encountering messages that contradicted the mandate. These messages formed a shadow reality, often unexpressed or overtly denied by all the adults in their lives, but visible to these young women nonetheless.

Some women acquired a skeptical view of traditional values as a result of painful experiences of being sexually or physically abused as children. Other women came into contact with the shadow reality as they observed the depression and unhappiness of their mothers, whose lives conformed to the fifties stay-at-home ideal. Josie, for instance, recalls feeling that marriage amounted to a "psychic death" for her mother, who had studied anthropology and deeply loved her work. Instead of becoming a college professor, she married one, giving up her plans for a career in order to raise her family. Josie says:

> My mother's life was absolutely traditional and I don't remember her being anything but small and folded in, living this very small, little life. I just couldn't see anything in the make-up of her life that gave her any real pleasure.

For Josie, observing the model of her mother's life instilled a strong suspicion of the traditional path that she was being trained to follow. She remembers:

By the time I was eighteen I can remember saying to myself that I never wanted to have a life like my mother's. Her life was absolutely traditional and though she would never say she regrets her choices, *I* regret her choices.

The older Josie got, the more depressed her mother became. Josie's choices, as she saw them being lived out in her mother's experience, were to follow in her mother's footsteps or to forge into the poorly marked and clearly dangerous territory of the never married. The result, for Josie, was a pervasive confusion. She knew what she *didn't* want, but she had no sense of other options being available to her:

By the time I was an adolescent, I felt absolutely at sea. I had no idea what was possible or impossible for me. I was just scared to death. As far as I could tell, women got married and died, psychically died. There would be no real life left. The kind of depression I experienced in my adolescence left me with so little sense of how to exist in the world that I didn't even have the courage a lot of people have to just say, "Well, I don't know what I want to do, so I'll hit the road."

Mary Catherine Bateson, daughter of anthropologists Margaret Mead and Gregory Bateson, has described the dilemma Josie experienced as a conflict between a woman's loyalty to her mother and her desire to avoid her mother's fate and live according to her own dreams:

Most women today have grown up with mothers who, for all their care and labor, were regarded as having achieved little. Women with a deep desire to be like their mothers are often faced with the choice between accepting a beloved image that carries connotations of inferiority and dependence, or rejecting it and thereby losing an important source of closeness.

For Josie, trying to forge a new kind of life on her own at age twenty, without any real role models, was simply overwhelming. Although her mother's experience had planted seeds of doubt about following the traditional path, Josie had no alternative vision. The prospects for a happy life as a single woman looked so bleak that, despite the obvious flaws in the way "every woman's dream" was being lived by her mother, Josie closed her eyes and jumped into the abyss, getting married as soon as she finished

college. Of the beginning moments of her first marriage, Josie says, "I remember waking up the next morning and feeling awful, as though somebody had just vacuumed out a part of my soul. I woke up as my mother, and
he woke up as his father—and that was a *bad* match."

SLIVERS OF LIGHT IN THE SHADOW

Not all women were led to question the traditional path by observing painful
disillusionment in their mothers. Some received direct, positive messages
that actually encouraged their independence, ability, and potential. Elaine
remembers being told by her mother, "Go for it . . . be out front. Don't ever
be afraid . . . try to achieve as much as possible." Other women had mothers
who refused to be limited in their choices by traditional dictates. Julia's
mother rejected the expectations of her day in order to do what made her
happy: working outside the home. While her choice was not without a
price, it was clear to Julia that it was worth the cost. Of her mother's attitude,
Julia says, "Every once in a while, she would have an attack of fifties-style
guilt and go home for a while, pretending to be a housewife. Then she'd go
crazy and have to go to work again."

Other women also benefited from a blurring of the traditional gender line
drawn between what boys and girls could do and be. Although our culture's
perspective on this issue was fairly unequivocal, individual families sometimes imparted views that allowed leeway. Shawna recalls that when boys
came to their home during the winter asking to shovel their snow, her father
would respond, "I have able-bodied women here. They can do it." Leslie
explains that her family also directly contradicted the cultural norm. She says,
"I never knew that girls were 'less than' boys until I got to college. My
family never told me that." Myrna's experience was similar:

> I never, ever thought there was anything I couldn't do because I was a
> woman. As a matter of fact, when I was in the first grade, I thought I
> was going to be a priest. The priest called my parents to tell them he
> thought that they should have a little talk with me to explain that I
> couldn't do that.

When many of these women reached adulthood, however, they faced a
struggle similar to the one Josie described. They, too, had difficulty translat-

ing these alternative messages and models into blueprints for their lives. Although they were encouraged to be independent, few of them received any concrete, practical directions about how to forge a non-traditional kind of future. Megan says, "My mother gave me vague, covert messages not to get married, but she didn't tell me what to do instead." Shannon also encountered a similar lack of direction in the messages from her father:

> My father always said that he believed in women and that I could do whatever I wanted. His basic philosophy was, "Do whatever you want in life." He didn't communicate a fear of life and he wasn't critical of me ever, but he had no idea how to help me shape a life.

Chapter 4

~ •

The Mandate Goes Underground

The great enemy of truth is very often not the lie—deliberate, contrived and dishonest—but the myth—persistent, persuasive and unrealistic.
                                                                —*John F. Kennedy*

It's hard to fight an enemy who has outposts in your head.

                                                                —*Sally Kempton*

Pageboys, circle pins, Peter-Pan collars, and girdles—hallmarks of the days when the marriage and motherhood mandate reigned—have long since gone out of style, but the mandate survives, if under an assumed name. Today, its message is delivered "underground," through the negative images of single women conveyed daily by the media. These images surreptitiously communicate some of our culture's most traditional and destructive myths about women, marriage, and being single:

- Single women lead lonely, depressing, and incomplete lives.
- Their unhappiness increases exponentially with each passing birthday, because past a certain age a woman is "used up."
- All women are desperate to marry or remarry because marriage is their only real chance for security and happiness.

These myths are not harmless quirks of our collective personality. Masquerading as reality, they are erosive and dangerous. Television, movies, music, advertising, pop psychology, newspapers, and magazines adeptly perpetuate these myths. The author of a 1984 *Cosmopolitan* article, "Sketches from Single Life," for example, describes a single woman's home as a place

. . . where the nights are chilly and . . . roaches waltz insolently over the dish drainer, no matter how clean you are or how much poison powder you put down—and where breakfast is a baloney sandwich and dinner a bowl of cornflakes. This is where she feels loneliest—lonelier than the nights she and Paul are together and he doesn't speak, except to snap at her.

A later *Cosmo* article presents another a disturbing, cautionary tale of what can happen when a woman stops dating. The author explains that such a woman

. . . will discover that her Will to Date has been replaced by a will to eat. A few months down the line, she will find herself sitting on her huge butt in front of Kojak reruns eating injudicious amounts of ice cream. She will have similarly plump pals with whom she will discuss only one subject. "Why are all the attractive men either gay or married?"

In both of these articles, the message is clear: Single women do not have real homes, real furniture, real friends, real interests, or even balanced meals. Their lives are bleak, lonely, impermanent, and utterly depressing.

SINGLE WOMEN IN FILM AND TELEVISION: OLD MAIDS AND SINISTER SPINSTERS

At first glance, it would appear that television and movies present images of strong and successful single women. However, a closer look reveals that these women's achievements and adventures are treated as incidental events, which simply fill up the time until the "real" (read *romantic*) plot begins. For example, the central character in the TV drama, *The Trials of Rosie O'Neill,* is a skilled public defender whose professional life is packed with excitement and the struggle for personal integrity in an ambiguous world. Her personal life is enriched by close relationships with family and friends, most of whom ignore what she finds so meaningful in her life and focus instead on whether or not she has a date. In the 1992 season we were encouraged by publicity spots to cluster around our TV sets as the real goal of Rosie's life quest was finally unveiled. Why, it's not justice for the downtrodden, after all—it's a man, presumably to be followed shortly by marriage. What a surprise.

The same message is repeated over and over. After listening to a male colleague utter the time-honored message that love is so important, you must grab it no matter what it costs, another successful female character, attorney Grace Van Owen of *L.A. Law,* abandons her law practice to reunite with her husband, who emotionally and physically abandoned her after she suffered a miscarriage. Even the otherwise competent and content character of Maggie on *Northern Exposure* periodically becomes obsessed with the search for a mate. Until recently, her quest resulted in the death of every man with whom she ever had sex—undoubtedly a commentary on the fate of men who are attracted to competent women.

In films, single women are either temporarily single heroines on their way to "happily ever after" or permanently single characters on their way to the asylum. The image of the single woman as a sinister and dangerous distortion of what women should be has become a cornerstone of the film industry. Perhaps the most frequently cited example of the potential depravity of a single woman pushed to the edge is that of Glenn Close's character, Alex Forrest, in the 1987 megahit movie *Fatal Attraction.* There are, however, an abundance of others. The short trip from depressed lady-in-waiting to crazy single woman was artfully illustrated by Michele Pfeiffer's character, Selina Kyle, in the 1992 film *Batman Returns.* Selina begins as a near caricature of the stereotype of the depressed single woman. She holds a "little" job as a secretary, bumbles even the most basic of tasks, and is constantly humiliated by her rich and powerful boss. She lives in a small, dingy apartment decorated with stuffed animals and other mementos of her childhood. Each night, when she returns home, she calls out in a sing-song voice, "Honey! I'm home!" . . . only to be followed by her confrontation with the harsh reality: "Oh, yeah, I forgot, I'm not married." Her life is so empty and lonely that her main interpersonal connections occur with her answering machine and her cat. However, by the end of the movie, this depressed little mouse has metamorphosed into a dangerous and vengeful Catwoman, seeking violent revenge on the men of the world.

A similar transformation occurs in the character of Helen Sharp played by Goldie Hawn in the 1992 film, *Death Becomes Her.* Helen is a single woman approaching midlife, whose hopes of marriage crumble when her "best" friend, an aging actress, steals her fiancé. Without a man or hopes of marriage, Helen becomes grotesquely obese and utterly mad. Barricaded in her apartment, she subsists on canned frosting, accompanied only by a clutch of cats. Each day she obsessively and endlessly replays scenes from a film in which her actress friend is murdered. Finally, she is carted off to a mental hospital, where she remains until transformed by the realization that she herself could do away with her old friend and steal back the husband who was rightfully hers.

The 1991 box-office hit, *The Hand That Rocks the Cradle*, follows a similar theme. Although this movie was most widely censured for its critical message about working mothers, it also presented a disturbing portrait of the danger posed by women without men or children in their lives. In this film, a woman, Claire Bartel, makes a public complaint against her gynecologist for having sexually molested her. When she comes forward, a number of other women also begin to disclose similar abuses suffered at the hands of the same doctor. As a result, the gynecologist eventually commits suicide and his young wife, Mrs. Mott, out of her grief miscarries what would have been their only child. Without the roles of wife and mother to ward off insanity, the now single Mrs. Mott launches a vendetta to destroy the happily married Mrs. Bartel, whom she blames for her husband's death. Her goal is to do away with Mrs. Bartel and usurp her position as wife and mother. There are no limits to Mrs. Mott's vengeful attempts to recapture these cherished roles: She takes a job as Mrs. Bartel's live-in nanny, secretly nurses her baby so that the baby bonds not to his mother but to her, turns Mrs. Bartel's young daughter against her, tries to seduce Mrs. Bartel's husband, actually murders her best friend, and finally tries to kill her.

Ultimately, *The Hand That Rocks the Cradle* ends in the same way as *Fatal Attraction:* The good wife and mother finally kills the evil single woman. Films like these masterfully pit our allegiances against the single woman, communicating the message that women without men or children are capable of horrendous, vindictive violence. Such films leave viewers with the impression that, if single women cannot be avoided altogether, they are best treated with caution and suspicion. For single female viewers, the price of such a movie is high. They are battered by the repeated underlying message that, as Susan Faludi phrased it, "the best single woman is a dead one."

For the most part, women who become single through divorce are not portrayed as pathologically as never-married women. In fact, divorced women are rarely presented in any terms at all (unless it is to display the overwhelming and utterly asexual existence of single mothers struggling to survive against impossible odds). In the 1970s many popular television shows and movies depicted women leaving marriages and successfully facing life and motherhood on their own. As Susan Faludi, in her book *Backlash*, has observed:

In films like *Diary of a Mad Housewife, A Woman Under the Influence, An Unmarried Woman, Alice Doesn't Live Here Anymore, Up the Sandbox, Private Benjamin,* and *The Turning Point,* housewives leave home, temporarily or permanently, to find their own voice.

In the past decade, however, examples of women who chose to leave their marriages to strike out on their own simply disappeared. The message of the eighties was clear: The status of "married woman" had been reinstated as sacred.

PUNISHMENT FOR THREATENING THE SANCTITY OF THE FAMILY

There always have been a few female characters who present a more optimistic view of singlehood for women, but it is invariably made clear that each of these characters has paid a high price for her independence and deviation from the cultural ideal. *Murphy Brown* is perhaps the best current example. Although, like most single female characters, she is portrayed as more than a little flawed (overly aggressive, chronically critical, and a recovering alcoholic), she is also one of television's few relatively satisfied, likeable, single, career women. However, when Murphy chose to have a child on her own, her decision was viewed as so radical and so threatening to the moral fiber of our country that she received criticism of unprecedented proportions from a large segment of the population. Vice President Dan Quayle even took the time and the trouble to denounce Murphy publicly. She is, he implied, a threat to the very sanctity of the family, an example of the moral depravity of our times, and a slap in the face of the fathers of this country. While Dan Quayle can hardly be said to speak for us all, his pronouncement reflected the culture's powerful reaction to independent single women: The behavior of a *fictional character* was deemed sufficiently influential and alarming to warrant the attention and criticism of the *Vice President* of our country!

Two of the most noted and controversial female characters of the past decade, *Thelma and Louise,* paid an even higher price than vice-presidential censure for their revolt from the mold of accepted female roles. In this twentieth-century version of Butch Cassidy and the Sundance Kid, to the delight of their female audiences, Thelma and Louise blazed a trail towards independence, leaving behind constricted lives and abusive men, actively pursuing both revenge and adventure. And yet, at the end of the film, unlike Butch and Sundance, who clearly had a chance to survive their plunge into a canyon, Thelma and Louise faced the Grand Canyon. Escape was out of the question. As women, they were forced to choose between imprisonment and suicide. This cautionary tale makes it painfully clear that women who cut loose from conventional roles are angry women who are a great risk to themselves and others. If women pursue independence and autonomy, their rage will lead them into nothing but trouble. Fish better swim. . . .

Some television shows and movies depicting happy single women, or women in the process of escaping the constraints of marital roles, encountered a different response than *Thelma and Louise,* which at least attracted a large audience. These shows and movies paid the price of obscurity, going largely unnoticed by mainstream culture or unrewarded in the film industry. One of the stars of television's *Designing Women,* a series based on the lives of four women on their own, wryly noted that, although their show had maintained high ratings for years and dealt with a full range of women's issues from inequality to sexual harassment, the only Emmy the show ever won went to the casts' hairdresser. The film *Shirley Valentine,* an upbeat and funny tale about a middle-aged woman striking out on her own, received little, if any, promotion or recognition, compared to films like *Fatal Attraction* and *The Hand That Rocks the Cradle.* A similar fate befell an endearing and profound movie called *Leaving Normal,* which told the story of two women who chose to leave neglectful and abusive relationships with men and live together, quasi-adopting two adolescent boys to form a slightly bizarre but nurturing family.

BEING SINGLE *AND* IN MIDLIFE: A DOUBLE BURDEN

While single women over the age of forty may be considered less of a threat to society, the overall negative bias against them nevertheless increases as they age. Single women past the age of thirty are frequently confronted with the question, "Why aren't you married?"—a thinly veiled version of the question, "What's a nice girl like you doing in a place like this?" As midlife approaches, the question changes ever so slightly but ever so significantly to, "Why didn't you ever marry (or remarry)?", clearly implying that the woman is now "over the hill" and it is simply too late. Even as the question is asked, the unfortunate woman put on the spot in this way can look into the inquirer's eyes and watch the theories race by like the fruit spinning in a nickel slot machine: Which tragic flaw prevented her from being CHO-SEN? If she isn't too plain, too fat, too bossy, or too loud, then the unfortunate quality must be less observable—perhaps she is too demanding, too selfish, too sexually unreceptive, too sexually receptive, or too choosy. If she was once married, they speculate, no doubt she was an impossible or at least disappointing partner who could not hold onto her man.

Some people put a little more effort into coming up with an explanation, usually based on a pop psychology theory that accounts for the inability of the woman to get or stay married. Her parents must have had an unhappy marriage, which left her unable to create a good marriage herself. Maybe she was damaged by some trauma or loss in childhood and is now incapable of experiencing sustained intimacy and commitment. Perhaps she is one of those women who frittered away her marriageable years pursuing an unfeminine career; in that case, she made her own bed and now she should lie in it, quietly. Whatever the explanation, the inquirer clearly communicates that the woman in question is both odd and hopeless because, at midlife, she is simply the victim of her own aging body, undesirable appearance, "dysfunctional" childhood, or dubious priorities.

As long as women are young, appear busy with the task of looking for a spouse (and, of course, are viewed as having some hope of finding one), they are accepted and even "helped" by friends and acquaintances who parade an array of fix-ups past their bewildered eyes. Once women are past thirty, their single status becomes suspect. Once they are past thirty-five, their single-hood is regarded as a chronic and depressing problem; by age forty, friends have stopped offering to fix them up, family members have stopped asking questions about who they are dating, and employers feel free to ask them to work late, since they clearly have no social life or family demanding their presence and attention.

This message that single women in midlife have little chance of marriage or remarriage, and therefore little chance of the slightest hint of true happiness, was strongly reinforced during the late eighties by the now infamous Harvard-Yale marriage study. Although a more complete examination of the facts revealed that the research design was seriously flawed and the conclusions grossly exaggerated, the so-called "findings" were cited and then sensationalized almost beyond recognition. *Newsweek* magazine went so far as to point out to midlife single women that they had a better chance of being attacked by a terrorist than of finding a mate. Other media published reports recommending cities to which "older" single women could move to maximize their dwindling chances of marriage.

AGING IN TELEVISION AND FILM

Television and movies present the same dark view of women who are aging. For example, Shelley from *Northern Exposure* expresses the views held by many as she warns Maggie about her upcoming thirtieth birthday. Shelly, who is dreading turning twenty-one, cannot believe that Maggie is neither depressed nor demoralized by the impending disaster of hitting "the big 3-0." When Maggie insists that she is truly looking forward to her thirties and forties, Shelly proceeds to give her a detailed account of her imminent physical decline:

> Yeah but thirty! You get crows feet and chicken chin and your nips start heading south and your bum turns to yogurt. And the competition's coming up and gaining on you, quick. Who's going to look at a chick who's twenty-four with all these teenage mall flies strutting their bootie and talking their trash. You'd think they'd invented spandex.

When one of the show's middle-aged male characters tries to reassure Maggie that thirty is "a slice of pie," Shelly is quick to remind him: "She's only got ten more years to forty! Then what's she going to do?"

The movie *Death Becomes Her* also presents another message about women and aging. In one of the opening scenes, beautiful Meryl Streep moans "Wrinkled, wrinkled little star," while she obsessively examines her face in a mirror. Later, both she and Goldie Hawn trade their souls, appropriately symbolized in our society by a check for a large sum of money, for vials from the Fountain of Youth. This elixir provides physical beauty and life everlasting, but does this pair little good because in their spiteful anger they continue to try to destroy each other. They may have eternal life, but they are trapped forever in a struggle with one another inside their battered, semi-dismembered bodies. Through their absurd antics, the film pokes fun at women's obsession with their physical appearance and their attempts to deny the process of aging. The only character who manages midlife gracefully is the man they fight over, played by Bruce Willis. Willis finds "real" immortality by refusing the artificial elixir of youth in favor of another one, that is, marrying a much younger woman, who bears him six lovely children—an option all the women in the audience are painfully aware is not open to them. The film *never* presents even a glimmer of hope that a woman could make it through midlife with her body, not to mention her integrity, intact.

The culture's double standard of aging portrayed in movies like *Death Becomes Her* is well summarized by the familiar saying: "A man is as old as he feels, but a woman is as old as she looks." It is not surprising that many women approach midlife with some degree of dread. They know what to expect. They have seen advertising images implying that wrinkles add character to the faces of men, while signaling the need for Oil of Olay (or even plastic surgery) for women. As Michelle Pfeiffer pointed out during an interview with Barbara Walters, Sean Connery may be labeled the sexiest man in America at the age of sixty but she is highly unlikely to receive such an accolade in her sixth decade. A woman's increasing age is treated by the media as a serious liability, something shameful she should try to hide. In a society in which women are primarily valued in the roles of wife, mother, ornament, or possession, few women past the age of forty have found a completely comfortable way of dealing with the issue of their age. As Janet Harris said, "Reared as we were in a youth-and-beauty-oriented society, we measured ourselves by our ornamental value." It is no secret to women that men value youth and physical attractiveness in their selection of mates. They have repeatedly been told that a woman's looks have a major impact on her fate. If they are young and beautiful, the world is theirs. If not, too bad. As Warren Beatty once said, "My notion of a wife at forty is that a man should be able to change her like a bank note for two twenties."

Our society's rejection of single women is sharpest at midlife. The message to midlife single women is that their fading desirability will close off one of their two primary routes to fulfillment, and if they have never had children, their biological clocks will soon cut off the other. Even if they have had children early in life, they are about to find their nests empty. Because they have lost or squandered their chances to find an eligible suitor, because they either have failed to bear and raise children or have completed this life task, their only possible remaining pleasure might be that of spoiling their grandchildren, providing that they were fortunate enough to have children in the first place. They are, in the mirror society holds up to them, laboring under the weight of a double burden. They must cope not only with the negative stereotype of the single woman as defective, depressed, and desperate, but also with the stereotype of the middle-aged woman as undesirable and useless. In short, being middle-aged and single in our society has been viewed as similar to, and about as desirable as, having a degenerative disease.

CONFRONTING THE SELF-FULFILLING PROPHECY

Through the myths it has spawned, the marriage and motherhood mandate continues to cast a long shadow over women and particularly those in mid-life, standing in the way of their efforts to create satisfying lives of their own design. The strongest of women still experience difficulty freeing themselves from the grip of this mandate. Poet, author, and feminist Tillie Olsen discusses her own struggle to begin to write after many years as a full-time wife and mother:

> The habits of a lifetime when everything else had to come before writing are not easily broken, even when circumstances now often make it possible for the writing to be first; habits of years: response to others, distractibility, responsibility for daily matters, stay with you, mark you, become you.

Even those women who become, as Gloria Steinem phrased it, the equiv-alent of the man they once wanted to marry—successful, economically se-cure, and socially mobile—find themselves struggling with the power of these covert and insidious myths. If seen and heard often enough, these myths can function as compelling prescriptions, causing satisfied single women to doubt the validity of their own experiences. Looking into soci-ety's mirror, they find their happiness distorted or simply invisible. Kelly, a never-married forty-three-year-old woman, struggles to express this self-fulfilling prophecy:

> Many people think women in my situation are unhappy and plodding through life. Well, maybe society is *telling* them that they're plodding. But if society stopped trying to convince them that they were plod-ding, perhaps they would feel differently.

Even if single women are able to hold onto the feeling that their happiness does, in fact, exist, the media tells them that it is a fleeting and momentary happiness, a temporary fluke that will quickly fade as the years slip by. Women who continue to insist that their life satisfaction is real and permanent are either dismissed or labeled as odd, deviant, and not "real" women. Psychologist Rosalind Barnett, in the book *Lifeprints* with Grace Baruch and Caryl Rivers, explains what she has observed in her clinical practice:

> Many single women are upset, not because they feel miserable without a man, but because they don't! What does it say about their femininity, they wonder, that their lives are going well without a permanent intimate relationship? Is there something wrong with them? Are they less than complete women?

Moreover, if single women do experience any discontentment or unhappiness in their lives, they are made to feel it is a direct result of their unmarried status. Clearly, they are unhappy because they are unmarried. Rarely is it suggested that some occasional unhappiness might be a normal part of living that even married women experience from time to time. Certainly it is never suggested that their unhappiness might stem, in part, from the hostile climate our culture creates for them, based solely on their marital status. Instead, single women are told there is one remedy to any feelings of unhappiness they may face: marriage.

The negative cultural images spawned by the marriage and motherhood mandate can affect not only women's feelings about themselves, but also their feelings about their relationships with men. Women may assume that they must be pliable, deferential, and ever accommodating in order to increase their chances of snaring a member of the ever shrinking pool of eligible bachelors. There is no shortage of books and articles available to help women learn these lessons, if they haven't come by them already. In an interview in *Harper's Bazaar*, Helen Gurley Brown advises single women what they must do, "You must be a living doll. If you want to enchant a man and eventually marry him, you are good to him, easy with him, adorable to be around. The difficult, neurotic creature loses men. They may enjoy her in bed, but they don't marry her." The interviewer continues:

> [Men] do marry the woman who researches their lives, asks them about their success and well-being and then listens to their answers with "total concentration" . . . they do not, Brown says emphatically,

marry the woman who constantly pushes, whines, nags, or brings up the subject of matrimony first.

Another article, in *Ebony* magazine, entitled "25 Ways to Find a Good Man," advises women to increase their chances of "catching" a man by wearing skirts, keeping a clean house, and learning to cook:

[Men] want to see legs, body and hair. Don't hide them . . . a man looking for a wife certainly doesn't want a woman who can keep house no better than he can. . . . With the availability of microwave cooking, gourmet frozen foods, and other convenient edibles, many men feel there is no excuse for a woman not being able to produce a good meal.

Most importantly, however, this article advises women to learn to be less "demanding" in their relationships with men. "You are not a 'perfect' woman," the author chides, "so why expect to find a flawless man?" From these types of articles as well as from television, movies, and advertisements, women learn that they should not have even semi-high expectations of the men in their lives; it is not only unwise, but arrogant, to do so. It is a woman's job to please and accommodate, and a man's job to simply be the prize. There are few instructions to women about how to get *their* needs met, or how to keep and value a sense of self in their relationships. It seems incredible that our popular culture is still promoting the same role for women about which Virginia Woolf wrote in 1929 in *A Room of One's Own:* "Women have served all these centuries as looking-glasses possessing the magic and delicious power of reflecting the figure of a man at twice its natural size." Try to imagine anyone publishing an article on twenty-five ways to find a good woman in *Gentleman's Quarterly* or even *Playboy.*

By continuing to live under the tyranny of these myths, single women may worry that their lives are deficient and incomplete simply because they are unmarried. Taking to heart the barrage of cultural messages about their inadequacies, they may end up feeling guilty about and ashamed of their "abnormal state." Never-married women may search their backgrounds and psyches for reasons explaining why they were unable to commit to a "real" relationship, however deep and lasting their friendships or relationships with lovers may be. Divorced women may carry the belief that their shortcomings alone caused the dissolution of their marriages. As Sandi explains, "When I first got divorced, I felt embarrassed. I somehow felt as if I were wearing a mark of failure." Sandi's feelings are also reflected in the words of Ruth, who describes the shame she experienced when her alcoholic husband left her for a younger woman: "I felt like a failure. If I had only done it right somehow. I felt like I wasn't good enough." Both divorced and never-married women may dismiss potentially satisfying aspects of their lives—work, friends, personal interests—as insignificant simply because they are not married. Little by little, they may begin to compromise their expectations and standards, even considering marriage to men whom they find neither attractive nor interesting—truly a recipe for disaster.

The dire messages to single women also affect their married sisters. While single women are encouraged to make whatever accommodations are necessary to get married, married women are encouraged to make whatever accommodations are necessary to hold onto their coveted status. They are urged to count their blessings, lower their expectations, and find ways to make their ailing marriages work. Lacking supportive messages and models, many married women find they are unable to push for change in their relationships or leave hopeless situations. In her provocative book on women and depression, Dana Crowley Jack describes the thorny trap that is created for women:

> A woman who believes that she cannot make it on her own does not challenge the status quo of her unsatisfactory relationship. She does not say: "This is how I feel and these things have to change or I will leave." She does not test whether her partner is willing to change. Instead, she hides her feelings behind false compliance.

Images of single women as desperate and depressed have successfully persuaded married women that anything would be better than going through life on their own. As a result, married women may stay in marriages that are unrewarding, abusive, or without discernible signs of life; they may feel unable to negotiate a better balance in their relationships; they may bend over backwards to save their marriages, even at the cost of their own integrity—simply out of fear of the dreaded condition of BEING SINGLE. The sad thing is that, in so doing, they cheat themselves *and* their partners by being less than genuine and by not realizing their own potential.

Considering the continuing power of the marriage and motherhood mandate and its myths, it may seem impossible for any single woman to get her life off the ground, much less make it soar. But many single women have surprised even themselves by using serendipitous opportunities to take their lives into their own hands, redefining what is important to them and creating their own happiness. Their journeys towards more satisfying lives began with making a profound change in their attitudes towards themselves and their lives, a process we call "giving up the dream."

Journeys without a Map

Chapter 5

Giving Up the Dream

The need for change bulldozed a road down the center of my mind.

—*Maya Angelou*

My sister and I sat in the theater at the end of *Cinderella* with tears streaming down our faces because we had believed in that story at one point in our lives and, oh, the truth is *brutal*.

—*Miriam*

Laura, a fifty-two-year-old woman, plaintively expressed the bitter sense of betrayal experienced by women who "bought" the marriage and motherhood mandate but couldn't make it work:

Marriage was HARD! And I worked so hard at it. And I'm angry that I didn't live HAPPILY ever after like THEY promised. I did EVERY-THING that THEY said I SHOULD do . . . I worked so hard at it!

Laura did, indeed, work hard at making her marriage work. She nurtured her husband and three sons, following the two Cardinal Rules for the preservation of marriage as she understood them: "Always look pretty when your husband comes home from work," and "Be loving!" As simplistic and superficial as these rules may seem when spelled out so plainly, they nonetheless gave meaning, security, direction, and predictability to life for generations of women. Laura, like many other women, was stunned, distressed, and profoundly confused when her marriage dissolved, unraveling her life plan. But she gamely pressed ahead trying anew to find the dream, going through several serious relationships with men—relationships in which she was promised a marriage that never happened, no matter how hard she worked to hold up her end of the bargain. Laura recently experienced yet another crushing disappointment when the man she thought she was going to marry abruptly terminated their relationship to date a younger woman. Severely depressed but determined to do something different with her life, Laura tentatively began her journey down the road to *giving up the dream*.

All women who are single for any significant part of their adult lives have to confront what Laura calls "The Dream"—the happily-ever-after life promised by the fairy tales beloved by most little girls. The Dream, of course, is the mandate all dressed up in the guise of romance. While the details of this blueprint for happiness have changed from generation to generation, The Dream itself has remained central for women—and for good reason. Hopes and dreams are as important to life as food and water, and it is from fairy tales and other dreamy stories of success, approval, and even adulation that we acquire the raw material for our aspirations.

In formulating their dreams, few young women focus on the advantages and possibilities inherent in being single. Being single and female has rarely been the stuff of which dreams or fairy tales are made. It is difficult to imagine Ariel, the little mermaid, trading her voice for a scholarship to medical school, or Cinderella being transformed by the chance to travel abroad. Young women cherish The Dream because it is romantic and exciting, and because they have been systematically conditioned to believe that romance is the essential spice of a good life. They also cherish The Dream because it was the path their parents encouraged them to follow. Most parents have dreams for their daughters, and these dreams usually begin and end with "happily ever after." If a woman chooses to abandon part of The Dream—if she seeks "happily ever after" minus the man—or even if she is forced to abandon it due to divorce or to being widowed, she is deluged with feelings of guilt and failure over disappointing her family. Leslie, for example, whose husband abandoned her and their infant son, was considered a failure by her family. "I came from a family in which nobody in our history, according to my mother, had ever been divorced. It didn't matter that *he* left *us*. They saw my divorce as a very evil thing." Morgan, who left her husband and never remarried, reports that before her mother died she whispered, "I don't want to die until I know there's someone to take care of you. *If I had it to do over again, I'd raise you to be more dependent.*"

The Dream's allure can be found not only in its promise of romance, not only in its protection against social censure, but also in its "guarantee" of some real and lasting benefits. Central to The Dream is the intoxicating lure of being "in love"—which can be the most exciting, expansive, and exhilarating flying any woman ever experiences. Certainly, having a loving relationship is a highly desirable state for anyone, male or female. In addition, The Dream is grounded in the primary biological and psychological drives for mating and parenting (which, until recently, have been reserved for those who are married). With enough economic and social support, The Dream can deliver a great deal of what it promises. Men and women who are able to create and sustain fulfilling marriages are, in general, happy and satisfied. The big *but* is that the number of men and women who are able to live The Dream over a long period of time is much lower than has been generally acknowledged. Therefore, despite the fact that few women intend to live their lives singly, an increasing number are finding themselves on their own at midlife—and are learning to like it.

There are many paths that women take to reach midlife on their own. Yet, regardless of the particular path, each woman eventually confronts the choice to either relinquish the aspirations she was taught to revere as a child or to hang onto them and feel deprived and depressed. Giving up The Dream requires that women give up the fairy-tale promise of "happily ever after," a truly painful rite of passage. Dreams, after all, are always harder to give up than reality, which has its thorns and prickles even when you are the heroine of the tale. (Consider the lives of our modern day princesses, Di and Fergie.) So women adjust as best they can to the actualities of their situations, but leaving The Dream behind altogether, even perhaps temporarily, is quite another feat. Because there have never been acceptable alternative paths for women, giving up The Dream can feel like stepping into an abyss.

LEARNING TO FLY: AN AFFIRMATION OF SELF

Seventy-year-old Lila made it crystal clear to us why giving up The Dream is such a crucial developmental task for single women. She told us she had given up on "happily ever after" after her second husband left her, not because she thought marriage was hopeless but because she wanted to concentrate on enjoying her life. After her divorce she surveyed all the men who might be interested *in her* and interesting *to her,* and noted with some surprise that they were old enough to be at significant risk of getting sick and needing care. A wiry and energetic woman herself, despite a heart attack and a bout with cancer, she decided that she would rather give up the idea of growing old with someone than run the risk of having to put aside her dreams to care for a sick husband. She is now busy traveling to the many places she had always dreamed of seeing but couldn't in her earlier years because she was too busy raising children and keeping house. Her discovery was that *giving up The Dream is not acceptance of deprivation but rather an affirmation of the self.* Lila recognized that there are choices and trade-offs in life, and that she had to relinquish the cherished notion of growing old with someone in order to pursue another sort of dream. The results for her have been spectacular. She is so pleased with her life now that her attitude is, "Why didn't I think of this earlier?" Even now, however, Lila does not rule out marriage as a possibility. After all, in her travels she could meet someone as energetic and full of life as she is. She tells us that what she really let go of was the idea that being married was the only way she could be happy, or even the best way for her to live.

The more we thought about Lila, the more it appeared obvious that the women we interviewed who had learned to fly solo had gone through a similar process of reevaluating what they needed to be happy. Although they often were not aware of this reevaluation process and didn't speak of it in those terms, clearly most of them decided at some point to stop waiting for their prince and take charge of their lives. Their stories show that, while there is always sadness in giving up any valued dream, there is also a special kind of joy, an opening of possibilities for the self. Having leaped or been pushed into the abyss, these women discovered that *they could fly.*

PRINCE WHO?
OWNING OUR CHOICES

Single women who have successfully given up The Dream report that a crucial step was recognizing that they had been making choices all along that have contributed to their remaining single. Even if it was only making the choice *not* to marry a man with a particular set of problems, they recognized that making such a decision constituted a declaration to themselves that they were not willing to accept marriage on absolutely any terms. Many women initially find it hard to acknowledge, even to themselves, the significance of the choices they have made. Some secretly fear that there is something wrong or even shamefully unnatural about them because of their ambivalence toward pursuing The Dream. They hide their satisfaction with being single behind the clichéd complaint that "all the good men are either gay or married." They continue to cling to The Dream consciously, even while taking steps toward becoming more psychologically and financially independent than traditional marital contracts have allowed.

For single women, the decision to endorse and enjoy being single is so radical that it is often only seventy-year-old women like Lila who are able to acknowledge openly that they have made such a decision. Sooner or later, however, single women begin to recognize that they have always been making choices, no matter how much they thought they were just filling up their time until the prince arrived. They realize that they are in a better position to feel good about their lives if they can see that they have, in fact, chosen a path that is well suited to them, rather than having been forced to walk it against their will. One of the authors, Carol, had the following experience when she was thirty-eight years old.

I remember sitting in a sidewalk cafe in a small town on the Amalfi coast in the south of Italy with a friend of mine. I was bemoaning the fact that there were no more "good men" out there; they were either married or gay, too passive or too domineering. My friend asked, "What would you be willing to give up to be married? What would you give up to be in a full-time, permanently committed relationship?" I can remember looking at him, utterly startled by his question. *Give up?* It never entered my mind that I would have to give up anything. Suddenly, it was like a kaleidoscope had turned and all of the pieces fell into a completely new and more coherent picture. Of course, I would have to give something up—but I had never acknowledged it. After that revelation, I began to see that I was not a victim of fate, bad luck, or anything else. I had *chosen* my path and I was *still* choosing it.

In retrospect, I'm not totally sure I know why I chose not to marry—I certainly had my chances. I think I instinctively knew marriage would not be good for me. I knew somehow that I would lose myself in the relationship, partly because, in those days, I had too much of a desire to please, too great a tendency to accommodate, too little ability to handle conflict and still stay intimate. I found it too easy to sense what a man wanted and give it to him, so the two of us would end up being *him*. I always found it hard to be what I thought was a "good partner" and not lose myself.

Carol suddenly became conscious of which goals she was pursing and which ones she was avoiding. She recognized that she had been making choices all along. She had done far more than merely *avoid* marriage out of fear of losing herself through over-accommodation. She had spent far more time and energy developing a successful professional career than she had ever spent cultivating a relationship that might lead to marriage. She had chosen to work hard when she could have been playing; she had chosen to give up troublesome relationships but not troublesome jobs. *She had chosen the set of problems she was willing to accept.*

The whole question of choice is a complex one, pondered for centuries by philosophers. To what extent is anyone really free to make choices in life? From a straightforward, pragmatic point of view, it would appear that we have only so much control over certain aspects of our lives; the rest is apparently controlled by forces greater than ourselves, commonly thought of as luck, fate, or God. If a woman is looking for a romantic relationship, she cannot control whether she will meet a man who fits her needs exactly: one who is sexually attractive to her, a good match in terms of values, interests, and education, and who will allow her autonomy and freedom while still providing her with a safe, stable, loving relationship. If a woman yearns for fame and fortune, she cannot control what job opportunities open up at precisely the time she needs them, or whether or not she is chosen for the scholarship she needs to pursue her educational dream. Nonetheless, women can exercise control over the goals and attitudes that shape their actions; where they concentrate their time and energy; and how prepared they will be for opportunities, should they arise. Women can decide whether they want to be married badly enough to go out of their way to try to meet an acceptable man; whether they are willing to do what is necessary to assist fate, be it attending parties alone or putting an ad in the personals. They can decide whether being married is important enough to make whatever concessions may be required. They can also decide whether being successful is worth the time and energy involved, or whether they would rather spend their time raising children, gardening, traveling, helping other people, or whatever. As a friend of ours is fond of saying, "You cannot prevent the birds of sorrow from flying over your head, but you can prevent them from building a nest in your hair." In other words, there *are* some things women can control. They *do* have the freedom to act on opportunities and to make choices.

LOOKING BACK AT SMALL STEPS

Once a woman has recognized that she is always making choices for which she is responsible, she is ready to begin the process of giving up The Dream. The particular *steps* of this process will vary from woman to woman. There is no preordained formula, no "seven steps" to a happier singlehood. Women's experiences differ depending on whether they have always been single or, if they have been married, whether they chose to leave their marriages or were divorced against their will. For women who have never been married, it is rarely a case of never having had the chance to marry. Rather, as Carol recounted, it is more a process that starts as an underground movement, as steps *away from* the mandate, an acting on motives as yet unconscious. For women who have been divorced against their will or felt compelled to leave abusive or intolerable husbands, the process also involves recovering from the traumas suffered before any real choices about life direction can be made. For women who chose to leave their marriages, some aspects of the transition are typically made while they are still married—sometimes on such an unconscious level that, once divorced, they are surprised to find that they feel relieved and have little or no interest in remarrying.

The women we interviewed all had very different experiences with this major developmental step. A few seem to have shed their childhood fantasies about "happily ever after" relatively effortlessly, while others tried again and again to make them work. For most, the passage from one state of mind to another was rarely a smooth one. As Adrienne Rich has observed, "The awakening of consciousness is not like the crossing of a frontier—one step and you are in another country." Giving up The Dream is not something one does on a sunny afternoon after an epiphany, such as Carol described. In truth, Carol's epiphany was just one more step among many she had already taken, and was more a first-time acknowledgment of the path she had traveled for some time rather than a turning point in her life. Lydia, a thirty-eight-year-old divorced woman, describes how giving up The Dream was a gradual process for her as well:

This is a very vivid memory. My anniversary was January 31 and I was sitting in my house thinking, "Brace yourself, your anniversary is coming this week." And then the day it came, I can actually remember going into the fetal position in the corner and just sobbing. In the sobbing was all my anger, all my fears. I was really feeling sorry for myself. It was like, "Look what this man did to me, look at what the world did to me. My life is nowhere. I'm almost thirty years old and I don't even know who I am."

Then I remember the next year and I didn't sit in the corner. Then the following year, the anniversary came and I missed it! I didn't even know it! I said to myself, "Whoa, you're getting better!" It was not a bright light or anything spectacular. Just the quiet knowledge that I had grown.

No one we interviewed described awakening one morning to declare herself "free at last" (although, endorsing being single is radical enough to qualify as a breakthrough in civil rights for women). Even those who had been in bad marriages experienced a great deal of ambivalence, a reluctance to give up the sweet and promising if unrealistic aspects of The Dream. And no one equated giving up The Dream with taking a vow to never marry or remarry. Instead of marking a moment in which The Dream died, women tended to talk about how unexpectedly content they began to feel. Louise voiced this well:

I'm happier now than I've ever been in my life. I thought I was very happy when my husband and my sons and I were all here, and everything was going well, but you see, I have matured since then.

The maturation Louise notes is not a rejection of men, but rather an affirmation of her capacity to create what she needs to find satisfaction in her life. It is the satisfaction that Lila talked about, the pleasure of taking steps towards oneself, not away from others. It is a flexible position that includes an understanding that things could change; The Dream could reappear in a more realistic form and again become a part of their lives. *But their happiness does not depend on it.*

Chapter 6

~•

No More Waiting for the Prince:
Tales of the Never Married

When people ask me how we've lived past one hundred, I say, "Honey, we never married. We never had husbands to worry us to death."
—Bessie Delaney, age 101, referring to herself and her sister, Sadie, age 103

Some luck lies in not getting what you thought you wanted, but getting what you have, which once you have it, you may be smart enough to see that it is what you would have wanted had you known.
—Garrison Keillor

Of all the old maid's blessings, the greatest is carte blanche. Spinsterhood is powerful; once a woman is called "that crazy old maid" she can get away with anything.
—Florence King

W omen who have never been married have had one hurdle to leap which they do not share with their divorced or widowed sisters: the worry that they are thought of as unlovable or as failures. For them, giving up The Dream involves an element of overcoming the fear of how they might be judged. As a result, many continue to act as if they are pursuing The Dream long after they have given it up as a serious goal. Many women commented that, had it not become so much easier to be single in the last two decades, they probably would not have had the courage to keep flying solo.

SHANNON'S STORY: OVERCOMING THE FEAR

Like many never-married women, Shannon began her adult years acutely conscious of the stigma of remaining single. She had to overcome the fear of seeming "less than" before she was able to perceive being single as anything but second rate. But ever since adolescence she had been taking small steps that eventually helped her endorse being single, steps away from dependency and towards autonomy and self-sufficiency. She told us that the foundation for these moves was established in childhood, as she was encouraged to become something other than the traditional wife and mother. Shannon's mother died suddenly when Shannon was four years old. Soon after, her father remarried a much younger woman with whom Shannon never really bonded. From an early age, Shannon learned to rely primarily on herself. She explains, "I didn't have anybody remotely taking care of me, so I ended up developing the independent part of my spirit a lot." This independence was reinforced by Shannon's early identification with the ways in which her relatives described her mother. In their memory, her mother was "a strong, bright, self-determined fighter who was extremely outspoken and who believed in fairness." Shannon also identified with her father, whom she describes as "strong and independent." He used to tell her that her older sister was "really going to be a great mother," adding, "but you're smart, you can do anything you want."

Unfortunately, when it was time for Shannon to go to college, she found her father had saved no money for her education and, in fact, was opposed to her leaving home, expecting her to content herself with going to a local junior college. Instead, Shannon took the first of many steps to move away from accommodation and towards autonomy and independence; she fought for the right to go to the state university, and to do so, paid her own way. She was rewarded when she got to college:

> I was just in heaven. I loved it. I adored it. I loved the freedom. I loved the independence. I was really poor and that was stressful, but I had my own life. I could study Shakespeare, I could learn and nobody could control me anymore. So there was something exciting about being on this adventure by myself.

Although at that age Shannon probably had little understanding of what the terms *self-definition* and *autonomy* meant, her decision represented an intuitive shift in that direction; and the satisfaction she felt reinforced her journey in the pursuit of those goals.

Once in college, Shannon struggled to define a direction for her life. Her difficulties were typical of those experienced by many women at that time. Finding a job in the business world in some capacity other than as a secretary or bank teller was so difficult that many women married in part to avoid the struggle of starting a career that would have a chance of succeeding. Shannon had hoped to dodge the business world by becoming a college professor, a strategy that coincided nicely with her plan to marry the man in her life at that time, who was also interested in an academic career. Her grand vision of the future broke down as she experienced a series of disappointments. Amidst the social upheavals of the sixties and seventies, Shannon witnessed many of her role models leaving their academic careers. Also, she became disillusioned with her boyfriend's attitudes: "Clearly, we both assumed that we would have careers. We met totally as peers, but I remember somehow thinking that my role was to back him up." With the internal and external support for her decision to enter the academic world crumbling, Shannon took a series of practical, short-term steps that promoted her independence and gave her a sense of direction. She broke up with her boyfriend, moved to New York with her sister who was getting a divorce, and after a six-month stint in a terrible job, found a position in the publishing industry that made use of her academic background. She has been happy and successful in her career ever since.

Shannon describes herself as liking men and having many close male friends, most of whom are married. Like many of the women we interviewed, she originally had no intention of staying single for life. She says, "Certainly in my twenties and thirties, I just assumed marriage was around the corner." When we asked her why she did not marry during all those years of dating, Shannon emphasized the influence of the era in which she came of age:

I always assumed I would get married, but I was a teenager when the women's movement was starting, and I didn't feel like it was my *job* to get married. It was assumed that I would get married, but I wasn't sent to college to get a man like women who were five years older than I were. I didn't ever feel I had that thrown at me. It felt like I went to college to get an education and try to find some kind of career. It wasn't so clear how to do the career part.

Shannon also clearly expressed an unwillingness to compromise her sense of what a marriage should be like:

> I haven't married because I never met anybody who really stimulated me and added something to my life. I have felt unsatisfied, not fulfilled in the connections I have made. I have a great appreciation for men, but I've never met a single man who I felt was my soul mate—or at least strong enough, bright enough, and interesting enough to engage me. That's been a disappointment to me most of my life.

Despite the clarity she now has, during her twenties and thirties Shannon continued to hold onto The Dream of marriage and motherhood as essential to make her life complete. She was shocked and dismayed to find herself approaching forty, still unmarried. With the goal of finding someone to marry while she could still have children, she placed an ad in the personals. Shannon met a man, Erik, whom she liked very much, but ultimately she ended the relationship because Erik could not accept the importance she placed on her relationships with her many friends. He was particularly jealous of the relationship she had with one very close female friend. Shannon questioned the significance of his demand that she sacrifice this relationship. Was her friendship with this one person the first of many compromises she would have to make to keep him happy? She perceived her autonomy as being threatened:

> He wasn't worth the sacrifices. You know, it sounded reasonable. All he was saying was end one friendship, but it was really like cutting my heart out. So I ended his and my relationship instead and I have never had regrets, even though I certainly grieved the loss.

Shannon's relationship with Erik was important in that it allowed her to relinquish the romantic myth of marriage. She came to see that "happily ever after" is never as simple as the fairy tales make it seem and that having even the "best" of relationships is not without some cost:

> I had so built up the fantasy of what life would be like when I met somebody I wanted to be with. My relationship with Erik sort of blew the myth of what it is to be with somebody. When I saw that the cost was too great, I was able to let it go and feel whole and not feel desperate to meet somebody. It felt like something was healed in the

process of that relationship and being able to let it go. Today, I don't have as much of an illusion that getting married would make me happy.

Another liberating aspect of her relationship with Erik was having the experience of a man really wanting to marry her. She felt that, by virtue of having been asked—in fact, pressured to marry—she had passed the invisible test that all women must take, that of being woman enough to BE CHOSEN. She felt as if she had "passed through the eye of the needle. I got into 'the club' and I was judged to be normal because somebody really wanted to marry me." It may seem incredible that even women who are accomplished and happy with their independence care as much as they do about what the invisible "they" think. The stigma involved in being unmarried has been so powerful that, in order to be happy single, women have to find some way of getting over the feeling of being fundamentally flawed. Some conquer the stigma of their status, like Shannon, by getting close enough to marriage to feel they have earned the social credit that certifies them as a *real woman*. Others move past the point where they care what others think; in fact, had Shannon not received a proposal, she eventually might well have stopped caring.

At forty-two, Shannon acknowledges that being single is not her preferred choice. All things being equal, she would love to have a partner with whom to share her life. However, she is also confident that she can be happy on her own. Being single is no longer tainted by a sense of hopelessness or shame. She has developed a highly successful career, has cultivated a strong circle of friends, has remodeled an old house into a beautiful home. She is beginning to travel around the world to the many places she has always wanted to see. She says with a smile, "I'm proud of my capacity to have a rich life without a mate."

MEGAN'S STORY: THE CONSERVATION OF SELF

Many of the never-married women we interviewed shared Shannon's experience: They never consciously struggled to give up The Dream until they approached forty and saw their chances to have children begin to disappear. Others report that they wrestled with the issue most of their adult lives but were only able to come to peace with it as they entered midlife. Megan, for instance, has thought about the pros and cons of marriage since adolescence. From an early age, she made choices based on what she perceived as the compromises inevitably involved in maintaining a close, committed relationship with a man. As she approached midlife, however, Megan began to think about these choices in a new light, in ways that allowed her to commit to a life on her own with a greater sense of pride and enthusiasm.

Megan inherited a vision of independent thought and social responsibility from her great-grandmother, who was a member of the socialist Fabian Society in England. As the story goes, this great-grandmother had to be talked into marrying a fellow Fabian by no less an influential man than George Bernard Shaw. She married but remained ambivalent about the decision the rest of her life. Megan believes that her own mother told her stories about her great-grandmother to nurture in her a streak of independence. To Megan, her mother never seemed to be having a very good time in her traditional roles as wife and mother. Although her mother had maids to help with Megan and her three siblings, and charity boards to occupy her time, she simply did not radiate the sense of well-being that "having it all" should have provided. With a laugh that betrays no trace of resentment, Megan says, "I don't think she was very happy as a mother. I always felt like we were preventing her from doing something more interesting than chasing after kids. She was actually happiest when we grew up and my father lost all his money and she got her real estate license and became a hot-shot broker."

Her perception of her mother as discontented left its mark on Megan. She remembers her life at home as frequently chaotic and often unhappy; she was glad to go away to boarding school when she was sixteen. At this private girls' school, Megan found her first role models of women who had something to offer society:

> In some ways, the school didn't prepare us to be anything more than interesting wives. But there was something very powerful, I think, about being with all females during those formative years. It really gave me a sense of women as having something important *inside* that was worth saving, instead of just giving it away by supporting *someone else's* career. I definitely got the message that women were important, but it wasn't clear what to do with that message.

Megan had difficulty figuring out how to prepare herself for a career that would bring her satisfaction as well as a good income. Part of the problem was her upbringing: "Growing up in an upper-middle-class family that enjoyed so much privilege for so many generations, I never saw women earning their own living." Even the women in her family who managed to maintain their integrity could do so only because they had the financial wherewithal to pursue other interests. But, again, part of the problem was simply the times. The confusion Megan experienced was shared by most of today's midlife women who tried to chart a course for themselves in the sixties and early seventies. They found themselves at sea because all the "givens"—the accepted values of the previous generation—were toppling and new ones were yet to emerge. Neither Megan's mother nor her mentors could help her plan an economically and emotionally feasible course for herself in such rapidly changing times, so she simply muddled along, making a string of decisions, one by one, which eventually began to coalesce into a satisfying life.

At boarding school Megan had discovered that she had talent as a dancer and an artist. "People were always moved by my dancing. It just shocked me because I was always sort of quiet and shy." After college she became a professional artist, becoming "moderately well known." However, like many artists, Megan was unable to support herself on art alone and had to supplement her income with a succession of "day jobs" such as waitressing and housecleaning. In her late twenties, she decided she needed more stability in her life than art could provide. She returned to school to acquire training in a profession that would provide a steady income. Today, Megan is on her way to greater financial security and is deeply fulfilled by her work. She has close relationships with her colleagues and the freedom to be creative. She has fun and finds satisfaction in helping people have better lives.

Megan's decision to change careers reflected a deepening commitment to remaining single that she has continued to build on since that time:

> In the past few months, I have realized that the choices I have made, I made for good reason. I am beginning to respect that reason. I never quite thought of it that way before. Although singlehood is supposedly a choice made by default, it's actually a choice I made at fifteen that I have kept renewing every year.

Respecting her own choices means that Megan no longer falls prey to the negative stereotypes of never-married women. At forty-one, she believes that her single life is not a sign of personal pathology, but rather the best fit for her own needs and goals. She explains, "I have a solitary temperament. I need enough time alone to think and process. It's like food to me." Megan is aware that her alliances with men, however pleasurable, have consistently presented two distinct but related problems. The first is a conflict over time and energy. She complains that she never has enough of either to support both her work and the demands of romantic entanglements. Whenever she entered a relationship, she felt a strong need, almost a compulsion, to make herself consistently available to her partner. But doing so, she then felt cheated of the time and energy she needed for her work and for participating in her community of friends. She explains her predicament, describing the men she got involved with as

> . . . very loving, but always wanting more time together, which I felt I should give. I thought, "Well, I guess I should see what it's like to be coupled." But ultimately it never worked. I would get so exhausted, trying to fit the man into my life, which always seemed fuller than his. I had created a full life for myself and there wasn't much room for the kind of intensity that occurs in the early stages of a relationship. I guess I just felt that what the man seemed to be offering me wasn't really worth it.

The alarm bells would ring early in Megan's relationships with men, signaling the arrival of her second problem, closely related to the first: that of the erosion of her identity:

> When I get involved with a man, I go into this mode that's not really me, that I don't really recognize. It's some "cultural me" that is part Sleeping Beauty and part nonsense. It's always very exciting at first, though. There is all the physical contact and someone adoring me and me adoring someone else. Then, after a while, there comes that normal stage of pulling back into yourself. I always have a hard time getting back to my priorities. I say to myself, "I've got to go back to work now. What was so important to me in my work before he came along?"

For Megan, being in a relationship awakens something in her, which she dubs paradoxically *Sleeping Beauty*—an impulse that propels her to forfeit her own priorities in order to make the man and his needs central to her existence. For Megan, this pattern has created an ongoing struggle in every relationship she has had with a man. She does not blame the men in her life.

Rather, she sees it as an inevitable clash between her need for intimacy and her need for self-expression. She does not see herself as a superwoman with an infinite capacity for juggling her own needs and those of others. She feels there simply is not enough of her—not enough time and attention and energy available—to do justice to herself *and* a relationship.

Recently, Megan tried to find a solution to this dilemma by dating a man who lived in another state, hoping that he would make fewer demands on her time. She hoped that a long-distance relationship would translate into delineations of each of their identities and priorities, allowing her the best of both worlds. But she still felt seduced by the same tug-of-war between becoming immersed in her fantasies of "happily ever after" and what she knows are her own needs and priorities:

> A man I dated was a visiting professor from Columbia University. Sleeping Beauty took over. I began thinking, "Wow, he has kids. This is great. I can be a stepmother." Then he left and went back to New York. And reality set in and I thought, "Are you kidding?"

After Megan decided to end that relationship, she thought long and hard about the compromises that any marriage and any family would demand of her and consciously decided to commit to a life on her own in a way she previously had not. Although she remains aware of the seductiveness of The Dream, of the difficulty of giving it up altogether, and of the sadness that accompanies such thoughts, she also has developed a clarity about the choices that are best for her:

> Whenever I begin a relationship with a man, I begin to try on this marriage thing, in the hopes that it's going to fit into my life by some miracle without my having to give up anything. And then when I realize what I have to give up, the whole thing falls apart. There is a sadness that I can't fit in, but I trust my inner integrity that this is the right path for me.

ELENA'S STORY: COMPELLING CHOICES

Elena gave up The Dream early in life in favor of the chance to pursue dreams of her own. She can look back in her life and see, as Megan does, that being single is not something that simply happened "to" her. Now forty, she says of her never-married status:

> I didn't *plan* not to marry. But marriage obviously wasn't a burning desire in me or I would have done it; I've had opportunities. I no longer view being single and living alone as temporary. How can I call it temporary when I've been doing it most of my adult life?

Elena does not see herself as a passive recipient of life's experiences. When we asked her if she felt she had drifted into being single at midlife, she explained that she had made a conscious choice to pursue an alternative path. With amusement she recalls:

> I remember right before I turned thirty, I actually wrote down resolutions. The last two points on the list were, "Stay single" and "Be happy."

Elena added that her decision to create a life on her own had actually begun much earlier than her thirtieth birthday. At age nineteen, she made the unconventional decision to break off her engagement to her college sweetheart and have an abortion, despite the weight of social expectations to marry and have the baby. Although this step was not a conscious step towards singlehood, Elena was even then moving intuitively towards a life that was self-defined and autonomous.

Elena's childhood experiences instilled within her a strong sense of independence and suspicions about traditional choices for women. Her ability to resist social pressure in her late teens may have been due to her somewhat unusual upbringing. Elena believes the messages she received from her parents, along with her experience of their divorce when she was twelve, mediated the power of the marriage and motherhood mandate. Both of her parents had careers in the arts and had many friends with alternative life styles. She did not get strong messages from them that her future inevitably lay in marriage. Their divorce, in fact, provided a painfully real example of how The Dream could crumble. Her mother also regularly told her, "If you don't aim for the stars, how are you going to get there?" She meant this rather literally. Elena's grandmother had experienced an unusual degree of adventure and independence in her life, marrying three times, traveling a lot, and performing as a pianist. Elena's mother was also a professional singer who went on tour to China when she was nineteen. She had a varied career and always worked—as a singer, actress, director, and producer. Her ambition for Elena was that she become an actress like herself and, at least potentially, a star—a possible but somewhat unlikely short-cut for Elena to money, power, and prestige. Her aspirations for Elena also included the college education she herself had never had.

Elena set off for college and was doing well until her mother died during her sophomore year. "When I lost her, I felt so confused. I almost dropped out." Six months after her mother died, Elena became pregnant, which in retrospect she views as a desperate act to somehow replace her mother, an unconscious desire to recreate the bond she had lost by bonding with a child of her own. But Elena also had to deal with the internal pressure she felt from her mother's aspirations for her future. Her opportunity to immediately have The Dream through marriage and motherhood would mean disrupting her college education and giving up her mother's hopes for her. She distinctly remembers the impact of her mother's dreams and of her own feelings about women who give up on themselves:

> I couldn't drop out of school and get married and have this child. Then I would have been like one of my cousins my mother had disapproved of, who had to get married because she got pregnant. You just didn't do that. "Be more, do more," was her motto. She believed it was hard to have a strong career and a family, that it was hard to have it all. And her life was evidence of this. I felt that the responsibility of raising children had actually held her back in her accomplishments.

Bereft from the loss of her mother's guidance and support, Elena was left with only her father, whom she describes as egalitarian in his approach to his children: He was not particularly ambitious for them, no matter what their sex. She did not view him as able to help her much with her decisions. The father of her unborn child, an under-employed ex-Marine, was a good man, but not one whom she had any particular desire to marry. Nevertheless, she almost did because it was the alternative her culture had conditioned her to choose:

> We went together to the abortion clinic and he turned to me after I got my blood test and said, "Let's get married." And I said, "Oh, okay." My Prince Charming had arrived and we walked out of the clinic. We walked around for a while, and then I remember that our car had a flat tire. I sat in the car like a helpless girl and watched him

change the tire, thinking to myself, "This is the man I'm going to be with for the rest of my life." I was kind of in a fog. I listened to him make all these plans, and in the three hours it took to get home, I became more and more silent and more resolved that I was going to have to go back to the abortion clinic the next weekend.

Elena realized that she could not limit her choices or her future in the ways she believed an early marriage would have:

> I was with him long enough to know that I was holding myself back in order to be with him. And that didn't make sense and I knew it wouldn't work in the long run. Even though it was hard, when I finally let go, I was on to bigger and better things for myself.

Elena made a choice that allowed her to begin to define her own direction. At the time, she saw the decision as being so influenced by her mother's desires that it was hard to claim it as her own. It was difficult to reject The Dream, even a version she felt was totally wrong for her. Also, the decision to have an abortion is often a painful one that can stay with a woman throughout her life. But, looking back from midlife, Elena realizes that, even at the age of nineteen, she was intuitively moving towards the independent life she wanted: "It is clear that a certain direction was being established when I did not take the route of marrying him."

Elena's choices certainly would not be right for every woman, but she feels they were right for her. She, in fact, chose to have another abortion ten years later because she did not want to raise a child alone and did not think a marriage with the man in question would last. Even though these are tough choices, she believes strongly that women should have such options available to them.

> If I got pregnant accidentally now, I would have a hard time having an abortion. But that is not to say I regret my abortions. I don't. I don't really have any sense of guilt about them. I made the decisions I made, and I'm glad we have the right to make them. We *should* have the right to make them.

On her own, Elena has created a life that works well for her. Shortly after college, she decided against being an actress and instead has had a varied career in the arts, including becoming a freelance writer. Her career path has not afforded her financial security at all times, but it has provided an enormous amount of personal freedom and satisfaction. She has become very successful and enjoys her work:

> I know that something is always around the corner. I've learned to appreciate my free time and I really value being able to structure my own time. When I'm working, it feels less and less like work all the time—which is great.

Elena has had many satisfying, interesting, and sexually gratifying relationships with men over the years. She has never felt compelled to marry any of them, although she has twice chosen to live with a man. Most recently, she has been involved with a man, Art, whom she describes as "warm" and "funny." Of their relationship, she says:

> We pretty much just share the present together. We goof off together, have meals together, go to the movies, have long walks. We do simple things together like go to parties, dancing or concerts. We don't really have an intellectually based relationship. It's emotionally based and a good sexual relationship. But there is actually a lot in my life that we don't share.

There have been times when Elena has entertained the idea of marrying Art, but she has always decided against it. She is not committed to being single as a cause, and certainly does not experience it as a moral imperative, but she values the many advantages of living on her own. She does not expect Art to meet all her needs:

> You don't really get it all from one person anyway. Each relationship is valid, each friendship is valid. There is nothing wrong with experiencing different people in different ways from a base of privacy and independence. It keeps relationships cleaner.

Being single gives Elena the time she needs to sustain a diverse network of friends that spans all parts of her life—with some friends even dating back to kindergarten! Being single also allows her to have friendships with other men and to enjoy the possibility of experiencing romantic adventures without having to think about being dishonest with a husband. Basically, Elena explains, being single "allows me to pick and choose how I spend my time

with integrity." While Elena acknowledges that there are trade-offs to living
a single life, she is confident that she has created a life that suits her own
needs and dreams:

> I have a trick I play, which is to ask myself, "Pretend you have a
> million dollars in your bank account. What are you going to do with
> your day? Would you do anything differently from what you're doing
> with your day now?" Pretty much, my answer is no. I think that's a
> good place to be.

Chapter 7

Broken Dreams: Women Pushed
into Lives on Their Own

I thought my life was going in this wonderful direction. I was happily married, having a baby, and I had the career I wanted. A year later, I had lost the baby, my husband, and my job. I was starting completely over. It was as if someone had picked me up and dropped me on Mars. My whole life, all my dreams were gone.

—*Nell*

Sooner or later, the way you thought your life was going to be changes radically. Navigating through that critical time is one of the most formative experiences a person can have.

—*Apryl*

Most people who get married sincerely believe they are doing so for life. A glance at today's divorce rate, however, shows us that keeping The Dream going has gotten more and more difficult as social pressure to make marriages work, no matter what, has diminished. Many married women whose lives hold predictable satisfactions suddenly find themselves "dumped off the truck" by their husbands for reasons that seem spurious and unfair. Their experience of having a marriage of many years suddenly terminated is not unlike becoming the victim of a catastrophic accident. Women wake up genuinely baffled as to what hit them, feeling a lot like the heroine of the 1977 movie, *An Unmarried Woman,* who, in shock over the sudden wreckage of her life, says, "My husband went to Bloomingdale's to buy a shirt and fell in love." Women ask themselves, "What did I do to deserve this?" as they try to pick up the pieces of their lives even while drowning in confusion, self-doubt, and grief.

Most of the women we interviewed who were left by their husbands reported an initial feeling of "spinning like a wheel out of control." Few had the time or opportunity to plan thoughtfully how they would manage by themselves. And, if they did have the time, most did not have the emotional stamina to focus on such a task in the middle of a major crisis. They found themselves traumatized by the complete destruction of their life plans, unable to function as the women they had always been brought up to be. These women had achieved The Dream and now they had to survive its obliteration. Witnessing the annihilation of a lifetime dream is an ordeal, particularly when it is accompanied by self-blame, a feeling to which women are particularly vulnerable. The initial aftershock almost always includes a period in which a woman feels either too numb or too hurt to do anything more than get through the day. It is an excruciatingly difficult time of mourning losses and allowing healing to begin.

While divorce is usually a nightmarish experience, most of the women we interviewed reported that changes in attitude and perspective, which have so enriched their lives, began when they were mired in the crises of ending their marriages. Most did not immediately grasp that living singly was even a feasible alternative. After all, marriage and feeling worthwhile as a woman are so linked in women's consciousness that, once the initial period of paralysis has lifted, it is natural to search for another "prince" who can rescue them from the humiliation of defeat and help them reconstruct The Dream. Most of the women we interviewed, however, having been left by or forced to leave one "prince," felt that looking for another would be too dangerous or just plain foolish. Instead, when they had recovered sufficiently from the trauma of the separation, they took an inventory of their feelings and their personal resources. They noticed that, although they had expected to feel devastated and despairing for the rest of their lives, they were beginning to feel okay—at times even downright good. While it took years for some women to recover, others reported actually feeling alarmed by the speed with which they had begun to enjoy their new freedom. As they exited the fog, they encountered a choice point: They could focus on feeling deprived of their marital status and all that it implied, or they could build on the autonomy that was now a part of their lives. Although the particular steps each woman took differed with her circumstances, each successful journey began with a determination not to succumb to bitterness, but instead to explore what they could do with their newfound, even if largely unasked for, freedom.

SANDI'S STORY: "I CAN DO THIS"

Many women who divorce do so before they reach midlife. For them, The Dream disintegrates before it ever really matures. Frequently, they must cope with the day-to-day responsibility of at least one child, with insufficient child support, inadequate education, and little work experience to aid them. To their surprise, they find they can build a life for themselves and their children that is rich in satisfaction. Sandi is an example of a woman who, despite being wounded by an unfaithful husband, decided to give up The Dream she had once cherished and raise her children alone. Doing so was enormously difficult and required that she "stretch" herself in ways that she never knew were possible for her.

Sandi openly admits that she gave very little thought to what path her life would take, accepting the general consensus in her family that, because she was female, her destiny was to be a wife and mother. "I really did a lot of coasting the whole time I was growing up. My mother was such a dominant, guiding light that I just assumed that I would follow whatever path she chose for me." Sandi followed that path religiously. She married at the age of twenty-three and had two children. Although her relationship with her husband was empty and sterile, she hardly noticed because she believed this was the way life was supposed to be. She accommodated his needs and his career completely, as she had been taught to do:

When I was married, I saw myself as incorporated into a unit, as part of a partnership. As far as thinking of what *I* wanted for myself, I didn't even think about it. My husband was drafted into the Army a year after we married. We lived in Kansas because his job took him there. I really went along, and was more or less in tow. We lived on Army bases and women on Army bases are not people—they are appendages. I didn't really think about where I was going with *my* career, what *I* needed, what *I* wanted. His job naturally came first.

Sandi accepted the fact that, because her husband was in the military, they would be uprooted frequently. Unable to become a part of a community, put down roots, and develop interests outside the home, Sandi focused her attention on her duties as a mother. She probably would have continued passively accepting this life plan if her husband had not had an affair that was so outrageous she could not ignore it:

I was devastated, absolutely devastated, when my husband became involved with another woman. I am a very trusting person by nature. I knew he was miserable—he hated everything in his life. I said, "I think it's you, you know, I think you've got some issues if you hate everything." I removed myself from the situation for a while; I decided to take the kids for a visit with my father. When I came back early, I was horrified to discover that my husband and his mistress had been carrying on in *our* house, sleeping in our bed. He even had two towels hung out, and they had invited the neighbors over for dinner!

His charade uncovered, Sandi's husband simply refused to discuss his behavior. Instead, he told Sandi "there have been other women for years," and promptly abandoned her and their children, leaving the state with his soon-to-be second wife. In the midst of this total breakdown of her life, Sandi sank into a paralyzing depression. "I was totally blown out of the water. I went through a grieving process that was incredibly intense." She had a hard time believing her dream could have turned so ugly. Like many women, she was overwhelmed not just with the shock and shame of being left for another woman, but with the sheer logistics of having to maintain a life for herself and her children:

When I suddenly found myself no longer married, I thought "This is so crazy." I mean, I never thought about raising children by myself, maintaining a car and a house by myself, living two days' drive from the rest of my family.

The first step Sandi took towards giving up The Dream was to learn to function on a day-to-day basis. In the beginning, she was unable to plan more than a day or two ahead, and certainly could not think about how she was going to support herself and her children over the long haul. First she had to learn that she could survive by simply putting one foot in front of the other. Starting over for Sandi was complicated by the fact that she had not taken college seriously and had dropped out to get a "little job." While she was married, Sandi attempted (timidly, by her own report) to sell her own art out of her home, but with little success. Consequently, when her husband abandoned her, she lacked not only a college degree but also any professional experience in the work world. As she gradually became capable of productive functioning again, she became increasingly aware of her isolation:

> I got to a point when I realized I was very disconnected; I needed to grow, I needed to be out in the world, I needed to be in touch with other adults. I was not going to be the kind of parent to my children that I wanted to be if I was home alone all the time. So there was a lot of searching: How am I going to overcome my shyness? How am I going to bridge the gap between my home life and the outer world?

Sandi decided she had to overcome her shyness and market herself:

> At times it's been really scary. But I realized that I wouldn't be able to raise two children and do the things I needed to do if I remained shy and timid. That's been the biggest challenge—realizing that I'm capable, I'm intelligent, *I can do this*.

Part of getting over her shyness and bridging the gap to the world beyond her home involved approaching her father for funds to complete her college degree. It was difficult for Sandi to ask her father for help. Neither he nor she had ever really taken her talent seriously, and she didn't feel right asking him to pay for the education she felt she should have gotten when she was younger. Nevertheless, she made up her mind to pursue the degree in fine arts that she really wanted whether she got any help or not. Not only did her father come through for her, but in the process of doing all this Sandi learned how to stand up for herself and market her work. Eventually, she landed a job that has allowed her to keep her dream of being an artist.

In discovering how to create a life for herself and her children, Sandi realized that remaining passive and compliant usually left her feeling helpless and depressed. She also came to understand that the shame she felt when her husband left her actually belonged to *him,* the person who could not live up to his commitments. Sandi now rates her life as a nine on our ten-point satisfaction scale. When we asked her why she gave herself such a high rating, she answered:

> I have my *own* life. It's not tied to anybody else's, even though my children are really important to me and they will always be a priority.

But it's my life and I like not having to consider someone else's decisions or feelings. A lot of the fear about where this is going and wondering what's next is gone.

While the wound of her husband's betrayal has been slow in healing,
Sandi has not ruled out marriage categorically. Now, eleven years later, she
has begun to make some efforts to meet available men. But in the meantime
she has learned that marriage is not necessary for a good life. When comparing her feelings about her life when she was married with her current satisfaction, she says:

It seems like an eternity since then. I'm not at all the person I was then.
I think I've really discovered myself. Some of my friends who are more
secure but have not had my experience—who had a smoother path—
are envious. I feel *whole*. I feel so liberated and free. I can do *whatever* I
want to do. I am coming into my own power and it feels great!

ALETA'S STORY: THE NEW AMERICAN CLASSIC

Norman Rockwell style portraits of American families celebrating holidays
usually included three generations, with Grampa and Gramma smiling be-
nignly at their brood. Grampa and Gramma were always together, firmly
anchoring the family in a solid, unshakable union. Today, a great many of
those family portraits would feature Grampa with his new wife and a child
the same age as his grandchildren, with Gramma sitting alone at the other
end of the table. The classic American story of a woman's life, in which she
marries and has children and is honored by those children and their children,
is facing stiff competition from a new story in which the marriage collapses
after fifteen or twenty years and the woman is left to fend for herself.

Aleta's story reflects the experience of many women divorced in midlife.
Like these women, Aleta worked to make "happily ever after" a reality, only
to be rudely awakened by the announcement that The Dream had been
cancelled because her husband no longer wanted to play his role. Aleta, too,
is an example of what can happen if a woman chooses to focus on the
opportunities inherent in her new life rather than dwell on her losses. Fifteen
years after her divorce, she says, "I was forced to confront being on my own,
despite the fact that I was kicking and dragging my feet all the way. But the

experience has enabled me to find out that it's okay, I'm really okay."

Unlike many women who had childhood dreams of being a ballet dancer or movie star, Aleta had dreamed only of being a wife and mother. Raised in an upper-middle-class family in which her mother's frail health made servants a necessity, Aleta's expectations of womanhood were entirely traditional:

> I looked to my mother as an example without realizing it. Because she was ill a lot, we had live-in help from the time I was eight years old. So my sense of being a woman was a sense of being like my mother: being a gracious hostess, having a beautiful house, having a husband who worked a lot, having some of my own interests but basically being attached to my husband's world, centering my life around the home. I had no sense of working, or of developing myself in anyway. I had a fairly static sense that, once you get married, that's it.

Aleta married a man who was as devoted to his career as her father had been to his—and as she intended to be to hers as wife and mother. Of her expectations, she says:

> My father was a very prolific writer and a teacher. His work was everything. It took precedence over the family. I knew that he loved me but that I wasn't anywhere near the center of his interest or attention in life. So then I married a guy who told me straight out that his work was more important to him than our relationship. Although that disappointed me, I thought, "That's reality."

Unlike her mother, Aleta raised her children without the help of servants. She had never realized the degree to which her mother's serene air of graciousness was made possible by the presence of domestic help. Aleta was totally unprepared for the day-to-day grind of domestic life and the profound feelings of loneliness that plagued her:

> I was very alone during those years. I was not prepared for the extent to which I would be alone as a parent. I liked being in a beautiful house, but I really didn't like housework. I liked eating wonderful meals, but I didn't like to cook either. It wasn't satisfying. It was one more thing I had to do.

Like most women who lived through the sixties and early seventies, Aleta was exposed to ideas that changed her perspective on being a woman long before divorce was even a remote possibility in her mind. She began to envision a place for herself in the world outside her home. She realized that, for her own good, she needed to continue to develop as an adult—an idea which, only a few years earlier, would have been totally foreign to her. Although she went back to school to finish her bachelor's degree and get her master's, in no way was she consciously preparing herself to "go it alone." She was stunned when her husband abruptly asked for a divorce. It was not a contingency she had even considered:

I never thought that divorce would even be possible in my life. Never. The divorce was absolutely beyond anything I could conceive of as happening. I mean, divorce was as possible for me as the sun rising in the north. It just couldn't happen. When it did, it totally reorganized my universe.

Like many women suddenly faced with the possibility of divorce, Aleta would have preferred to try to work out a reconciliation, but her husband simply wanted out. Faced with the intractability of his position, Aleta was forced to let go of her "sort of happily ever after" dream. If another man had been waiting in the wings to take her husband's place, she might have gravitated toward him as a source of comfort and support in her time of need. However, like most forty-plus-year-old women in her situation, Aleta found more comfort in her friendships than in romance. Although over-whelmed with a myriad of distraught feelings, she also simultaneously experienced a sense of well-being she had not previously felt. Beneath her panic was a sense that, in time, she would get through the storm of feelings she was experiencing and be more truly herself than she ever had been. It was not an easy or instant transition. "It took me a long time to get over the wound of the divorce," she says, but adds, "I don't feel so wounded now. Both the wound and the marriage seem distant and long ago."

Aleta decided to concentrate on using the freedom she had gained rather than mourning the loss of the status, security, and at least the minimal sense of intimacy that marriage had afforded her. When her older son left for college, she began to exercise her options as a single person. She sold her house, moved to a small town outside New York City, and invested herself in her work, exploring ways to find happiness and meaning that did not depend on being married.

Today, Aleta exudes a sense of comfort with herself. Although still struggling to become financially secure and save for her retirement, she has created a life she enjoys. She is close to her sons, sees friends frequently, and has been romantically involved a couple of times since her divorce. While she has enjoyed these liaisons, her attitude toward relationships with men has changed dramatically: "A relationship doesn't seem to be the key to my own evolvement at this point in my life. For countless years, I believed it was." Like many other women who have grown to value the advantages of flying solo through the experience of forced liberation, Aleta does not rule out the possibility of remarriage—but she also does not depend on it. She says:

> The resistance to being on my own was enormous at first, and the pain was very great for a long time. Now there is no pain at all. In fact, I think I would find it inconvenient to have somebody else in my bathroom, to make room for somebody else's schedule. If I met the right person, I know I could love someone very deeply and find that quite wondrous, but I also don't miss it—I don't feel anything is missing.

Since her divorce, Aleta has undergone many changes—changes she believes other women possibly could make while they are still married, but which she personally would not have made unless forced to become a woman on her own. For her, giving up The Dream has become a celebration of self and an affirmation of life:

> I saw myself as less powerful, less accomplished than my husband, which was accurate. I saw myself as far less free to literally leave the house, to go out, to accomplish things, and see people. Now I feel very free. I feel very powerful. I can't imagine not having the freedom of doing whatever I want whenever I want. I express myself in a way I didn't fifteen years ago. I am creative in a way that I didn't know I could be. I would say, as a generalization, the whole experience of my life has been a journey from living a life of obligation and "putting up with" to experiencing real joy, pleasure, excitement, and *expansion*.

APRYL'S STORY: DERAILED BUT DETERMINED

Like other women who were pushed out of their marriages against their will, Apryl has found many ways to make life on her own soar. Rating her life an eight or nine on our ten-point satisfaction scale, she says:

> I'm very happy with my life. I don't know when I stopped feeling that my life was derailed, when I stopped wailing, "This isn't what I want . . . my heart is broken . . . I'll never be the same." But I did, and I discovered so much to explore: my own capacities, my own interests, my own strengths, my own needs. I would say that freedom and not having to be accountable to anybody are what I value most.

Apryl's ability to cherish her freedom was not a product of her upbringing. Like Sandi and Aleta, she was trained to honor the dictates of the mandate:

> My mother was a traditional homemaker and that was what I always expected to be. My life certainly is completely different from what I had ever expected. The women's movement happened when I was in college. I went to college as if it were a finishing school, but then, all of a sudden, I began to think, "Whoa, I could have a career. I could have a lot of other stuff in my life that I never expected."

In spite of this near-awakening, Apryl married right after college:

> I couldn't quite derail myself. It was like the train was already moving. I thought, "Well, when I finish school, if I don't get married, what will I do?" I didn't have the confidence to go out in the world.

Ironically, she ended up going out in the world to work anyway. In the tradition of so many wives who have supported their husbands during graduate school, Apryl worked to put her husband through law school. She got a job in a mental health agency in which she helped formulate public health policy. She spoke with great pride and clarity about her achievements while holding this position, and, in fact, it was through this work that she began to see a future for herself that included not only being a wife and mother, but also being a lawyer like her husband. Even though she was beginning to have a dream for herself other than the traditional one and did enroll in law school, there was no confusion about whose dream came first. Her husband promised her that when they both finished school they would move on to the next part of The Dream: buying a house and having children. So when he finished law school, Apryl readily quit her job and transferred to another law school to follow his career opportunities. After buying the house, something that neither of them could have predicted happened:

> I finished law school and got a job with the government. I was trying to get pregnant when my husband went through something that has never been explicable to either one of us, despite many years of therapy: he had a "thirties crisis." He decided that he didn't want to be married, that he didn't want to be a father, that he didn't want to be a lawyer—he wanted to be a Greyhound bus driver. So that was it! We got a divorce, out of the blue.

In our interview, Apryl never did say whether her husband pursued his somewhat bizarre version of *Easy Rider*, but her statement that he still has a considerable income would lead us to think not. Given the transient nature of his particular plan, Apryl might have weathered the storm of her husband's premature midlife crisis, but she felt so overwhelmed by his depression and desperate for "some joy in my life" that she initiated the separation by moving out. She decided to leave because she could no longer passively allow *his* unhappiness to decide the fate of *her* life. Out on her own, however, Apryl found joy a long time in coming. "I was just totally annihilated by the experience. The whole rug of my life had been pulled out from under me." She sank into her own despair and, although she showed up at work every day, she makes it clear that she "certainly wasn't doing much." At first, she thought that she would pull out of this fog by remarrying, simply because she "really enjoyed being married" and "really wanted to have a child." But a prince worthy of the role failed to materialize. A year into the process of separation and divorce, Apryl moved to another city and spent months taking an inventory of her life. Living off her pension fund, she says, "I went into a big cauldron of reconstructing myself. It was a very important time." She emerged from these months to get a master's degree in social work, enabling her to combine her legal knowledge with her commitment to social issues in marketable ways.

Apryl has since launched a highly successful career that has allowed her to become part of a supportive community of people who share her interests and social commitment. Apryl's work, however, is only one part of the satisfying life she has built for herself. A few years ago, she decided that motherhood was the piéce of The Dream she did not want to give up, and so she adopted a child. Now that she is a mother, she laughs, "I need a servant or a partner right now. All things considered, I would rather have a partner than a servant, but I may just wind up getting a servant first." Apryl is surprised by her own relaxed attitude about the issue of remarriage and her feelings of peace and even pleasure with being single. Since her divorce, she has had some serious relationships with men, but none compelling enough for her to give up her single life for marriage. She says, "If it happens, it would be nice, and if it doesn't happen, it will be fine. I can't believe I'm saying this, because I never thought I would get to this point. But it's true."

Chapter 8

Leaving Normal: Women Who Have Chosen to Leave Their Marriages

I never believed that I could be the traditional kind of woman, so to some degree I always felt like a fraud, like I was *pretending* to be a good wife and mother. It wasn't that I didn't love my husband or that I didn't care for my children. It was that I realized I just could not be that kind of wife. I tried to do the usual kind of homemaker things, but I always felt that, sooner or later, they were going to find out that I was faking.

—*Julia*

The choices I made were based on the way I grew up, but it was a *non-fit* for me from the very beginning. I don't think it was ever so much about marriage per se as it was about marriage not fitting *me*, personally.

—*Terry*

Women have to summon up courage to fulfill dormant dreams.

—*Alice Walker*

S ome of the women in our project chose to leave their traditional roles because the roles never really fit them. In doing so, they were leaving more than their marriages—they were choosing to leave the safety of well established lives to try their "wings" in unfamiliar skies. These women usually found it easier to adapt to being single than those who were forced out of their marriages by their husbands' actions or decisions. Much like some of the never-married women we interviewed, who never embraced The Dream wholeheartedly, these women also experienced early doubts or had always had alternative dreams of their own competing for their attention.

Their decisions to marry represented detours from these early dreams; getting divorced—while painful—often simultaneously felt like getting "back on track." Thus, women who chose to leave their marriages not only had the advantage of not feeling rejected, but perhaps more importantly, they had the advantage of never having fully accepted The Dream or of having given it up, bit by bit, for years before they left. In fact, most of them could be said to have left *because* they had already uncovered the disappointing illusions of The Dream.

But even these women usually had a long journey to the place where they experienced being single as a positive choice, rather than something thrust on them. Most had not only to mourn the loss of their marriages but also to overcome harsh criticism for their unconventional choices. When Glenda chose to leave her marriage, she did so in anger because she felt her husband had let her down. It took some time before she could view her decision as a positive move toward a preferable life for herself, one that provided her with opportunities for education and a career. Arlene had a clearer vision than Glenda about the ways in which her marriage failed to provide her with satisfaction, but it also took her a few years before she was able to find a way to make a better life for herself. Julia went through many months of marital therapy and a painful process of grieving lost hopes before she was able to give up The Dream and commit to a life on her own.

GLENDA'S STORY: REDISCOVERING THE SELF

Glenda had unusual opportunities as a child to establish her individuality and build self-esteem. She was the sixth of seven children in a second-generation immigrant working-class family. They were staunch Catholics who sent all their children to parochial school. Her father worked as a truck driver, and the women in the family stayed at home, living very conventional lives. Glenda describes her mother as living "in a very small world." Glenda, however, happened to be born at a time when all the other babies in their large extended family were male. Since all her relatives lived in the same neighborhood, she played with her male cousins and was granted some of the freedom typically reserved only for male children. She attributes much of the feelings of independence and competence she experienced to this fact and to her relationship with her father:

My father was a big influence in my life. He used to take me to union meetings. He would wake me up at 5:30 in the morning and we would go to church, then go out for breakfast, and then we would go to the teamsters meeting hall. He used to tell me, "Now listen to this, this is about people who work for a living. Don't listen to any of the curse words (laughing), don't listen to those. Just listen to what the men are saying."

Glenda took away more than just lessons about unions. She took away the message that her father thought she was special and that she could do all sorts of things that were not defined as within the province of women at that time. Whether it was her father's encouragement, her natural inclinations, or a combination of both, Glenda started learning how to "fly" early. She began ballet lessons at age four and was good enough to be teaching ballet to younger children at age twelve. She played football and baseball and was the first woman in the city to learn Judo and earn a brown belt. Her adolescence was marked by power struggles with her tradition-bound parents, particularly with her mother. Glenda is proudest of her struggle to be allowed to attend public high school. She insisted and persisted to the point where her parents relented on the condition that she maintain straight A's. Her sisters resented Glenda being given this freedom, failing to see the lesson of fighting for your own dreams. "I told them, 'You have a choice.' They said, 'No we don't.' I said, 'Yes you do.' "

Glenda's head start toward autonomy and independence was brought to an abrupt halt a few years after graduation from high school when she decided to marry her high school sweetheart, Paul, rather than pursue an education. Looking back, she feels she "clipped her own wings," perhaps unnecessarily, but at the time she believed that no one in her family would support any choice for a female other than getting married and having children. While she had been able to create choices earlier in her life, of her decision to marry she says, "When you don't think you have many choices, you just deal with what you feel you have to do." Shortly after her marriage, Glenda became pregnant and gave birth to her first son. She discovered (to her surprise) that she liked being a mother so much that she chose to have another child, again a son. Her "just do it" approach to life asserted itself and carried her through the challenges of managing a home and raising children.

Her summary of her fifteen-year marriage is succinct: "I didn't realize how independent I was and how dependent my husband was until I got divorced." Despite external conformity to the traditional model of marriage, Glenda found she was in charge of everything except Paul's job.

Life proceeded relatively smoothly until Paul lost this job. Glenda's response was characteristic: she "plugged the hole in their boat" by getting a job herself as a director of a senior citizens center. After six months, Glenda decided to apply for a better paying position and, in the process, had a life-changing experience:

> I was so nervous driving to this interview. The woman who interviewed me was totally intimidating. She was all business, asking me all of these questions, with no warmth whatsoever. After struggling to answer for a little while I thought, "Oh, the hell with this. I'm just going to say what I feel like saying." I got home and ten minutes later the phone rang: She offered me the job! That job did a lot for me.

Glenda loved her job, but working and keeping her home afloat were wearing her out without any help from her unemployed husband: "He was checking this out and that out—job interviews and school applications. I'd come home and the kids would be here unsupervised and he wouldn't be anywhere around. And then I'd find out he was out at the swimming pool." The situation escalated to crisis proportions when Glenda found a box in the basement filled with the applications for work and school Paul had supposedly completed and returned. She was furious. She had traded in the ambitions she had harbored for herself early in life for the roles of wife and mother, and now Paul was wasting his chances to improve himself in ways she would have welcomed for herself. Her anger was very useful; it got her through the guilt of initiating a divorce despite her Catholic upbringing:

> My husband had no intention of going to school. He had no intention of working. I had to accept that, but it took me a long time. Coming from the Catholic background I did, it was overwhelming to face the fact that he was not going to change and that I was supposed to stay with him for life. I sat back and thought, "Well, it's almost insurmountable." I mean, it felt like, "There's no way." But then I reached the point when I just couldn't do anything else. I guess I had to get angry enough to make the change, whatever the consequences.

Glenda had to rediscover the buried part of the woman she had started out to become so many years earlier. Like many women who married young and focused their energy on their homes and children, she had to begin building a life for herself and her children on the shaky foundation of an inadequate education. Then it occurred to her: Why hadn't *she* thought of returning to school? She sought admission and scholarship support at a local university and received both, only to find herself struggling to get off the ground on these unfamiliar runways: "Oh, I was so overwhelmed in school, it was unreal. I mean, I was very thankful for the opportunity, but at first I was so discouraged." It was a long struggle, particularly financially. "One year we lived on six thousand dollars—and that was *before* taxes. Luckily my kids were still in school because they got lunch for free. I only ate every other day." Eventually Glenda found a job that allowed her to support herself and her children while going to school—a job she still had when we spoke with her. She was grateful to have had it when she needed it, but she is now ready to take her degree and search for a job that offers more challenge.

Clearly, Glenda did not focus her energy on finding another husband and trying to rebuild The Dream—a dream that had not dominated her childhood in the first place. At one point, she did become engaged to a physician who lived in a neighboring state, but she broke off the engagement because she felt she was not enough of a priority in his life to negotiate with him from a position of strength. Now that her children are leaving for college and she has finished school, she is writing a book about her family and is indulging her favorite hobby, fishing. She is feeling deliciously free, as if all the weight of responsibility is being lifted and she is finally free to *fly*.

ARLENE'S STORY: HAVING IT ALL WAS NOT ENOUGH

Arlene was married to an attorney. They had everything: an expensive house, three children, and a respected position in the community. Nevertheless, after years of marriage she felt emotionally bankrupt. She felt her "soul was shrinking and shriveling," so she made the painful decision to end her marriage.

Arlene grew up in Chicago in the midst of a large extended family of Jewish immigrants from Poland (similar to the one featured in the television show, *Brooklyn Bridge*). Aunts, uncles, and cousins all lived in the same apartment building. The women in the family were powerful in their own way: "They led the family, they were very outspoken, they kept the traditions." But roles were clearly defined. "Males were put up on a pedestal. They were expected to go out and become doctors, lawyers, engineers. Women were encouraged to succeed intellectually, but we were also expected to be mothers and continue the traditions of our mothers." Arlene feels that growing up in such a traditional family was not an encumbrance to her development of a sense of self. "I always felt that we were *all* special, but the boys were just a little more special." Arlene perceived her mother as discontent with her lot in life but, like so many women of her time, unable to envision having a choice about how she would live her life. "The message I got from her was, 'I want you to have more than me.' "

Arlene cherished two dreams simultaneously, but did not have the experience to see that fulfilling one could preclude the other. In one dream she was a musician; in the other, a wife and mother. Along with all the female cousins with whom she grew up—most of whom have gotten advanced degrees and have careers—Arlene went to college, where she majored in music. Her ultimate goal was to be a concert pianist. But the long arm of family tradition reached out and ambushed her, cutting her off from her ambitions before she had time to make them materialize. "I didn't expect to be married as early as I was, and I didn't expect to have children when I did."

Arlene's surprise at her own decision to marry is a testimony to the power of The Dream. She believes her decision was less a case of being carried away by romance than it was a logical decision: She had found someone who could support one of her dreams and somehow she would find a way to sandwich in the other between her duties as wife and mother:

> I was twenty-two years old, a year out of college. I had goals and clear ideas about where I wanted to work and what I wanted to do. We both had the same value system, and there were a lot of things we had in common. Two years after we were married, I got pregnant accidentally. So I was still pursuing my dreams, but it was hard to focus on my music once I had a child. Part of it was that we were moving every two years. My husband's degree was more . . .

Arlene never finished this sentence, but we could finish it for her. Jonathan's career as an attorney was more important than hers as a musician, so Arlene accommodated herself to his needs. She decided to have another child quickly and "get her childbearing over with," and she did—and then another. Between moving and motherhood, Arlene's dream of becoming a musician slowly died.

Arlene does not regret a moment she spent as a mother, nor does she think of herself as having made sacrifices for her husband's career. She was simply postponing her career to concentrate on their mutual commitment to having children. Even now she says, "What I miss most about my marriage is not the man that was in the marriage, but the family that we created. And I think we did that really well. We created a very good family." Her attitude of seeing the years she devoted to motherhood as being an acceptable choice is typical of the women we interviewed. They evaluate their experience of motherhood separate from their experience of marriage. They cherish their children, but devotion to children makes devotion to a career more difficult, a problem that, no doubt, will take generations to resolve.

Arlene tried to find her own resolution to this problem by "making do" with a lot of volunteer service. Finally, when she was thirty-six, she decided the time had come to revive her original dream, at least in part. Thinking that she would have a better chance of success if she used her recent life experience with raising children, she opened a music school—a job she felt would utilize her natural skills with people. Her hours were flexible, so she was able to tend to her children's needs, as always. Despite the care Arlene took to accommodate herself to her family's needs, the results were disastrous in terms of The Dream:

The irony of my life is that once I was successful in my profession and feeling really good about myself, my marriage deteriorated. People ask me, "Did your school break up your marriage?" I think the marriage was dead before that, but when I started to succeed, my husband started to withdraw. He did not like the competition. I had a traditional midlife crisis at forty, and I did a most untraditional thing. I left the house and got an apartment nearby.

Even though Arlene saw her children every day and knew they were doing well, she had committed an unforgivable sin for anyone raised on The Dream. Women simply don't move out and leave their children behind, no matter how poor they are, how affluent their husbands are, or how close to their children they stay. Arlene explains:

I was ostracized by my friends, male and female alike. I had no support system after that. I worked even harder and I did well, but it was very stressful, emotionally and financially.

Arlene had to bear the burden of knowing that when she left her husband she left not only her own and her daughters' visions of The Dream, but also the dream of her immigrant parents for their daughter to "have it all" as the wife of an attorney. Although her daughters soon moved into her apartment, and her son, the youngest of the children, still spends a great deal of time there, forgiveness for her original sin was slow to come. Even her career suffered because she no longer had the same social network and therefore lost many referrals. Of her decision she says, "I'm not sure I thought about it logically at that time. It was a deep, *emotional* response."

Arlene soon discovered that she no longer wanted to run a music school. The problem was, what to do next. She visited a career counselor and discussed her situation with the few friends with whom she still had contact. One friend, an ordained rabbi, told her about a synagogue some distance away that needed help:

> He said that he couldn't fill the position but that maybe I could. I said, "Oh gosh, I don't think so, how could I do that?" He said, "Why not?" It was true, I had always been involved in the feminist move- ment for Jewish women, and I had conducted services in the syna- gogue here, and I had encouraged women to participate. But it was something I did on the side. Well, I could use the money, I thought, I could use a break. So I interviewed with them and liked them. I told them I'd do it for a few months. But the more I did it, the more I liked it. I looked forward to going there. They said, "Well, you're the best thing we have going here. How would you like to do this on a full- time basis? And we'll pay you well so you can commit to doing this." I was very surprised. I was flattered. Here I was—a woman.

Here she was, indeed. She returned to discuss this development with her rabbi friend, who not only encouraged her to take the position, but to apply for seminary as well:

> I was struck by the thought of following in my father's footsteps. Actually, my father and my grandfather were both rabbis. My father stopped practicing during the Depression; he went into his brother's business. It was the one thing he always regretted, giving up his con- gregation. Becoming a rabbi was not possible for women during the time I was growing up. I had no role models. None. So, in a way, the

pleasure of it is that I am following in my father's footsteps, I am completing something he himself did not get to do. It feels boundless.

The odds that Arlene faces to actualize this dream are formidable, but she is ready to take them on. There are only two seminaries in the country she can attend, both a considerable distance away. She plans to commute by air to Cincinnati, attend seminary three days a week, and then return home to tend to her congregation and her children the other four days. In addition, she has to find financial support not only for tuition but also for her commuting expenses. But her passion for the dream of becoming a rabbi makes surmounting all these obstacles worthwhile. And, her choice of profession is mending the wound caused by her divorce in her extended family:

The divorce was very hard on my family—my children, my parents, and my sister. But this job made everything okay again. I've gotten a lot of support, especially from my father and mother, who are giving me all these positive strokes about, "You can do whatever you want to do." Even my children are extremely supportive and proud of me. So I'm getting green lights from everybody, including the women in my life who thought I was terrible for leaving my children.

Arlene is certain that she never would have been able to even consider becoming a rabbi if she had she stayed married. She characterizes her ex-husband as non-supportive. "Whatever I did, I had to do on my own, and he'd negate it. It was just such a struggle." She takes her new life seriously, especially her sense of herself as a role model:

So now, divorced and single, having left the "good life"—a good lawyer and all that stuff—I'm finally becoming my own person. But it's also a very hard responsibility. I need to watch what I do. I am now a role model. I've got to succeed. But I really don't feel I have a choice—this is the best option for me. No matter how hard it is now, it was harder before.

JULIA'S STORY: BEING A CAT IN A DOG'S WORLD

Even in high school, Julia imagined a life that was not solely oriented around marriage and motherhood. She was an extremely bright and motivated student who dreamed of going to college to build a rewarding career:

> I always figured I would have some sort of career. It never occurred to me that I wouldn't. I just never thought I would be a housewife. I didn't really think that much about having kids either.

She laughs now as she recalls how she started with the *"A's"* in formulating her career plans, envisioning herself as an *art* historian or perhaps an *archaeologist*. Unfortunately, she hadn't made it much further into the alphabet when she began to receive staunch opposition from those around her. As mentioned previously, when Julia told her school guidance counselor, Mr. Palmer, that she wanted to go to Barnard College in New York as a first step towards a serious career, he discouraged her, insisting that women developed careers only "to have something to fall back on." His response was only one of many negative reactions in her world:

> The idea that a woman might have interests of her own that she wanted to pursue, that she might have career aspirations of her own, simply didn't cross the minds of most of the guidance counselors and many of the teachers and ninety percent of the parents of my generation.

With little support for her plans from either her school or her parents, Julia began to drift, waiting to apply to college until April of her senior year. "It was sheer passive resistance—I didn't want to go to the state teacher's college." Finally, Mr. Palmer and her parents "strong armed" her into applying to a large university in a neighboring state. She went for one year and then transferred to a smaller, private university to study English. It looked as though Julia was finally on her way to getting the education she wanted, but then in the summer of her sophomore year she discovered she was pregnant. The following semester, she dropped out of school, got married, and had a baby girl. Two years later, she gave birth to her second daughter.

Staying home with two young children was not the life Julia had imagined, but she tried to make it work. Admittedly, it was not easy. She constantly felt like a failure and a fraud because she did not feel comfortable in her role as traditional wife and mother. She recalls:

> I didn't know what it meant to be a wife. I didn't know what it meant to be a partner to anybody. All I knew was what my parents did— which wasn't what I wanted—and what was shown on TV. I think I had a lot of expectations of what marriage was supposed to be like, what I was supposed to feel. When those feelings didn't happen, I figured I just wasn't doing it right, that there was something lacking in me.

Julia relied on her determination and intelligence to learn how to be a mother to her daughters, although it was hard in the beginning. "I didn't really think I could do it," she admits, "and then suddenly here I was, a mother." Julia began to watch Mr. Rogers with her children and to read about parenting and child development. She soon realized that she could mother her children on her own terms, taking what was meaningful from these sources and applying it in a way that was right for her. Her success at parenting surprised her. "It turns out I was not a bad mother at all," she laughs, "I was actually pretty good at it. I really liked it." She also learned that she didn't have to feel like a failure because, as she says, "I didn't have those feelings that the books, the magazines, the baby cards said you were supposed to have."

Creating a comfortable role for herself in her marriage was, however, another story. Although she tried to fulfill the image of the ideal wife she had seen on the *Donna Reed Show* as a child, she and her husband were becoming increasingly unhappy with one another. Tensions between them began to rise:

> I could see that my husband was not happy, although he didn't deal with it overtly. When he was unhappy, he would simply say, "It's because you're bad in bed, it's because you're a lousy cook." There were times that I was so miserable, I was so sure that I was a failure, that I thought about suicide. At one point, I seriously considered it. Then I thought, "Boy, is that dumb! I don't want to do that!" I mean, I was thinking everyone would be better off without me. The kids would be happier. My husband would be happier. Then I thought, "No, I can make them happier some other way."

Long before she was able to leave her marriage, Julia began to understand that, while fulfilling The Dream can be wonderful for many women, following such a path was simply not suited to her. Initially, she felt guilty about this realization, much as Adrienne Rich described herself in the following lines: "I had a marriage and a child. If there were doubts, if there were periods of null depression or active despairing, these could only mean that I was ungrateful, insatiable, perhaps a monster." It took Julia some time to believe that she was not unnatural or abnormal because she found marriage a poor "fit":

There are dogs and there are cats. Dogs are pack animals; they like to be with people, with other dogs, in groups. Cats do not. They hunt alone, they like to be alone. They may form close relationships and bond with people or other animals, but by nature they are not group animals. In my marriage, I figured out that I was a cat and not a dog.

Julia increasingly realized that she could not develop into a real person within the structure of her marriage. She did not know what else she wanted, but she knew she needed the chance to find out. She explains:

I felt as if the choice was between going forward and growing into someone I wanted to be, or staying where I was and changing myself into someone I knew I could never truly be. So, it was really a survival choice for me.

Looking back, Julia realizes that giving up The Dream was a crucial part of being able to leave her marriage and move towards a life of her own. This process was very difficult for her because it meant committing herself to a life ungraced by the protections of tradition:

In order to leave a marriage and move on in a positive way, I think you have to let go of a lot of illusions, you have to let go of a lot of hopes. Some of it had to do with accepting the fact that I was not going to be a traditional woman, that I was not going to have an easy life. It's hard to accept a choice that will make your life *more* difficult. For me, being married meant having a good income, being able to work if I felt like it but not having to work, being able to go to school while I was being supported in a reasonable manner. Those things were very nice. And I was a safe person because I was a married person. People knew how to deal with me. I could be Mrs. So-and-So at parties or at business gatherings. It was easy, clear-cut. Recognizing that I had to walk away from that meant recognizing that it would not be so easy, that I would probably not have much money for a long time, that sometimes people wouldn't know quite what to make of me. That part of it had to be dealt with and it had to be accepted as the price I was willing to pay for something else I really wanted to have—which was a higher degree of *personal freedom*.

Being able to give up The Dream and all it entailed involved a process of mourning which Julia described as similar to her experiences of grief after the death of a close friend. Her pain and sorrow were intense. Fortunately, she was able to experience her grief in a healing way over a period of time:

I did a lot of the grieving and letting go of illusions while I was still married. The marriage ended over a long period of time. We had gone through some counseling, and I did a lot of soul searching about what I wanted to do through that period.

Ultimately, Julia decided that she needed the chance to pursue a dream of her own. She left her husband and moved out with her two daughters, then eight and five.

At first, life on her own with two children was frightening and over-whelming. Julia had not finished college and she had little sense of how she was going to support herself and her daughters. But she sustained herself with the knowledge that she would finally be able to create a life that fit her own goals instead of trying to fit herself into someone else's. Although more difficult, it would be a life *she* chose, one that was true to herself:

At the time I left my marriage, I was not a strong, fulfilled, "self-actualized" person. I was very much a struggling embryo of a person. But I knew I had to develop in a different direction if I was going to become the person I wanted to be.

Julia returned to college and completed her degree. Soon after gradua-tion, she landed a job as an assistant buyer for a department store. It took some long hours, but eventually she became an executive with the company, a position that affords her a good salary and feelings of being successful and respected by her colleagues and staff. In her spare time, she loves to write and

paint and plans to do more of both when she retires. She also enjoys a
relationship with a man whom she has known for the past nine years; it is an
alliance that meets her needs for intimacy and sex without infringing on her
independence.

Julia is proud of the changes she has made in her life and the role model
she has become for her daughters. Overall, she feels her life has an integrity it
did not possess when she was married. She says, "I really am very, very lucky
and I appreciate everything I have been able to do."

Midlife: Charting a New Course

Chapter 9

Midlife's Gifts to Single Women

The ambition for middle-aged women must be to render the present "lovely," which means not that it is calm and without pain—such contentment may be found in a front porch rocker—but that it offers its own intensity, and is experienced in non-nostalgic relation to the past.

—*Carolyn Heilbrun*

Like so many women of my age, about thirty-five, I started feeling better. It was like convalescence, a slow midlife cure—as if we were taking tiny homeopathic pills marked Enlightenment, Energy, Self-Delight.

—*Margaret Morganroth Gullette*

I know women who freak out over turning forty. They're always looking at their lines with a microscope. But I say, "Honey, I've earned those lines. I'm here and I'm looking good. . . ."

—*Debbie Allen*

The overwhelming majority of single women we interviewed told us that, for them, midlife has been a time of renewal; it has been a time of giving up leftover dreams, finding new and unexpectedly sweet ones, and fulfilling old ones long forgotten. Women experience midlife not as the beginning of the end, but as the advent of a time of great potential, a time of coming into their own. For them, it is an era dominated by the delicious task of figuring out what they have always wanted and going after it with a vigor and a certainty of purpose they did not have when they were younger. They describe feeling an intriguing mixture of inner contentment and a new willingness to "stretch" themselves by taking more risks.

The tales single women tell of the benefits of midlife include both minor advantages they never would have missed had they not stumbled upon them and major life-altering shifts in identity. They talk of discovering qualities they never knew they possessed, such as courage, determination, and patience, and of developing a sense of pride in the things they have been able to accomplish on their own—a feeling they would have missed if they had continued as "number two" in a two-person team. Julia summed up the feelings of the women we interviewed:

How do I feel about being single at this time in my life? I love it. I think it's great. For me at my age, this is like a whole new life starting. I am really having a lot of fun and part of that has to do with the fact that I am single. I wouldn't have that sense of renewal, of having a new opportunity to begin and make decisions for myself all over again, if I was in a marriage.

Their stories tell of freedom, adventure, self-satisfaction, ease, and an increased capacity to appreciate moments of joy and discovery—a gift so rare and unexpected that many experience it as a feeling of spiritual regeneration or transformation.

TERRY'S STORY: EIGHT QUILTS, TEN
JOURNALS, AND A SENSE OF SELF

Terry's story is particularly explicit about the unexpected gifts of being single at midlife:

For me it isn't a matter of a midlife *phase*. It's more like *being born*. I've finally been birthed into this process of—I keep coming up with the word *choice*. You know, at the age of fifty, I've probably got twenty more years of this renaissance, and I wonder what it will bring. It's not like I've scripted it. It's like *anything* is possible. And I've never said that before in my life.

Terry's opening statement to us was, "It's peculiar that I have ended up single." She explained that her parents were committed to the idea of staying together for life, and she grew up without ever having known any single women in her family—or anywhere else, for that matter. When she got a divorce, her parents ceaselessly reminded her that no one in their family had ever done so. "Everyone in my parents' community stayed locked into relationships. That I was divorced with little kids, and would stay single *by choice,* was totally mystifying to them."

Terry had gotten married not because she dreamed of being a wife and mother, but because she didn't know what else to do. She simply had not been raised to consider any other possibilities in life, except, possibly, becoming a nun. Confident that a nunnery was not for her, she spent a year at Berkeley at the time of the "free speech" movement. As she was exposed to radically new ideas and options, the intensity of the times had a reverse effect on her. Instead of being swept along with "the times they are 'achangin,'" she was catapulted backward, grabbing in fear for the familiar. She wasn't ready for revolution, for violence, and for "all those dirty, unwashed people protesting all those lefty causes." Instead, she "ran into marriage for protection."

Once married, Terry tried to be a dutiful wife in the traditional ways she had seen her mother practice. She matched the towels, had dinner on the table at six o'clock, kept a nice garden, and greeted her three sons with milk and cookies after school. But the more she tried to fit into the mold of what she thought was the perfect housewife, the more she began to feel "incredibly crazy." The seeds of revolution planted by the frightening students she had fled at Berkeley were beginning to flower, whether she wanted them to or not. She became increasingly aware that the scenario she was trying to live was not a good one for her. "I don't think it was ever so much about marriage per se as it was about marriage not fitting *me,* personally." Almost against her will, she began to think of opportunities that might await her outside her marriage. She admits she had little idea of what she wanted, but had come to know clearly that she *didn't* want what she had. When she was only twenty-nine, she told her husband she wanted a divorce:

I had absolutely no sense of where I was going, no sense of the enormity of the decision that I had made in relation to myself and my kids, no sense of the enormous difficulty I would face trying to raise three kids on my own. What I did feel was the most incredible sense of freedom I had ever experienced in my life. I felt real fear, but I also felt an almost euphoric sense of freedom. I really liked being single!

Terry had attended college for only two years before she fled into marriage. When she separated from her husband, she finished school and worked as an urban planner while she raised her three children. Although

Terry never questioned her decision to leave the marriage, those early years on her own were challenging ones. She and her sons had very little money and the work of raising them alone when they were small was relentless. Terry laughs as she looks back on those years now, recalling that "there were some years when my kids thought they would never get anything more than macaroni-and-cheese and hot dogs." Both Terry and her sons were somewhat relieved when they were older and could fend for themselves and, when the time came, leave home.

Since she was only in her late thirties at this time, their departure threw Terry into the exigencies of a midlife "something" earlier than most women. Now that she had time to focus on her own life, she realized how discouraged she had become with her job. Describing that time Terry says, "I couldn't figure out where I wanted to go, what I wanted to do. Life felt really flat—not depressing, just flat."

By this time a new and unexpected role model entered Terry's life—her own mother. She believes that part of her ability to capitalize on the advantages of these vital midlife years stemmed from witnessing her mother's own renaissance in midlife. Growing up and as a young adult, Terry had always seen her mother as a model of those attributes—*waiting* and *accommodation*—which are so highly valued by the marriage and motherhood mandate. Although her mother did not run off to Greenwich Village but remained steadfastly married to her father, Terry reports that in midlife she did begin to blossom:

My mother began to make choices. Before, she had been a very dependent woman. My father was the wage earner, she kept the garden and the house, she didn't drive, and she never asserted herself. To this day, I don't know what sort of transformation occurred, but suddenly she was driving, she began to express herself, she got involved in art and became a very accomplished artist. She was in her fifties. I got luckier and went through this transformation it in my late thirties.

Terry is certain that being single worked to her advantage by pushing her to stretch toward independence and self-discovery at an earlier age than her mother. Terry's response to her children's coming-of-age and her new freedom was remarkable. She took a year off and lived alone in an isolated cabin on the slopes of the Eastern Sierras. "Pieces just fell into place" to make it possible for her to have this adventure—such as a friend loaning her the cabin. Having worked summers for the National Park Service at Yosemite,

Terry was comfortable in a wilderness environment, but nothing could have prepared her for the isolation:

> The first few days in the cabin I didn't think I was going to last. But what began to emerge was a real sense of self, a deep sense of what I wanted in my life and where I wanted to be. I realized that I could survive solitude—in fact, not only survive it, but begin to grow in it.

Terry deliberately chose to be alone to confront herself. She wanted to take full responsibility for her choices. Because she knew she could hide her head in books for the entire year and not think a single self-reflective thought, she brought very few books with her. Instead, she kept journals and made quilts, activities which facilitated an inward focus. The experience was truly transformative for her. She emerged at the end of the year with eight quilts, ten journals and a decision to move across the continent and commit herself to a new career.

Midlife had extended its invitation to a dance of renewal, and dance she did. Terry left California to return to the East Coast where she was raised, enrolled in graduate school, and emerged with a new profession. The changes she made have brought her the incredible gifts of selfhood and joy. Not all midlife women would want to spend a year alone in an isolated mountain cabin like Terry, but many can muster the courage to take advantage of the gifts midlife has to offer.

THE GIFT OF "WIDER MARGINS"

Certainly, the women in midlife we interviewed are aware of the fact that they are no longer young. The rhetorical question they begin to ask themselves in midlife is, *So what?* They readily admit that some aspects of aging in our youth-centered culture are not joyous. However, they choose not to allow their time and attention to be consumed by worries about wrinkles, graying hair, and cellulite. Regardless of the shrieks of panic inspired by the marketing moguls of Madison Avenue, they do not spend their time and energy searching for remedies to help them hold the line against the inevitable tide of aging. And if they spend hours in the gym working out, it is more likely because they are in training for an anticipated climb up a mountain than because they are frantically attempting to remain attractive to the opposite sex. Instead of mourning their empty nests and sagging flesh, they have chosen to change their attitudes about aging by seeking opportunities, challenges, and advantages.

This indifference to the national obsession with youth and beauty is indicative of one of the most delicious gifts of midlife: freedom from the burden of the traditional expectations that dominated women's early years. At midlife, women become more impressed with and concerned about their own opinions than those of others. Erika explains the shift that occurs:

> I don't care about what anybody *else* thinks would make me happy. I don't care about what anybody else even thinks in general, because I'm finding out what *I* think. I have to think about what will help *me* and make *me* happy.

Terry told us a story about a hiking trip she and Tom, the special man in her life for the past ten years, took along the Appalachian Trail. It is a story that links her newfound feelings of excitement and joy with midlife and the ability to let go of concern with tradition and the opinions of others:

> In the south, the Appalachian Trail goes all through these little towns that are very traditional, very redneck, very desolate. As we walked into one of these towns one day, my friend looked around and said, "Well, this would be a perfect place for us to settle. I'll publish the newspaper and you can be the town eccentric." His comment made me realize that there will be people in my life who will look at me differently because of the choices I have made, because I can pick up and go, because the conventions are not important, and because the margins of my life are wider.

THE GIFT OF THE WAKE-UP CALL

Midlife gives women a loud, sharp wake-up call, focusing their attention on the need to take charge of their own life journeys and find deeper meaning in their lives. There is an increasingly urgent existential need to examine the meaning of decisions and behaviors. When postponing dreams no longer makes sense, priorities change. Everything goes up for grabs—relationships, careers, previous decisions, and outdated commitments. Women feel challenged to pursue the experiences they once only passively waited and hoped for, be it taking classes, taking trips, or taking "time off."

In the context of all these opportunities, the downside of midlife seems much less noteworthy than its wake-up call—particularly for women who have been living on "automatic pilot," women who have been working too hard to be perfect, women who have not yet rediscovered and made peace with their own power. Midlife's wake-up call does not advise these women to hang their heads in shame at putting on a few pounds and slowing down a bit. Instead, it announces, "If you are ever going to do something for yourself, *now is the time.*" For example, at the age of fifty-three, Aleta says:

> I see myself as a late bloomer, and I think a lot of women are. I know that my creativity will only increase in my fifties and sixties. I anticipate just being on the edge of much fuller self-expression.

At fifty-two, Ruth agrees. "I really have a whole life now to create for myself." Ruth has decided to go into a new business, opening a book store with a close friend. She says, "I think I've become much more adventurous. I'm trying this new business and I'm very excited about it."

For some women, the wake-up call comes slowly, through the unmistakable physical changes that accompany midlife. We all know the signs. You never needed glasses and, one day, you suddenly can't read the print on the cereal box. You get backaches or muscle spasms after exercising. Constant vigilance is required where food is concerned because your body shape changes all too easily now. You begin to notice the subtle changes in skin texture and tone that accompany menopause. These signs, typically viewed as negative, can have a profoundly positive effect. Alerting women to their own mortality, they can increase the appreciation of the sweetness of life, and they can motivate women to chart new courses for their futures or to recognize and appreciate the ways in which their lives are already rich and full. Megan explains:

> The older I get, the more I realize how fragile and transient life is. I've stopped putting my life on hold until *x, y,* or *z* happens. I really appreciate what's in my life *now.* My life at this time is complete and perfect in its own way—and *I'm* in charge of it.

For others, midlife's wake-up call comes suddenly and dramatically through experiencing the illness or death of a parent or a friend. As painful as they are, these losses bring a greater awareness of the value of reaching out affirmatively for life. Describing such an experience following her mother's death, Hillary says:

> I guess I started doing as much as I could for myself three or four years ago, when my mother died. That's when everything started to come into focus. That's when I began to realize that I'm not going to live forever and I'd better make sure that I do a whole lot of fun things.

The death of a parent sometimes places a woman in the position of representing the oldest generation in her family, or even being the last remaining member, imbuing her with a new sense of authority over her life. For Elaine, the loss of her father catalyzed a radical shift in her inner attitude towards herself. Suddenly she had an increased appreciation of life's fleeting nature, which helped her to confront the parts of herself that were timid or fearful. She began to see herself as an autonomous woman capable of self-authority, perhaps because her father's death relocated her in the "senior generation":

> After my father's death, I thought, I'm not part of a family anymore. I'm really an individual and I have to look at things differently. I didn't realize how much a part of my nuclear family I considered myself to be. I hadn't really defined myself as an individual. I think my father's death gave me the final nudge I needed to start taking charge—not drifting but *directing*.

For many women, times of loss are times when they find within themselves the resources to make important and sometimes quite dramatic changes in their lives, which prove to be highly beneficial even though imposed by undesired circumstances. Consider Heidi, a woman who lived her life as the archetypal heroine of The Dream. For Heidi, midlife brought more than a wake-up call; it was "like the explosion of a terrorist's bomb." Her world dramatically changed one morning when her husband died without warning from a heart attack in his car on the way to work. Suddenly, she faced overwhelming loss, an acute sense of her own mortality, the devastation of being single for the first time in more than twenty years, and the prospect of aging without the long-term companion on whom she had always counted. The years through which she had believed she would gradually and easily coast—the years of transition from active parenting to retirement—abruptly crystallized into the most difficult challenge she had ever faced. Her response to this challenge is a dramatic example of the ways in which the experience of loss can transform a woman in midlife.

Heidi was raised in a farming community in which a woman who was not married by the age of twenty-one was considered an "old maid." She grew up as part of a large extended family that included six brothers and sisters, twelve aunts and uncles on her father's side, and fifteen on her mother's. This background instilled in her fairly traditional expectations of life, and she "just didn't plan on living alone."

> Where I grew up, you didn't plan on living independently, especially if you were female. Females *have* to form some kind of attachment; they *have* to have someone to take care of them. It's hard to get out of that mold. Parents tell you that marriage is the goal, the place to finally rest yourself.

Like many farmers, Heidi's family was poor. There was always plenty of food on the table, plenty of hard work, and a marked shortage of money. Heidi remembers that her father was "a woman-chaser, a carouser" who caused her mother a lot of pain. She also recalls that in midlife, her mother (like Terry's) became more independent. While her father seemed to enjoy her mother's independence, he also became more subdued, perhaps worried that his wife might respond belatedly to his former habits of drinking and womanizing by leaving him. Of her mother's newfound independence, Heidi says wistfully, "I wish she would have been that way when she was younger."

While Heidi's older sister remained single all her life, breaking off several marriage engagements and ultimately escaping to the "big city," Heidi followed The Dream and got married:

> I was very dependent on my husband. I let him tell me, "We're going to do this and we're going to do that." And, "I think we should buy a house. I think we should buy a new car." I usually went along with whatever he said because I was just a young farm girl and he was from the city. From the beginning of our marriage, he knew more than I did.

Heidi is one of those lucky women for whom The Dream delivered what it promised. For over two decades, she had a satisfying marriage and four children whom she was happy to raise as a full-time mother:

My life was very satisfying. I enjoyed my kids; I loved watching them grow up. We had strong family ties, we always took vacations together and planned our lives around our kids. My husband was a good solid family man.

Kevin died when he and Heidi were already staggering from the recent deaths of his parents, who had been very close to both of them. Heidi plunged into a grief so deep she did not believe she could survive it:

> I wanted to pull the covers over my head and say, "Okay, my life is over." There were several times—at that point I was swimming a lot at night, on my own. I'd think to myself, it would be so easy, you know. I thought about suicide a lot. For the longest time I was angry at Kevin for leaving me. It took a long time for the anger to subside and for me to say "Okay, maybe he didn't want to die." It wasn't his choice, but I blamed him.

When Kevin died, two of her children were already married and one was living with his girlfriend. Heidi was left with one almost-grown child and a potentially empty life. She could have sought solace in her children and grandchildren, but she sensed that path would not work as an answer for her future. She could have caved in and let her older sister, who had insisted on moving in with her after Kevin died, care for her and tell her what to do and how to live. Instead, she chose to assert herself for the first time in her life. Sending her sister back to her own home, Heidi began looking for a job. As the months passed and she found she could make a life for herself, her entire self-image changed:

> I assert myself a lot more than I used to. Before, if someone said, "Heidi, sit down," I would sit down; "Now, you fold your hands," I would fold my hands. It's been *hard* to come out of that mold and say, "I don't have to sit down. I don't have to fold my hands." I would talk to myself and say, "I am a responsible person, I can do this." It was *hard*.

Single against her will, Heidi was forced to awaken from The Dream as she and her husband had lived it and take charge of her life. Taking an inventory of her ingrained attitudes and making peace with her old dreams, she recreated her life in an entirely different mode that required her to find new paths to fulfillment. She now has a rewarding job; she sold the home she had shared with Kevin and bought one that better suited her current needs; she takes vacation trips when and where she chooses; and she has flaunted convention by having a lover twelve years her junior. Would she trade it all to be back with Kevin? Of course, but she can also say:

> I would give anything to have Kevin back, but I know that's impossible. I like my lifestyle. I like being my own boss, doing my own thing, being in charge, paying my own bills, being responsible for my own livelihood. It's a good feeling to sit back and say, "This is mine."

THE GIFT OF FREEDOM

When children leave home, they are missed. Fortunately, nature makes them teenagers first to ease the pain. Nevertheless, there is a sadness or nostalgia for a time and a way of being a family that has ended. The women we interviewed acknowledged this sadness, but they also reported that there are serious advantages to this period of their lives. As Lillian Rubin suggested in her book, *Women of a Certain Age,* "It's no big news to women who live it that the empty nest syndrome doesn't exist for most of them." Our women described their years with growing children as a time when they were doing little more than "keeping their heads above water." Now, the so-called empty nest of midlife has finally given them a chance to *breathe.* Freedom from the massive caretaking responsibilities that had dominated their earlier years gave them the time (and money) to fulfill some of their own secret desires. Any negative feelings they experienced were more than balanced by the relief and exhilaration that came from their diminished sense of responsibility coupled with their new feelings of accomplishment. Having worked hard to raise their children, and having done so reasonably successfully, is a major source of satisfaction for midlife women. Peggy told us:

> Even though I've been very career-oriented all my life, what gives me the most satisfaction is the fact that I've raised two kids and that we have a good relationship.

Audrey, after years of caring not only for her children but for her aging father as well, welcomed turning fifty and finally having time for herself:

My children were thriving, self-sufficient, and happy. I had given it my
best shot with my parents, and now that was over. I didn't need to beat
myself to death with what I didn't do. Everything was okay.

The experience of feeling liberated is particularly common among those
women who spent their twenties and thirties focused on adjusting, psychologically and economically, to both parenting and divorce and life on their
own. The early years demanded a relentless focus on the needs of their
children and, often, on finding a way to make ends meet. These women find
the self-reliance and autonomy forced on them can be used in their midlife
years in whatever way they choose. They often report discovering parts of
their identities that had been placed "on hold" by the duties of motherhood.
They experience a new sense of spontaneity and freedom simply to enjoy
life. Sandi, who raised her two daughters on her own, says: "I've done the
things I needed to do. I've had my nose to the grindstone at work and at
home; now I can step back and soak up the sunshine a little bit." Glenda,
who raised two boys on her own, explains: "Life is so simple when you get
to midlife. It is as if all the major responsibilities are lifted off your shoulders,
at last." Julia, whose youngest daughter just finished college, agrees that the
midlife years finally gave her a chance to focus on herself:

> I like the new freedom I have. After twenty-some years of taking care
> of somebody else, I'm thrilled to take care of just *myself*. If I don't want
> to make dinner, I don't make dinner—I just get some corn chips. I
> have this little golden island of time when my kids are gone and my
> parents haven't moved in yet, and I want to make good use of it. I
> want to do the things *I* want to do.

THE GIFT OF CONTEXT

Regardless of women's marital status, midlife brings an opportunity to view
life from a new vantage point. While women tend to view their struggles as
personal, during midlife they develop a greater appreciation of the fact that
their personal histories have occurred in the context of the political and
social history of our society. The programs on public television, designed to
provide a historical perspective on today's social issues, are no longer a look
at the remote past. Instead they become a glance over our shoulders, an

exercise in "where were you when you heard. . . ." It becomes possible for women to place themselves in a particular era, to see themselves as part of a history still being lived. Today's midlife women have lived through a turning point for women in our society—an awesome context which helps women understand and accept their own personal choices and relationships. For Susan, 1993 has been a year of remembering:

> This year being the twenty-fifth anniversary of 1968—that year that numbed us all with its violence—we have been inundated with programs forcing us to look back. It was also the twenty-fifth anniversary of my graduation from social work school, and I attended the reunion. As I listened to a good friend talk about her experiences in the civil rights movement in the South prior to moving North, and her struggle to trust that we wanted to be her friends, I realized how little I had understood her at the time. The night wore on and we talked on, and I came to understand how little any of us had understood not only each other but ourselves. We knew we were against all forms of oppression and, of course, we were against the status quo, but we had very little idea what we were *for*. We were a collection of misfits, women for whom the dream never fit. We were all so lost and scared inside that we couldn't admit it even to ourselves. Day after day, we filled ourselves with bravado and, like the refugees in Bosnia picking their way through the bombed-out buildings, we picked our way through the confusion, looking for fragments of meaning with which to build our lives and our loves. Only now can I feel any sympathy for us, trying to build structures for our lives knowing only what we didn't want them to look like; and only now can I see the courage, strength, and perseverance we have shown ourselves to possess.

For single women, or women considering becoming single, coming to terms with the past in the context of this historical perspective is an integral part of redefining their lives. At midlife, asserting their right to make choices for themselves in their own private lives can be seen as part of a much larger movement of all women to have more control over their lives. Women can look back on the struggles of the women's movement in the sixties and seventies and see their own personal struggles as a mirror of their times. At midlife, women see themselves not as misfits, but as *women living on the edge of cultural change*.

⌒ •

Chapter 10

Accidental Careers: Circuitous Paths, Recovered Dreams, and Midcourse Corrections

Our lives are littered with mid-course corrections. A full half of us divorced. Many of the women have had career paths that look like games of Chutes and Ladders. We have changed directions and priorities again and again. But our "mistakes" become crucial parts, sometimes the best parts, of the lives we have made.

—Ellen Goodman

It is now time to explore the creative potential of interrupted and conflicted lives, where energies are not narrowly focused or permanently pointed toward a single ambition. These are not lives without commitment, but rather lives in which commitments are continually refocused and redefined. We must invest time and passion in specific goals and yet at the same time acknowledge that these are mutable.

—Mary Catherine Bateson

Work . . . always has been my salvation, and I thank the Lord for inventing it.
—Louisa May Alcott

Discovering the significant role work can play in creating a satisfying single life has been a source of surprise and delight for most of the midlife single women we interviewed. Forced to redefine themselves either by the termination of their marriages or by never having married at all, these women have discovered that work can be far more than a way to pass the time or to put food on the table. In fact, for single women who have left traditional roles behind, work becomes an increasingly important source of self-satisfaction, as well as a basis for rich relationships with others.

Most women now at midlife never really planned to have a career, at least not a "real" one that mattered. Brought up in the heyday of the marriage and motherhood mandate, they were rarely taught that a career could become an organizing force in their lives, a source of identity, self-esteem, and confidence. At most, they were encouraged to develop some skills to fall back on "just in case" something happened to their prince. But more commonly, they were discouraged from even thinking about their futures beyond how their lives would be decided by the circumstances of their marriage. Julia's story about her guidance counselor, Mr. Palmer, disparaging her plans to study art in New York City captured this reality, as does Myrna's story about her response to being asked what she wanted to be when she grew up. "I want to be nothing," she answered, "just like my mom."

Under whatever circumstances women now in midlife joined the work force, the process was commonly one of "falling into" a job that, over the years, turned into a valued career. Some fields such as teaching, nursing and social work were particularly conducive to this accidental pattern because precedents for promoting women already existed, as did precedents for accommodating the need for flexible hours in relation to child care. Most fields, however, were not. The few women who ventured into male-dominated fields, becoming physicians, lawyers, police officers, government officials, and stockbrokers, found doing so a formidable task. While they took pains to acquire the education and training they needed, they had no female mentors in these fields, no one to teach them how to survive as women in a very male culture. And yet, despite the obstacles women encountered in traditional and non-traditional fields, all of the women we interviewed have succeeded in redefining the importance of work in their lives. Necessity may have propelled these women into the workplace, but the fulfillment of doing a job well and the enjoyment of working with other people have kept them there.

AFTER THE BALL IS OVER

Those women who always planned to orient their lives around dreams of marriage and motherhood faced particular work challenges when their marriages crumbled. Their ball was over as abruptly as Cinderella's coach turned back into a pumpkin, minus the warning from a beneficent fairy godmother. They had to learn to take charge of their lives in unprecedented ways, often with the added complication of having to raise children. Women who had started and then abandoned careers at least had some sense of a direction to fall back on when their marriages ended, but most women had nothing. It never occurred to them that someday they might have to support themselves without any preparation to do so. All too often they found themselves under-educated and ill-prepared to compete; even those who had an education frequently lacked specific work skills and any sense of direction or career preference. The ways in which these women have managed to piece together jobs and careers out of resurrected academic interests or even hobbies, despite the demands of being mothers, is amazing. Their work histories reveal how they have had to focus and refocus their attention and commitment as the circumstances, responsibilities, and assumptions of their lives changed.

Audrey, for instance, had an education but no specific job experience when she and her husband divorced twenty-five years ago. Her upper-middle-class parents had sent her to an Ivy League college not because they were hoping she would discover her life's work, but because a good education was expected of a wife, mother, and member of their affluent community. Audrey put it this way:

> I grew up during the Eisenhower years. Everything was quiet, life was good. In the fifties you didn't do much thinking about where you were going because it was just pleasant. I think all of us assumed that we would have a wonderful time in college and learn good stuff and then get married and live the American dream: the white picket fence, two children and a husband who loves your mind. It didn't turn out that way for most of us.

Audrey was right. It didn't turn out that way for many of the women of her generation; however, as young women, they had faith in The Dream and envisioned their lives accordingly. Audrey, in fact, married her high-school sweetheart, Martin, within weeks of graduating from college. Because Martin was an aerial reconnaissance pilot for the Navy, he and Audrey moved around the country from one military base to another. What made this life style tolerable was being part of a tightly knit group of pilots and their wives. Audrey speaks with fondness about these early years of their marriage and their intense association with this group of friends. Despite the many moves, life was good. She and Martin were close and in rapid succession they had two daughters. Everything was proceeding according to The Dream, until the war in Vietnam began to erode their "happily ever after" foundation. Being a part of the military during an unpopular war put an enormous strain on Martin and, eventually, on their marriage. One by one they lost their support group, as many of their friends were killed in action or taken prisoner. Martin survived active duty and returned home, but when attending the funerals of their friends became a depressingly regular part of their lives, he withdrew from Audrey and the girls, drinking excessively and eventually having an affair. The situation deteriorated so rapidly that marital counseling could not save the union. Reluctantly, Audrey made the difficult decision to leave the marriage and return with her children to her native city, where she could have the support of family and friends.

Audrey, who never expected to work outside the home and had no specific job skills, was suddenly faced with the necessity of supporting herself and her children. This time period was extremely difficult:

> I never anticipated divorce. Suddenly my life was out of control. I had two kids, ages five and two-and-a-half, no means of support, and no assurance that Martin would keep me afloat for a while.

Audrey's choice of career was "pure necessity" and pure accident. Before her marriage had dissolved, a friend had asked her to help teach a Head Start class. She agreed and immediately discovered that she loved teaching children. When the marriage crumbled, Audrey remembered her experience in the Head Start class and went to her church's preschool in search of a job. "I threw myself at their feet and told them, 'I'm not worth much, but I like this stuff.' " She knew her salary would be low, but when it was combined with the money Martin had promised to send, she could make ends meet *and* she could be home with her kids after school and during the summers. She got the job and taught for seven years. As her children got older, she decided to go back to school and earn a master's degree in education.

Even though Audrey insists that she was never an ambitious person, she was regularly recognized and promoted for her commitment to excellence and outstanding work. At age fifty-three, she looks back on the years she has spent developing her career with a certain amount of surprise. After all, she never expected to work at all, much less create a successful career. Today, however, she is the director of a highly prestigious private school. The work she began out of sheer necessity has evolved into a truly satisfying career.

Although she is careful to maintain a balance in her life, spending time with family and friends and doing things to please herself, her commitment to her work has grown over the years, so that she now ranks it as one of her main sources of life satisfaction. She loves the responsibility she has, explaining "that's something I just seem to thrive on." She also enjoys the feeling of knowing she is working hard: "There's something deeply satisfying about knowing that you're doing the best job you can. I think that's my source of satisfaction—that I give it my best shot."

Audrey is not alone in either her success or the satisfaction she derives from it. Many women, who once dreamed only of being wives and mothers, have done phenomenally well at the game of catch-up, despite the daunting difficulties. Miriam, who grew up believing she would be a "nurse or a schoolteacher, in case something happened," now owns and manages a successful gallery that represents artists from around the world. Peggy put herself through graduate school at the same time both her girls were in college, earning a shot at a top job which she got and continues to enjoy to this day. Ruth not only created a successful consulting business, but has now embraced the risk of doing something "entirely different," recently opening a book store. Michele has become a physician, Marie a professor, and Lydia a lawyer. These women may have begun their careers accidentally, but their successes are no accident!

WORKING WHILE WAITING FOR THE PRINCE

Some women intended to marry but didn't, working hard while waiting for a prince who never came. After graduating from high school or college, they worked at jobs that were supposed to be "temporary," to occupy themselves until they married and got on with the real purpose of their lives. By the time they found themselves approaching midlife and still unmarried, most realized that their insignificant jobs had become important parts of their lives. They had fallen into areas of interest, and once there, had experienced an unexpected kindling of ambition and commitment. Without consciously trying to change their life direction, they awakened to find that they were no longer women waiting to be married, but had transformed themselves into women who were seriously committed to their careers. Pauline describes what it was like for her:

Somewhere along the line I thought, "Well, if I'm not going to get married, then I want the best there is for myself." I changed direction, put marriage aside. I don't know over what period of time this change emerged, but I really started looking out for myself in terms of my career and what *I* wanted to do.

Like Pauline, Erika never really planned to have a career but is now the first to admit that her work gives her enormous satisfaction. What started as a temporary job, which she took until she "settled down" and became a wife and mother, has evolved into a highly successful career in journalism. Erika developed a strong sense of ambition and commitment so gradually, she cannot pinpoint when the shift actually happened, only that it happened in a profound way.

Thirty-eight years old and never married, Erika is certain that nothing in her childhood prepared her for the role her career plays in her life. Her expectations were formed by witnessing her parents' marriage, which was so traditional it rivalled that of the parents on *Father Knows Best*. Her father unquestionably was king of their small castle, and her mother's job was to maintain it and him. Erika says, "There was no such thing as compromise in my parents' marriage. I mean, you did what my father said and that was it." Erika describes the emotional sacrifices she perceived her mother making:

When I think about my mother, I think about how she really gave up her independence when she married my domineering father. Some of the stories my mom tells me about her life before she married my dad and the way I see her react in situations now—I see this very active woman who then became passive because "a man's house is his castle."

Erika's parents, and particularly her father, strongly encouraged her to follow in her mother's footsteps. In fact, explaining what she believes would be her father's most important wish for her, Erika says, "Before he dies, he would love to know that there is someone there to take care of me, because he's not going to be there." All these years later, it still does not occur to him that she might be doing an excellent job of taking care of herself.

Despite her awareness of the compromises she saw her mother making, Erika accepted her parents' dream as her own. She grew up believing that it was only a matter of time before she took her rightful place in the comfort of hearth and home. Since she had not found Mr. Right by the time she finished college, she took a job on the staff of a magazine, thinking she would work there temporarily until she married. She explains:

Because there was no one around on a steady basis who was going to take care of me, I thought, well, you just have to do the best you can on your own, and you're only as good as your last article. I felt like I had to do a good job.

Erika did the best she could, which was very good, indeed. Over the years, as her all-important prince failed to appear, she simply continued to do her best. She worked throughout her twenties and thirties, and by the time we interviewed her, she had become a major success in her field—quite accidentally. Like many other midlife women, Erika never consciously competed for the opportunity to take on new responsibilities, but her superiors took note of the consistent excellence of her work and gradually she was promoted through the ranks. Today, Erika earns a salary she never dreamed of making. She is competent, successful, and struggles with her tendency to let her job take over the rest of her life. She loves her career and feeling competent and successful; she works with people whom she admires and respects and feels that her work touches the lives of others in important ways.

CIRCUITOUS PATHS: WOMEN WHO ALWAYS WANTED TO WORK

Not all women left childhood with no conscious career ambitions. Some women always had particularly independent personalities and dared to dream of something different. Others benefited from being exposed to the women's movement and the female role models it provided. Some women were even encouraged by their families to explore alternatives to marriage and motherhood. They received overt or covert messages from their mothers that the traditional roles were not as fulfilling as they were touted to be. Many also looked to their fathers for models of how to succeed in the world outside the home. After all, it was good old Dad who seemed to have the better deal, who seemed to be *happy* to leave for work each morning. Some of these women married, while others did not; all, however, intended to learn to fly. Unfortunately, however, they lacked a flight plan, a set of known coordinates, to guide them. Though they had career aspirations, their goals were often cloudy and unfocused. As a result, they were vulnerable to many detours, often following circuitous paths to realize their dreams.

For example, Alice always knew she wanted a career. Nevertheless, she had to struggle to create a professional life in a world that offered her little guidance or direction. Alice was fortunate to receive the active support of her parents, who worked to instill a sense of independence and confidence in her from an early age. When she turned twelve, she was sent to a special girls camp, where she continued to go each summer until she graduated from college. At this camp she was exposed to "a very rich set of role models," women who gave the message "that I could set goals, that I could be independent, that I could do things, and that I had a future as a person."

Alice was inwardly supported by these formative messages when she developed important goals for herself in early adulthood: She knew that she wanted to go to college, join the Peace Corps, and then go to graduate school. She did all three. She entered the Peace Corps after finishing college and spent three challenging years working and travelling in Africa. When she returned, she entered graduate school as planned, but it did not help her to identify what she *really* wanted to do with the rest of her life. She felt alone and lost, "without a vision of what I would do in the world." Unlike her male colleagues, she had no role models or mentors in the work world who could promote her career or provide her with examples of how to create such a vision.

Halfway through graduate school, Alice realized that she wasn't interested in the field she was studying, so she changed programs. When she finished her degree and took a job in her new field, she absolutely hated it! She recalls telling herself with a sinking feeling, "I've made this dreadful mistake. I'm in the *wrong* profession." She watched women around her react to the anxiety they felt about a life without direction by escaping into the structure and security of marriage. Alice, in contrast, renewed her search for some other dream. She took the entrance exams for law school, thinking she might change fields yet again. While waiting for the results, she was offered and accepted a job in business. This time she *loved* the work. Since then, she has developed a strong commitment to her career, willingly working however many hours it takes to get the job done. Quickly promoted up the organizational ladder, she now manages a staff of sixty-five people and is rewarded by the knowledge that the decisions she makes and the policies she establishes have a far-reaching, positive effect on others.

Alice's struggle to develop a career was shared by many divorced women as well. Josie, for instance, first mentioned in Chapter 3, traveled a circuitous path as she went through two divorces and many unsatisfying jobs before she was able to realize her early dreams of having a serious career. As a child, Josie watched her bright, capable, and creative mother "shrivel" into a chronically depressed state after giving up her chance at a career to be a full-time mother. Witnessing her mother's life instilled within Josie a commitment to find work that would be an important part of her life. This early goal was further reinforced as Josie saw how much her father's work as a professor of anthropology meant to him:

> The person who seemed to be having the best time was my father, and much of what made his life happy was that he got up and went to work every day. He deeply, deeply loved what he did. His work was more important to him than anything else in his life. I grew up with the impassioned idea that you picked work you loved, and it made you happy.

The books Josie read with enthusiasm, endless numbers of biographies of adventurers like Davy Crockett and Amelia Earhart, only confirmed her emerging dreams of a future that would give her something of value. By the time she was a teenager, Josie had vowed to herself that she would not have a life like her mother's. She knew her choice of career would be a crucial one. She explained her thinking at the time:

> No matter what, I was determined to fling my piton into the world. No matter how much I dangled there, I would *never* let go of the world because if I did, I'd end up in this black hole like my mother.

Although Josie had a head start on women like Audrey and Erika who never anticipated having a career, the process of creating one was more difficult for her in some ways. She had little help along the way and often struggled with her own doubts and depression. Like Alice, she knew what she *didn't* want, but figuring out what she did want was a different matter. She found herself floundering: "I just kind of made it up as I went along. For better or worse, I was very much on my own as I tried to develop some kind of dreams and ambitions." She spent her adolescence and early adult years "like a glider pilot," trying to catch updrafts and air currents in constantly changing wind conditions. She explains, "I really fell apart. I had no sense of how to make this transformation into an adult female. There were no models for that."

As noted earlier, at the end of her senior year of college, Josie jumped into marriage. She still intended to have a career, but in *what* she didn't know. She took a temporary job as a waitress and then later a more serious one as a librarian. When her husband went into the Peace Corps, she followed:

Sometime in the middle of our assignment the women's movement hit. We were living in this tiny town in Central America. I remember when a friend sent me a copy of *Ms.* magazine. I began to understand that something was going on in the world and that I had *missed* it. I knew that if I didn't give it to myself, I was going to be miserable. I didn't consciously think, "If I don't do this, I'll be like my mother," but all of a sudden, horizons were opening.

Ultimately, Josie chose to end her marriage and enter graduate school. She began searching for models of women who were creating unusual and imaginative careers for themselves, hoping for more inspiring visions than the ones she had been able to construct on her own. She feels deeply indebted to the women's movement for the inspiration to rebuild her image of herself:

I cannot begin to express my gratitude for the women's movement. No matter how crummy you felt, there was hope and there were visions and there were models. Models were being resurrected and made anew. I was virtually feeding myself with these images of women who were appearing in *Ms.* magazine saying, "The traditional life is not a life you have to live. It's not a life that's pleasant. There's a much better life."

Josie used these models to give her the courage to pursue a Ph.D. in her first "love," philosophy. She says, "I was doing at the age of thirty what people now do at seventeen. I was getting a life." She married and divorced again, this time realizing that she needed to be single to be fully herself. Although working had been central to Josie's well-being throughout her life, after graduate school she finally began the work that has given her the satisfaction for which she always yearned. Now, at midlife, as a respected university professor, she has created a career that reflects her true identity and her most cherished values. She speaks about her work with excitement, enthusiasm, and a sense of wholeness:

Philosophy is absolutely my passion. I can read and think for the rest of my life! I wanted a career in which I could be introspective for the rest of my life and I found it. What more could I ask for? I feel very complete.

A MATTER OF MEANING

The experiences of the women whose stories we have told in this chapter highlight an aspect of working that is of great importance to all women: work contributes significantly to their sense of independence, self-satisfaction, and self-definition. There are few experiences more gratifying than acquiring a sense of mastery over something that has been a serious challenge. Women find a variety of such challenges in the workplace, and the mastering of each brings with it a sense of increased personal efficacy and self-esteem. Women new to the work world often express surprise at how rewarding it feels to develop a sense of their own competence. Women who spend any amount of time working experience these gifts and opportunities in no small measure. The women we interviewed all reported that their work offered them a new and more secure sense of themselves as competent individuals who could establish their own priorities and apply them to their daily lives.

Not all the women we interviewed were high-level executives, doctors, lawyers, or other professionals. Women emphasized the simple but incredibly satisfying reward of knowing that they were capable of doing a job well, even if that job were considered mundane by others. As Pearl S. Buck once said, "The secret of joy in work is contained in one word—excellence. To know how to do something well is to enjoy it." Women who had not been able to pursue college and graduate educations, or who had spent many more years than most working as full-time wives and mothers, often did not have the opportunities to develop professional "careers." Yet these women still found great satisfaction in their work. Emma, for instance, has worked as a secretary ever since her children were quite young, making barely enough money to survive (last year her net salary was only $11,000). Still, Emma clearly takes pleasure in knowing that she does a job well and that people can count on her. She explains, "I feel great knowing that I give my best effort to my job. That's satisfying."

Some women reported that the sense of meaning and pleasure from their work increased as they got older. Divorced women who had raised children on their own reported that midlife had left them freer than ever to immerse themselves in their work. They felt that they were just hitting their stride and had not yet come close to realizing their potential. Morgan, who married in her early twenties and divorced nine years later, worked throughout her marriage and ever since. Yet at forty-eight, she feels that her career is really just beginning. With her children finally on their own, she is able to focus on her work with no distractions. She has not yet begun to do all the things she wants to do, knows she hasn't peaked, and is certainly a long way from wanting to retire. Even a few never-married women who have worked all their adult lives report that they did not appreciate how much their careers meant to them until these midlife years. Perhaps appreciation came late because they are only now reaping the rewards of their efforts; or perhaps, no longer waiting for a prince, they no longer fear appearing unfeminine by unfurling their ambition. These women heartily endorse Carolyn Heilbrun's observation that "the ultimate joy of middle-age is work."

Chapter 11

Turbulence and Tailwinds: The Challenges of Flying Solo at Work

To improve the lot of America's women, the pressing need is not an ever greater focus on the self. More good will come from swapping ideas about how to force employers to pay attention to women's needs, how to handle sex discrimination and harassment situations, how to get ahead despite the obstacles of sexism.

—Deirdre English

It's as if we women are in a totally rigged race. A lot of men are driving souped-up, low-slung racing cars, and we're running as fast as we can in tennis shoes we managed to salvage from a local garage sale.

—Naomi Weisstein

B eing single can be a serious advantage for women in the workplace. While single women are not on equal footing with their male counterparts in most organizations, they often have an edge over women who are married. Employers tend to view single women as having fewer demands competing for their time and energies, particularly if they do not have dependent children. They know that single women are less likely to quit their jobs because they have to support themselves, that they will only rarely leave because they are pregnant, and that they will never leave because their husbands have been relocated. Single women are seen as "fair game" for extra projects that require staying late or working weekends to meet deadlines. Employers assume that they should be dependable and available, and they often are.

Many single women who make themselves available in times of crises and deadlines move into positions of steadily increasing responsibility as their special qualities become evident. Having received little encouragement to be competitive, women now in midlife work cooperatively, frequently offer to help their bosses and peers, and are usually less threatening than their male colleagues, not only for the wrong reason (no one takes women as seriously), but also because they tend to engage in fewer overt power plays and be less invested in getting ahead at all costs. A fair number of the single women we interviewed were offered advancements they did not seek because someone noticed they consistently did outstanding work without being pushed. For example, Angela worked her way from a minimum-wage menial job to vice-president by always offering to help whichever colleague was in the next job up the ladder, thereby learning the tasks of that job. Single women, like Alice and Erika, devoted themselves to their jobs and were promoted as a result. In many cases single women prove to be such assets to corporations that, as Barbara Ehrenreich once suggested, they may start screening out women who cannot answer, with a firm no, a modified version of the standard loyalty oath: "Are you now, or have you ever, contemplated marriage, motherhood, or the violent overthrow of the U. S. government?" For single women who work hard and make themselves available when necessary, the rewards of their careers are many: feelings of competence, a sense of self-esteem, close relationships with colleagues, promotions, financial remuneration, invitations to travel as consultants and speakers, the respect of their colleagues, and generalized glory.

THE CHALLENGES OF FLYING SOLO

There are also some distinct penalties to be paid for being a single woman in the workplace. Despite three decades of efforts to change rules and behaviors in work environments, women—married and single alike—continue to face more than their fair share of difficulties. A *New York Times* poll in 1989, which asked women to rate "the most important problem facing women today," reported job discrimination by an overwhelming majority. In countless ways, women experience far more challenges in the world of work than their male colleagues. They can get jobs, but they continue to earn less than men for the same work, and they tend to be passed over for managerial positions for which they are equally qualified. They are more likely to be harassed and less likely to be believed when they report it. They can move

up the ranks, but usually not with the same speed, helpful mentoring, and
financial perks that characterize the careers of their male colleagues. Even
when they are part of senior management teams, little "slights" occur daily
from other women as well as men. For example, while secretaries routinely
ask their male bosses if they would like coffee, they assume a female boss can
and should get her own.

While all working women have to deal with the many sexist barriers and
impediments to their success, doing so effectively is particularly crucial for
single women. Unmarried women always face the harsh reality that they
have no one else to count on, that they must support themselves (and their
children, if they have any). If they get frustrated at work, or get fired, they
cannot "opt out" of the game in favor of staying home to care for their
husbands and children, still a valued option for at least some married women.
If single women want a comfortable life style and a feeling of security and
self-esteem, they must do their jobs competently at all times, earning the
respect and confidence of those around them. In addition to this eternal
pressure, single women face other obstacles as well. Many impose the burden
on themselves of negotiating all of these challenges without compromising
any of their feminine traits and behaviors, their ability to attract men, and
their ability to maintain rewarding personal relationships. They also must
deal with their vulnerability to becoming intimately involved with co-
workers. It is not an easy mission.

THE SEDUCTION OF WORKING
RELATIONSHIPS

Single women are more vulnerable to the romantic and erotic allurements
and pitfalls of close working relationships. After all, work is one of the
primary places where both men and women meet prospective partners and
marital candidates. Work can be much more fun when there is someone
around to whom you are attracted, and it is an infinitely better arena for
meeting and choosing a mate than the singles' bar scene. At work, a woman
has a fighting chance of getting involved with someone who has the same
interests, and she certainly has a better opportunity to get to know the man
before romance and sexuality become the focus. However, romance and
sexuality in the workplace are complicated issues, which have caused an

enormous amount of grief to women in general and to single women in particular.

When men and women work well together over long periods of time, it is easy for the boundaries between the professional and the personal to blur. Working together closely with a colleague who has the same goals and values is conducive to the development of intense relationships. Often, unintended intimate relationships ignite before either party has noticed what is happening. Even those who are happily involved in relationships in their personal lives can lose their bearings. As genuine fondness and mutual respect develop, the work relationship can become compellingly intimate, sexual, and *very* complicated. When the male in these office relationships is in a position to help the woman's career, as is often the case, other workers resent what they see as a woman taking unfair advantage of her relationship with her boss. Of course, some women *do* use the interest of a superior, married or not, to serve their own goals of advancement. It is a rare woman who is above using the influence she has gained through a personal-professional relationship, especially when she thinks she has good ideas and deserves advancement. While some of these same issues of undue influence have been noted in the case of the boss's "favorite" son, the sexual overtones of a male-female working team can lead to nasty resentments of the woman involved, particularly if she is single. Her access to the boss's ear gives her power she would not otherwise wield, however competent she might be.

Different complications arise when a man in the workplace is interested in a single woman who does not want to pursue a personal relationship. In such cases, it can be difficult to turn down advances gracefully without jeopardizing her career. Married women have a spouse to use as a defense, an excuse, or a threat. Single women cannot laugh off an advance by noting the presence of an insanely jealous husband. Men who feel rejected can sometimes make the workplace an uncomfortable place for a woman, whether they mean to or not.

No matter how they behave, single women are more likely to be the targets of office gossip, which can erode their credibility and, if chronic, undermine their long-term survival in the workplace. Attractive single women often find that accusations of using their sexuality to gain advancement are made, even when they are completely unwarranted. Over time, clever women learn to avoid most of these situations or to ignore them without letting them "get under their skin."

CAREER WOMAN OR "REAL" WOMAN:
THE FEMININITY DILEMMA, PART ONE

All single women who desire to advance to top positions within organizations must come to grips with simultaneously being females and serious competitive professionals. To succeed as power figures in most organizations, women must be less "feminine" in order not to appear seductive. These women are always in a bind, always faced with contradictory messages about how they should behave to survive and succeed in the culture of the organization. If women take pains to "play the game" the way men do, depending primarily on logic, raw competition, and undiluted aggression, they run the risk of being labeled as unfeminine, hard, or, worse yet, "a castrating bitch," even by female colleagues. However, if they operate in ways that are traditionally seen as feminine, they may be poorly evaluated as unassertive, lacking in self-confidence, and not commanding respect. Sometimes, women who try to preserve their feminine behaviors, who do not behave assertively, are seen as female versions of the Charles Atlas ninety-seven pound weakling, in whose face everybody is kicking the corporate equivalent of sand. And as we've already noted, if women act really "feminine," they run the risk of being seen as seductive and manipulative.

While all women worry about sacrificing their feminine traits to the corporate jaws, single women worry more. After all, the stereotype of the "lean and mean" career woman is always with her and she has no mate whose very presence at her side attests to her attractiveness and femininity. This vulnerability can be exploited by corporate power games in which anything goes. Consider one of Carol's experiences:

> I was arguing strongly with a male superior about how to handle an employee situation. Mind you, this is someone who had encouraged me to be more assertive. It was clear to me that I was right and I was not about to back down, so the discussion became heated. When it was clear that he was losing the argument on rational grounds, he became exasperated. He then resorted to what I'm sure he thought would be the most devastating attack, saying: "Boy, you're tough, I can see why you're not married. A man wouldn't dare get into bed with you."
>
> When I first reflected on this encounter, I considered what he had said and decided it was *his* problem. He knew he was wrong, so he

mounted a personal attack on me that was meant to hurt. Obviously he hoped a single woman at midlife would be sensitive about this issue, so he used what he could to make his point. It was only much later that I worried about the possible truth in his remark. *Was* I harder to get into bed with, since I had learned to play the game with "the boys"? As I took on more power at work, what had become of my softer side?

Some single women deal with this dilemma by deciding that they do not want to relinquish their traditionally "female" qualities in the workplace. They are comfortable with this style and believe it works better in leading and motivating employees than the more highly touted masculine qualities. They believe that sensitivity, the ability to be supportive, a commitment to collaboration and team spirit, and an ability to circumvent rather than confront resistance are strengths, not liabilities. They refuse to give up a style of relating that, for them, has personal *and* professional advantages.

However, many women who have worked in male-dominated career settings report that they pay a price for not following the male rules and styles of management and negotiation, even in situations when a woman's style would work better. Donna believes that the primary reason women do not advance as rapidly or easily as men "is because women tend to be more aboveboard; they directly address the problems and try to mediate and resolve them, which men don't do as well and therefore devalue." Julia has felt frustrated by a similar reality in her workplace:

In spite of the rhetoric, male values predominate in the work force. Men don't negotiate much. They don't solve problems by building consensus. They solve problems through power plays. I think I've become better at asserting my authority and getting my point of view heard, because I figured out, finally, that it was not helping me to *not* do those things. But I still don't like it. I'd still rather solve problems and address issues in a more cooperative manner.

Thus, women in positions of authority find that in order to succeed, they must take charge, be assertive, and play by the rules—rules that are usually made by men. Many also find that it isn't so easy to leave these behaviors at the door when you leave work. Single women who want high-powered careers but also want to continue to be active in the mating game are left in a quandary; they are forever trying to balance what they want to achieve with the price they will pay in the personal domain. Most know full well that power in a woman is not an aphrodisiac for men. Grace, first mentioned in Chapter 1, found that fewer and fewer men were interested in her as she became more successful and powerful in her career. She now says, "It's difficult once you get into my position. There's just not a whole lot of demand for police commanders. It turns a lot of men off when they find out what I do."

CALM AND CONFIDENT: THE FEMININITY DILEMMA, PART TWO

One specific aspect of the dilemma of whether or not to be feminine is *what to do with feelings*. Long regarded as the traditional domain of women, feelings are generally deemed inappropriate at work (unless, of course, they are negative and belong to the boss.) The question of whether to express or suppress feelings—and if expressing them, *how,* and if suppressing them, *at what cost*—is a difficult one. It is troublesome to both married and single women, but again, because single women are singularly dependent on their jobs to provide them with an income and a future, they *must* find a solution to this dilemma.

Lydia talked to us about this problem in her work life, saying that she recently learned the results of expressing her feelings the hard way. A few weeks before our interview, Lydia had received her annual evaluation. The areas of weakness her boss identified were particularly telling. First he told her that she became "unwrapped" too easily. Thinking that was some sort of legal jargon, we asked her what becoming "unwrapped" meant. "That's a good question," Lydia laughed. "What does it mean?" She had asked her boss the same question and learned that it meant she revealed her emotions too much at work. As an example, she explains:

> On a Monday morning two weeks ago, three clients called to complain. They must have had horrible weekends and decided to take it out on me. So maybe that Monday it was showing on my face that I was annoyed or that the day wasn't going perfectly. Some weeks I work sixty or seventy or eighty hours. Well, you begin to show that. I don't try to hide my feelings. If I'm angry, I'm not going to walk down the hall and call you names, but at the same time it's not my mind-set to say to myself, "I better hide this anger." I just walk down the hall

the way I am. If I'm mad, I'm mad. Well, I guess you're not supposed to do that.

Lydia was also informed that she had displayed what is probably the second most common "fault" of which women are accused at work: she was not sufficiently "self-confident." Translated, this so-called fault seems to mean that women are less willing or less able to bluff their way through a situation, trying to convince themselves and everyone else that they know something when they don't. The gender bind appears again: most women were trained in childhood to be reticent, to *not* express themselves aggressively, even when they know the answers; now, as adults in the workplace, this ingrained behavior is evaluated negatively by colleagues and clients as a lack of self-confidence. Lydia explains:

> Every year I get a very good report. I'm a terrific worker, but they always say the same thing at the end. "Lydia, you need to work on your self-confidence. You know, we want our firm to win. We want clients to say, 'I want Lydia to handle this case.' "

Lydia's boss tried to help her with this "problem" by advising her, "When you do not feel totally confident, act as if you do." This injunction to act confidently is a challenge for women who have rarely been encouraged by anyone to act as if they are even knowledgeable, let alone proud of their abilities and their work. Women in the workplace usually have to build the appearance of confidence from the ground up, starting with experiences in which they encounter problems, take risks, and find solutions. This is never an easy, pain-free process. Lydia describes one of her biggest challenges:

> My firm holds litigation group meetings every couple of weeks. You're supposed to report on what new cases you're handling that might be of interest to other members. The first time I had to say something in front of the litigation group, I almost died. My terror was very obvious. Afterwards our group leader came up to me and said, "You know, we really need to work on that problem of yours. You need to work on being able to talk." Every year it gets a little bit easier. I have my first jury trial next month, a milestone in my career. I'll be glad when I've done it. Public speaking is something I have to work on every day.

Even if women accumulate enough experiences to build a genuine sense of self-confidence, they still face the problem of having to walk the very fine line of being seen as confident but not cocky. Donna has attempted this precarious walk and has paid a price for wavering toward "too confident":

> I fully understand what women mean when they talk about a "glass ceiling." I know I can come across as overconfident and I think that was a problem when I was working at the corporation. The senior vice president for whom I worked was having an awful hard time with women. I don't know whether it was a glass ceiling or a brick wall, but it wasn't right. Suddenly, instead of running the marketing division, the president wanted me to move into the financial side. That didn't make any sense. I had been in marketing for over twenty years.

BOUNCING OFF BRICK WALLS AND GLASS CEILINGS

Because single women are so dependent on their jobs for support, they are likely to be invested in advancement and therefore to have had more than their share of experiences of bumping up against what has been dubbed "the glass ceiling," or as Donna put it, "the brick walls." Put simply, the top jobs in most large organizations continue to be reserved for men. All too often, hard-working women who have rapidly climbed their corporate ladders reach a point when it becomes clear to them that they will never be allowed to take the next step into upper management, let alone that final step to the top of their organizations. They are faced with a number of options: They can stay in their organizations while "swimming against the tide" and trying to change it; they can try to find other work environments in which women are treated differently; or they can leave the corporate world altogether to strike out on their own.

Some of the women we interviewed have remained in the semi-hostile environments of their corporate worlds and take pride in the changes that have occurred as a result of their efforts. They believe the years they have devoted to change have made the road smoother for other women who may follow. Kelly, for instance, feels encouraged by the new directions now being taken by her employer:

I can't believe how the company has changed. We've got a long way to go, but management is finally recognizing that family issues are a part of work; they are considering on-site day-care and recognizing that people need time off!

Other women have had less hopeful experiences. Even those women who have learned to play the corporate game well enough to move into major leadership positions report that their work environments are not friendly places, and that the higher they go, the less friendly the atmosphere. Valerie, for instance, who has spent her entire career in the corporate world, says it has never stopped being tough to be a woman in a man's world. Over the span of thirty years, she moved up from the clerical pool to a highly visible position as vice president of a division, making herself a modern-day female Horatio Alger. She negotiated what she describes as the "white Anglo-Saxon male-dominated" system well. At first she sought and received the mentoring she needed from a rising young executive, getting his support to go to school so that she could leave the secretarial ranks. When she finally made it into the professional stream, she worked long hours, meeting and even surpassing her own goals. Then, at midlife, not unlike many men who have worked hard all their lives, she reviewed her life and reconsidered the meaning and rewards of all her hard-won "success." As a result, she chose to move to a smaller corporation where she was given a position of equal status and pay, but less responsibility. She opted to be a big fish in a considerably smaller pond, a decision that has allowed her to work fewer hours and to focus on areas in her life she had neglected during her long climb to the top. "You get tired of fighting," she says, "I'm much more inclined to put energy into my personal life now."

Some women described the brick wall they encountered as an "empty feeling": They had achieved success, but neither their work nor their interpersonal contacts felt meaningful to them. In large corporations and corporate-like businesses, there is such a single-pointed focus on scaling the corporate ladder that few employees have the time or inclination to cultivate mutual and meaningful interactions with one another. While this sterile aspect of corporate culture has certainly been noted by many men as well, men don't seem to complain about it as much as women. Barbara Ehrenreich was probably right when she observed that, "There may be a poor fit between the impersonal bureaucratic culture of the corporation and what is, whether as a result of hormones or history, the female personality." Women tell us that a sense of purpose is very important to them in their work and that personal advancement, in and of itself, rarely provides this sense of significance. It isn't surprising that women, raised to give and receive nurturance in relationships, feel that something is painfully missing when there is none to be found. It also isn't surprising that single women, who often depend on their jobs to meet many of their interpersonal needs, find this environment particularly barren. Single women (particularly those who have never had children or whose children are grown) often feel compelled to do something about this lack of meaning in their work and work relationships because of the large role work plays in providing the satisfaction they find in their lives.

A considerable number of the women we interviewed have chosen either to leave large corporations and organizations or have never worked for them at all. Instead these women have pursued careers in which they are accountable primarily to themselves and in which they find the work inherently meaningful. Many of our single women described the independence and freedom in these work arrangements to be the most satisfying aspects of their careers. Their work, they explain, is an expression of their autonomy in every way. The women we interviewed in medical and mental health fields moved from large hospitals and health-care systems to private practices; women in corporations left to establish independent businesses or consulting careers; women in large law firms moved to smaller partnerships or legal-aid societies. We mentioned Angela, who chose to leave the corporation for which she had worked for over a decade to start her own business, because it had become clear that the top job was closed to her. She loves the freedom and independence of having her own business, and she also loves the meaning she finds in her work. She says, "My business is very rewarding. I help people. I can make their lives much more comfortable." Similarly, Donna finally got fed up with the never-ending obstacles of sexism in her corporate job and left her employer to create her own company. Nell, exhausted by the all-consuming work habits of her male partners that left her personal life vacant, solved her dilemma by buying their shares of the business:

These guys were like Donald Trump. I mean, they were *really* into it. They worked until eleven o'clock at night; they worked six days a week, and then, on Sunday, they would want to have a business meeting! They held business meetings at nine at night. Now, at last, I've got a personal life.

When these women go out on their own, it is truly a gutsy move. They usually have no second income to sustain them through the lean period when their new business is building a reputation. They are usually in need of the fringe benefits that come with working for corporations, such as health insurance and retirement plans, because they do not have spouses whose plans would cover them. For example, one of our friends recently told us that if she were still married she would leave the university where she works because of her vehement disagreement with their policies. But with three children to put through college and an ex-husband who is often less than responsible despite his large income, she feels she is a prisoner of her need for financial security. Another single friend recently spent months agonizing about whether she could afford to update the equipment she needs for her small business. Forced to purchase a new computer system in order to compete, she is holding her breath, praying for the necessary business to cover her loan payments before she falls in default on her mortgage.

A QUESTION OF BALANCE

The downside of all the success that single women frequently achieve, whether working for themselves or others, is the difficulty of maintaining a balance between their professional and private lives. It is very easy for single women to let their work consume them. Some women feel under such pressure to succeed that they fail to notice that they have allowed their support networks to atrophy, defining themselves more and more in terms of their jobs and the people they work with, and less and less in terms of their friendships. Women who feel they lack confidence in the area of socializing, or who are unwilling to participate in the singles scene, said that they sometimes used their work to avoid dealing with this area. But even single women who enjoy socializing are vulnerable to taking on heavy job responsibilities and long working hours. Some, like Grace, find great satisfaction in their busy schedules and many commitments at work; for others, however, the rewards of financial remuneration and the esteem of their colleagues do not compensate for the lack of time they have to devote to their personal lives. Lydia, for example, is in the process of taking a midlife look at her priorities. She loves being an attorney and for years she has revelled in the rewards of her professional success. She does a good job, loves to win cases, and has been working towards the goal of becoming a partner in her firm. Earlier in her career she readily gave up aspects of her personal life in service of this goal. For instance, she dated a man she had met in law school until her dedication to her job drove him away:

> He was a great guy. He would call and say, "Can we do something this weekend?" "Uh-uh, I'm working." "What about next weekend?" "Well, I'll let you know next weekend." And the next weekend would come, "I'm working." He finally told me, "Go take a hike." This pattern in my social life was characteristic of things to come. The past few years have been grueling. You've really got to prove yourself, you just do.

Now, however, Lydia is wondering if she wants to continue making the sacrifices necessary to achieve partnership:

> Work brings me a certain amount of fulfillment and happiness, but I know now that I don't want to be taking legal journals to bed when I want somebody to hold me. I want to have a *life*. I want to work and be the best I can, but I want to have a personal life. I don't want my life to become "all work and no play," with no friends and no quiet time.

Women talked to us a great deal about the importance of finding a balance between their work and personal lives. Helen insists on having time for herself. "I don't take care of myself by working ninety hours a week. I think that overworking and withdrawing socially are probably the two worst ways to take care of yourself." An orthodontist in private practice, Helen has never sought fame and fortune in a large organization, preferring to apply her skills as she sees fit within the context of a small and comfortable partnership with a few other professionals. When we asked her about her ambitions, she denied any desire for a high-powered career, saying simply, "What I want from life is fun and enough money to be comfortable and a reasonably pleasant job."

Repeatedly we heard women reevaluating the amount of time they have devoted to their work, particularly those women who spent their twenties and thirties devoted to their careers. For example, now that she has a son, Kelly says of her career, "I'm well enough established to take a back seat in my career. My attitude is, I haven't done it all, but I know how much it takes to get it all and I'm not willing to do that." For these women, the pleasure of midlife is feeling free to give attention to areas they haven't had time to explore. Women who have worked long and hard for success find they are ready to let work take a back seat to children, travel, or some other personal passion. Michelle sums up the views of many of the women we talked with when she says:

> You only have so many years and you might as well enjoy the ride. I don't see my work making a major impact on society. I do not have grandiose aspirations. I do want to produce something meaningful and to feel like I'm contributing. But on the other hand, I have no problem being on vacation.

IMPLICATIONS FOR THE FUTURE OF FLYING SOLO

Flying solo in the workplace, while not easy, holds many rewards. Achieving success and developing feelings of competence not only can positively affect single women's individual lives but can also transform the basic structure of our society. It is hardly surprising that those who revere the two-parent nuclear family as a sacred entity have vehemently discouraged women from making work a significant part of their lives. Many are threatened by the implications of single women becoming successful in the workplace. Charles Westoff expressed the fears of many when he wrote in the *Wall Street Journal*: "What is going to happen to marriage and childbearing in a society where women really have equality?" He went on to state his opinion that "the more economically independent women are, the less attractive marriage becomes." Like many, Westoff assumes that what holds women in the cherished roles of wife and mother is primarily financial dependency and that the traditional order will crumble if women have the opportunity to make their own choices. We disagree. Since women value relationships, they will undoubtedly continue to choose marriage, even if they are financially independent. However, we do believe that the rules of marriage will change when women are truly free to choose to make it on their own. Women who are no longer subservient, abused, or expected to carry the brunt of household and childcare tasks, *and* who have financial independence, constitute a force for the radical revision of gender in our society. Their increasing economic success will likely be the key to the *survival* of marriage and the family, not in its present form, but in one that finally embodies the principle of equality. The possibility of choice itself will allow women to negotiate the marital relationship in a way that is more likely to meet their needs.

Chapter 12

A Good Ground Crew: Intimacy, Friendship, and Community in the Lives of Single Women

> Women not only define themselves in a context of human relationship but also judge themselves in terms of their ability to care.
> —*Carol Gilligan*

> The loneliest woman in the world is a woman without a close woman friend.
> —*Toni Morrison*

> I feel my life is woven together with people who know me in the way, I suppose, a primary partner would. This certainly gives me a sense of being loved deeply, of being connected beyond what average friendship provides.
> —*Shannon*

Lydia was twenty-seven years old when she escaped from her marriage to Neal, an abusive and alcoholic husband. When she left, she had a high school education, no money, no place to live, and no job skills. "I left with nothing except my life and my child," she explains. "I didn't even bring my dog because we had to leave quickly." She was suddenly on her own, with little sense of who she was other than Neal's wife, and *no* idea of how to build a life for herself and her child without him.

Lydia had chosen to marry early primarily because no one encouraged her to pursue the academic promise she had demonstrated in high school. Her father was a machinist and her mother worked as a waitress in a local restaurant; no one in either of their families had ever attended college. When Lydia met Neal, she was impressed by how strong and self-confident he appeared. He seemed well equipped to take care of her in what she experienced as a frightening and ambiguous world. Once married, however, Lydia soon learned that with protection comes control:

> Neal had a sense of control about him that I felt I didn't have in my own life. Inside, I just felt out of control. I didn't know where my limits were, where I ended and the world began. Well, Neal began to set limits for me.

Increasingly, Neal took charge of even the most private parts of Lydia's life. He forbade her to wear certain clothes, to choose her own method of birth control, to take ballet classes. Lydia found her every move being dictated and criticized. Eventually he began to punctuate his comments and commands with body blows. Lydia tolerated his abuse and rigid control for three years; her self-esteem was so destroyed in the process that she came to believe her life was not worth saving. One afternoon in her kitchen, however, Lydia realized that her young son, Jeff, was also in danger, if not of being beaten, at least of growing up to become an abuser himself. With this chilling realization, Lydia found the courage to flee:

> Neal had one of Jeff's arms and I had the other. There was this baby in the middle! That was the moment I said to myself, "I'm out of here." I waited for Neal to leave. I called my girlfriend, I called the United Way, and I went to a shelter until I could get the plane fare to go home. To compare that moment with the twenty or thirty or fifty other moments I was in a corner, beaten and bloody, makes that moment seem like nothing. But it was the crucial moment. I did not want Jeff to grow up to abuse people and I did not want Jeff to grow up with a mother who had no self-respect.

Lydia looks back on those times with sadness and more than a little amazement that she was ever that vulnerable and dependent. "I was a shaky person. I don't know how I got to be so shaky." She is shaky no more. Eleven years after her divorce, Lydia is a competent and self-confident lawyer who lives with her son Jeff, now a teenager, in her own comfortable home. How did she overcome her insecurity and the chaos of a shattered life? How did she begin her recovery? Lydia, like so many women, discovered the seeds of her own courage and strength in making connections with friends and building a sense of community in her life.

A week after Lydia left Neal, she moved back to her hometown, where she could benefit from the support of family and friends. She took full advantage of the services and resources offered by the community, including subsidized housing. She also cleaned houses so that she could take her son to work with her, and she started making choices that would give her the ability to create an independent life style. Upon the recommendation of her United Way counselor, she enrolled in the local community college where, as part of her studies, she became a part-time work/study student at a women's center. The connections she forged there played a crucial role in her discovery of a sense of self she could value. "Getting involved with other women at the women's center made me realize that there was a *self* in here," she explains, tapping her chest. "It was like a light bulb suddenly turned on."

Lydia was given an opportunity to pass on what she had learned from her experience when she was assigned to lead groups for other separated and divorced women and women who had been battered:

I walked through that door so many times in the form of other women. They would come in and they weren't ready to talk about it, but you knew they had been through hell the night before. They would have bruised arms and black eyes, and they'd be wearing dark glasses—the same stuff I used to do.

Helping other women through their struggles aided Lydia in healing the damage done in her own abusive relationship with Neal. Equally importantly, she also began to weave a web of supportive friendships with the other staff members at the center. "We lived and breathed for each other," she says. "I would have done anything for any of them. They were my family."

Lydia's experience of the importance of close friendships in her life was shared by all the women we interviewed who were satisfied with their single lives. For some, like Lydia, friendship networks played a crucial role in helping them leave difficult relationships. For all, such networks made living singly possible. Indeed, these friends are the "ground crew" who make it possible for single women to take off and soar comfortably on their own.

VALUING ALTERNATIVE FORMS OF INTIMACY
AND SUPPORT: A TALE OF TWO WOMEN

Ignoring the fact that women experience intimacy in many relationships, the marriage and motherhood mandate has relentlessly equated intimacy, security, and support exclusively with marriage. This message has been circulated in a variety of ways, too often leading women to devalue their friendships and particularly their connections with other women. Recently, for example, Susan was browsing for birthday cards and found one of a young woman saying to a female friend, "I'll always be there for you." On the inside of the card, the woman adds, "Unless, of course, I have a date." These attitudes comprise some of the most powerful obstacles women must confront to create the "ground crew" they need.

Megan, like Lydia, is a woman who has been able to overcome these limited notions of the mandate in order to acknowledge the value, warmth, intimacy, and practical help in her friendships. "My female friends have replaced *family* for me. They are my real support." She refuses to minimize her network, even if the world around her does:

> Close friendships are not considered equivalent to intimate relationships. Friends are more often viewed casually, as people you go to the movies with. But it's never been that way for me. I guess not being socially sanctioned makes my network sort of *invisible*.

Contrast Megan's attitude with that of Nell, who is one of the least satisfied women we interviewed and one who has few relationships in her life. Unwilling to let go of her dream of traditional marriage, when Nell talks about the significance of spending time with her friends, and particularly her female friends, she portrays it as little better than treading water:

> I don't mean to be ungrateful, but spending my night with some girlfriend isn't my idea of heaven, you know. But that's where you are when you don't have a man and you're single. You just keep yourself busy.

Nell has not expanded her definition of intimate relationships and therefore underestimates the amount of support and joy women like Megan have found in a variety of social ties. While Megan recognizes that the webs of support she has created are worthwhile, even though they are undervalued by society, Nell continues to view a relationship with a man as the only real answer to all of her needs and the only real way of mastering life's challenges. As a result, she is unable to cultivate meaningful relationships with friends and so continues to feel isolated and empty within.

While Nell was unique in how tenaciously she held to the belief that relationships other than marriage are insignificant, her line of thinking was not totally foreign to some of the other women we interviewed. Many divorced women began their single lives with few close friendships of their own. During their married years, they had funneled all of their energy into the roles of wife and mother, and while they might have had friends, they seldom made these relationships a priority. Elena, who has never married, explained that she has become aware only recently of how she has neglected friendships while in romantic relationships in the past. She hopes to do things differently in the future:

> I wonder what it would be like to be in an intimate relationship and still maintain all the friendships I have. During my last relationship, I put a lot of these friendships "on hold," and I don't feel good about that.

Although valuing what we, as women, can give to one another does not receive societal support, most women who have lived on their own have learned, like Megan and Lydia, about the importance of developing friendships with other women. Some women explain that their relationships with other women are their most significant sources of emotional support, even when they are actively and romantically involved with a man. As Ria explained:

> Mark is my sweetheart, my lover, and my life partner, so he is central in my life. But in terms of my main day-to-day needs, I don't call him as much as I call my women friends.

Jean, who has many women friends, offered valuable advice on the subject:

> I would never think of underrating my women friends. They are my ballast! I am as attentive to my women friends as I am to a man I'm madly in love with. I mean, I'm as thoughtful and considerate and concerned about their well-being as I am about his. I take good care of the people I care about. I really believe that is crucial.

FINDING WHAT FITS: ELEMENTS OF A
WELL-FUNCTIONING NETWORK

A well-functioning friendship network supplies the intimacy and emotional support that lead to feeling loved and valued, as well as a general sense of connectedness and community. In the past, the sense of being part of a community was provided by neighbors and extended family, but increased mobility, anonymity, and divorce have changed the landscape of our social lives forever. Today, friendships augment and sometimes replace the role once filled by families and neighbors. For single women, in particular, friendship networks provide a sense of being connected to a community of people who care about one another. This net of security and community offsets the sense of vulnerability that otherwise accompanies living singly. After all, we may all be essentially *alone* in the universe, but life would be grim indeed if we had to constantly confront this existential fact. We must believe we would be missed if we disappeared tomorrow. We need to feel confident that someone will be there when we need to share our triumphs as well as our woes. Even when women choose not to call on their friends for help, they take comfort in knowing that a safety net would be available if they really needed it. As Elena expresses this, "Just knowing that my friends are *out there* makes me feel good."

Beyond these basic similarities, the networks of satisfied single women come in many sizes and shapes. During her years at the women's center, Lydia relied on the small, tightly knit group of other women who worked there. Many of the women we interviewed described similarly small and intense networks, while others described ones that were larger and more diverse. What seems most important is the "fit" between a woman's particular needs and expectations and the network itself. Some women, who describe themselves as private and solitary, prefer to forego the pleasures of a large friendship circle in favor of a few close friendships, carefully tended. Elsie explains that she feels very connected in her life, but that she can "count my really, really, really good friends on one hand." Louise also emphasizes the importance of a few close friends, explaining, "In this city, I have three women who are very dear to me. We look out after each other. I'm a very private person. I meter out my friendships because, in order for me to be a good friend, I can't spread myself too thin."

Quite a few women reported a strong need for solitude. For these women, tending a large network of friends would infringe on their need for time alone. Terry recognizes a tension in her life around this issue. "In order to maintain friends, you need to tend to them. A lot of the time I prefer solitude, but I know that my life would be incomplete without my friends." Jessie, too, feels this conflict in her life. "I have good friends who are important to me, but I am also very introverted. As much as I enjoy my time with other people, returning to myself is always a pleasure."

Other women seek large, diverse networks involving a lot of social activity. Liza, for example, thrives on an extraordinary number of friendships. From the time she was a little girl, Liza always wanted to be a part of a large family. As an adult, Liza's extensive network has more than made up for the deprivation she felt as a child with only one brother. Her network includes adults of all ages as well as the children of friends, with whom she plays the role of favorite aunt. She has a group of friends with whom she plays squash on Sundays and Wednesdays, a group of friends with whom she goes to the pool in the summer, a group of friends with whom she goes sailing, friends from high school, from college, friends from her first job out of college, a group of friends for a monthly bridge game, and many "volunteer friends" from various organizations with which she has been affiliated over the years. For her fortieth birthday this year, she could not even begin to narrow her list of friends down to the 100 people who could be accommodated at the party being thrown in her honor. Many women would find the need to maintain 100 friendships overwhelming, even if they were casual ones. Some might go so far as to say that such a network would be a burden, more trouble than it was worth. But Liza sees each of her friends as close; each has a special place and function in her life.

There is diversity not only in the size of women's networks but also in the people whom they choose to make up such networks. While most single women agree that friendships with other women are an essential part of their networks, they are not unanimous about whether they prefer cultivating friendships with women who are married or single. Again, the "fit" between a woman's choice of friends and her particular needs and priorities is what seems to be most important.

Some single women report that, in the face of the skeptical responses they receive from the wider culture, friendships with other single women provide a needed validation of their life style as well as an important sense of being part of a community of like-minded people. Moreover, these women often feel that other single women are better able to understand and relate to the challenges, struggles, and joys of their lives. Megan, for example, who in the words of a friend has "a real dignity about being single," explains that, as she has entered midlife, she has sought comfort and acceptance in friendships with other never-married women because they are facing similar questions and life issues. In this similarity, she finds the understanding of shared experience. She describes conversations in which they discuss their feelings about marriage, the kinds of relationships they want with men, whether or not to have children, and how to cope with loneliness and the other challenges of single life. She explains her connections with her friends:

> None of us was prepared to be on our own in our late thirties and forties. And though we are fully cognizant of the pros and cons, there are times when it gets really lonely and when it's scary being on your own in this world.

Connections with divorced women can also be particularly important to women going through their own divorces. When Marie's husband Jim left her after twenty-five years of marriage to pursue a relationship with one of his graduate students, she felt abandoned and alone. Looking back, she realized that she had been so focused on meeting Jim's highly demanding needs that she had never formed any real friendships of her own. "All the friends or people I associated with were contacts through my husband. When he left, I really had no friends of my own. None!"

Once on her own, Marie began to recognize the importance of connections with other women. She slowly started to reach out to some of the women with whom she worked. During her first holiday season on her own, one of her colleagues approached her at a school party and asked her where Jim was. When Marie revealed that Jim had left her, the woman responded quickly, "Oh, we've got to do something. We've got a support group. There are three of us who meet for dinner and you must join us!" This group of divorced women became Marie's anchor during the tumultuous months that followed, as she and Jim fought over their divorce settlement and she began to rebuild a life on her own. She says, "Those three women listened to my tales of woe to no end. It was just marvelous." Marie's experience was similar to Sandi's, who also explained that relationships with other women helped her get through the difficult times following her divorce. She says, "It's really been other women who have helped me get past the feeling that I'm all alone and that I have nothing to look forward to in life."

Many women reported that their single women friends are particularly important parts of their lives because they are the ones with whom they share everyday pleasures and activities. Married friends are often less available to go to movies, plays, concerts, or to share meals and other adventures such as travel. As Erika says, "I don't always get to see my close married friends a lot because they have kids and other agendas." While single women need very close friends to whom they can bare their souls, they also need "activity friends," casual friends or acquaintances who have some of the same interests and needs. They may never tell these friends their fantasies, troubles, or dreams, but that doesn't make them any less important. Jean, who has many single women friends, explains:

When you're single, you don't have this cozy, self-contained home entertainment center in the form of a spouse. So you get to know enough people that there is always someone you can call up when you want to go to dinner, or to a movie or the museum.

These friends create a buffer against lonely times for single women. There is always someone to call should they wake up on a Sunday morning with no pre-arranged plans but with a desire to just "do something."

ACCEPTING OR REJECTING DIFFERENCE: ANOTHER TALE OF TWO WOMEN

Although single women need other single women, they also want friendships with married women, and particularly they want to preserve their long-term friendships with women who happen to get married. Some of the women we interviewed describe these long-term friendships as their most significant, since they involve a shared history that may date back to late adolescence or early adulthood.

Friendships with married women have their own special and unique benefits. Helen said that she *preferred* friendships with married women because she felt they were more dependable. "I find that women friends who are married are not as likely as single women friends to abandon you if they get a man. They've already got a man!" Married friends who have children also may offer single women the pleasures of family life, including them in Sunday dinners and holiday celebrations, and welcoming their help with child-care. In this way, single women who don't want to commit to raising children can still experience some of the joys of loving them, with the added benefit of being able to go home when they have had enough! Helen loves to go to the beach with her married friends and their families. Before she adopted her daughter, these outings gave her the opportunity to be with children in limited doses. Now they provide her and her daughter with a sense of extended family.

While friendships between single and married women have indisputable benefits, they also can bring very specific challenges: Single and married women sometimes have problems tolerating one another's lifestyles. The tale of Beth and Elena is one of two friends who took different paths. They have had one of those very special "best friend" relationships since junior high school. Even though they sometimes lived hundreds of miles apart, mutual interests and similar careers strengthened rather than weakened their friendship. They remained close throughout their twenties and thirties, spending a lot of time together, confiding secrets, cheering each other's victories, and comforting each other when comfort was needed.

The commonality of Beth and Elena's lives changed considerably when Beth got married at thirty-eight and then had a baby. Beth is no longer available to Elena in the same ways as she was in the past, and Elena is no longer a part of Beth's daily reality. Their priorities are now very different. Beth looks back on her single years and wonders what was so great about "being on an emotional roller coaster year after year." She acknowledges that it was exciting, but adds "enough is enough." She accepted the proposal of a very nice man, and they have since created a comfortable marriage. Everything in her life seems stable and secure, and she is thrilled to have it that way. Beth has a new appreciation of the meaning of family, and she enjoys belonging to a community where she is known and respected. Elena, however, still loves the freedom of her single life and the excitement and adventure of international travel and meeting new people. The transition in this old friendship has been hard for both of them, as it is for many women whose life paths diverge.

We asked ourselves, how can two friends who have treasured their relationship for over a quarter of a century have trouble accepting each other's choices? The fact that one woman may need and want to be married and have children, while another prefers to be single without children, has the power to threaten a friendship. Each woman must look at the other and see what she has had to give up. There are times for *all* women, married and single, when other choices seem appealing, so it isn't surprising that these reminders of the alternative oath are disquieting at best. Single women sometimes look with envy at the apparent joys of a happy family: the adorable children, a loving husband, the comfort of the familiar. The envy of married women can be no less intense when they see their single friends enjoying the freedom and excitement of travel, rewarding careers, and passionate, if impermanent, romances.

To defend themselves against these conflicting visions, women often disqualify or even denigrate what is different. The nature and expression of their friendship shift and old habits and expectations are relinguished with a sense of loss and disappoinment. Negative feelings about another's choices can be intensified by the fear of losing a friend because the gap of difference may become too wide to bridge. This fear has a basis in reality. Some friendships cannot make the transition from revelling in commonalities to enjoying differences. But women who are committed to each other in their friendship, who can acknowledge their feelings and take time to adjust, can affirm each other and maintain their relationship becoming enriched by the experiences and differences they discover through each other.

BRIDGE OVER TROUBLED WATERS: REACHING OUT AND GIVING BACK

Creating and maintaining strong, reliable, and satisfying friendships requires the same effort other gratifying relationships require: time, attention, commitment, and care. Liza explains why friends are so important in her approach to successful single living:

> I think friends are one of the most important resources you can have. But you do have to *work* at being a friend. You have to call people from time to time, be interested in what they are doing, and cheer their victories and console their sorrows. You have to *be* a friend in order to *have* a friend, really.

Jean agrees:

> You have to cultivate your friendships. If you're going to be single and *happily* single, then you have to create a life for yourself. It can't just be your job. I mean, work is a tremendous chunk of your life simply because you're there so much. But it's really crucial to have friends.

Cultivating the friendships that create a well-functioning network can be a lot of work, as Liza says. Once beyond high school and college, making friends usually requires that women go out of their way to reach out to others. As Audrey summed it up, "You don't wait for somebody to call you. You initiate things." But reaching out is difficult for many women, a problem which can be complicated by the sheer lack of time. The women we interviewed expressed the feeling that there is never enough time to go around. Helen, who is in business for herself and was in the process of adopting a child when we first interviewed her, admits, "I can't get around to visit my friends as often as I would like. I can't even find one free evening a month." Grace also struggles to juggle the demands of her career with the need to cultivate her network. She says, "I make time for my friends, but they all tell me I do too much. They don't get to see me when they want to." Lydia, who has a teenage son and who feels that her recent decision to work only six ten-hour days a week represents progress, also feels frustrated with her lack of time for friends. Of her friends, she admits, "They're out there, but I'm not real good at picking up the phone and saying, 'Let's do something Friday or Saturday.' " Lydia confesses that, by the time the weekend finally arrives, she either wants to spend time with her son or is simply too tired to go out with friends.

Lack of time is not the only obstacle to reaching out. Some women struggle with the belief that they should be able to survive on their own, that being single means doing everything *single*-handedly. They feel particularly guilty about initiating friendships primarily to gain practical support. They fear that their intentions are less than "honorable" in that they have an agenda attached to them—even though *all* relationships, intimate and otherwise, have an agenda. Nevertheless, many single women feel they must be able to move a baby grand piano up a flight of stairs, or perform its psychological equivalent by handling all of life's problems on their own. Perhaps it is because they believe that the only way *not* to be the dependent creature the mandate dictated is to be its polar opposite. In any case, total independence is an untenable position and an illusion. Sooner or later, single women find themselves in need of someone's friendship and help. As Tina says:

> I get upset with myself when I can't move a piece of furniture. I have to wait until I have somebody come over and help. I'm pretty independent and I don't like to ask people to do things, but sometimes you *have* to ask for help whether you like it or not. You have to rely on others.

Although Tina complains of being more dependent than she would like to be, she has learned that everyone needs friends who are not only available for leisure activities but who are able to help out in practical ways. These functional relationships can operate in a reciprocal way to everyone's benefit. The long-term results of being forced to ask for help are the formation of bonds of interdependency among friends, which help women to cope with both practical and existential problems. This recognition that they can and must call on others for help breaks down the barriers erected by false pride and allows women to form communities of mutual aid and support.

Fortunately, the strain of reaching out and asking for help is balanced by the experience of reciprocity. While nobody keeps score, asking for help is made easier by having given help when it was needed. In *Habits of the Heart*, the seminal study by Robert Bellah and his colleagues of individualism and commitment in American life, Ruth Levy describes the importance of reciprocity in building a sense of community:

> You need to put into the pot. You need to be there if something needs to be done. To make courtesy calls and sympathy calls and to deliver food. But the other part is that you are also the beneficiary and when you are stuck and need someone . . . when disasters strike, you have support.

After Kelly gave birth to her son, she often needed to call upon the support of friends. Although she was thirty-eight years old, as a new mother she knew little about all the minor symptoms and worrisome behaviors so characteristic of infancy and early childhood. Whenever she panicked or just felt concerned, she turned to her friends for information and emotional support. "He won't stop crying, what do I do?" she would ask. Her friends, who had been through their own anxieties when their children were infants, provided calming reassurance and practical advice. Being able to compare notes with friends makes a tremendous difference for new mothers who are married, but being able to do so as a single mother, solely responsible for an infant's welfare, is critical. Today Kelly's friends are returning to work as their children are getting older. Now it is their turn to ask Kelly for advice on how to combine parenting and a career. Being helpful to them during this transition in their lives is important to her. "I feel lucky to be able to pay them back a little bit for all the help and advice they've given me."

Despite the obstacles to reaching out and reciprocating, cultivating strong networks can have tremendous rewards for single women at midlife. Most of the women we interviewed told stories about how their networks have helped them to cope with not only the daily challenges of single living but with the unforeseen crises as well. When women flying solo have to make unexpected landings, it is their ground crews who provide comfort and support. Sandi, for instance, tells how, in the early years after her divorce, she had to plan carefully to have enough money to make it through the end of each month. One month, her older daughter got sick and she had to pay $35 for medication. She simply didn't have the extra money; it was literally a choice of medicine or groceries. She called her father to ask for help, but his response—"stiff upper lip, old girl"—didn't go very far towards feeding her children. Fortunately, his response was balanced by a caring network of friends. A day after Sandi complained to one of these friends about the frustration of always falling behind, no matter how hard she worked and planned, she came home to find two bags of groceries and twenty dollars on her doorstep. "It was wonderful," she recalls. "I really felt carried."

As single women approach midlife, another difficulty becomes more common: problems with health. Being sick is always a challenge for single women, but worries about serious illness become more pressing during the middle years. Some women know they could depend on extended family members to care for them if they were to become ill, but many do not have this luxury. Even then, if a single woman has been careful to tend her network, help usually appears. For example, a few years ago, Helen, who has been single all of her life, was diagnosed with breast cancer and underwent a mastectomy. Not only did her parents and siblings live over a thousand miles away, but she did not feel they were emotionally strong enough to come to her aid. Fortunately, over the years she had developed an extensive network of friends who rallied around her during her illness. Echoing the words of many of the women we interviewed, Helen states with feeling, "Somebody was always there for me. In a crisis, I never felt totally alone." Some of her friends drove her to and from the hospital and visited her after the surgery. A close friend who works in another state took time off to come and stay with her while she was recovering. Helen was amazed at how well she weathered the crisis and at how cared for she felt throughout the entire episode:

During the whole ordeal of waiting to have the surgery, having the surgery, and then recovering from the surgery, what I kept saying to myself was, "I'm amazed that I don't feel alone." Every time I walked in the house, someone called or knocked at my door. I never felt abandoned during that entire time.

It is not only women's health that becomes more vulnerable at midlife, but also the health of people close to them. There is no denying that the second half of life, for most of us, contains many more losses than the first. We come face-to-face with our own mortality more often and with greater intensity. No one can protect us from these experiences, but having friends to call on in times of grief makes the pain easier to bear. Consider Kelly's experience. While she was adjusting to being a new mother after the birth of her son, her father suffered a stroke. Her network, which has always been strong, became even more important as her father became increasingly incapacitated and Kelly felt she needed to find time in her busy schedule to help her mother care for him. This responsibility, even part time, on top of her full-time job and the needs of her son, became more than a little overwhelming. Simply being able to talk to her friends about the challenges of dealing with aging parents was a relief, but her friends provided more than sympathetic listening. They provided regular baby-sitting for her son, even during middle-of-the-night emergencies when Kelly was suddenly needed to take her father to the hospital.

What these women say about their friendship networks reveals an important lesson about closeness, support, and community. Women do not have to be married to have their needs for support and intimacy met; they experience love, connection, and a sense of community in their lives in a wide variety of ways. In this diversity, there is great strength. No one relationship meets all of their needs; no one tie is so crucial that its destruction would cause their network to fail. The women we interviewed are deeply aware that this strength, this diversity, this source of love and caring, cannot be taken for granted. They have put energy into developing friendships and supports which they nurture carefully over time. Together, these ties form the communities that sustain them, making it possible for them to fly solo.

The Problem of Men

Chapter 13

Men: The Icing, Not the Cake

I think there are lots of advantages to sharing your life with somebody. But for me, it's the icing, not the cake. If I had a relationship with a man, it would be great. But I don't *need* a relationship to have a full life.

—*Helen*

Why is it men are permitted to be obsessed about their work, but women are only permitted to be obsessed about men?

—*Barbra Streisand*

None of the women we interviewed bore any resemblance to society's caricatures of terminally bitter divorcées or man-hating old maids. They like men and they like to be "in love." They are aware that nothing quite compares with that particular state of grace, that sense that all is more than right with the world. Aleta summed up the feelings of many of the women:

If the right man came along, I know I would melt instantly. I know enough about myself and I've had enough experiences to know that falling in love can happen very easily and that there is a special joy in that. Love is love, and it feels better than not.

Those women who have a man in their lives are happy he is there; those who do not, all things being equal, would like one. In fact, many of the women who described themselves as unusually happy and satisfied—who rated their lives an eight or nine on our ten-point scale of satisfaction—said that a relationship with a special man would make their lives a perfect ten.

Shawna, who feels very good about herself and her life, acknowledged this missing element:

> Unfortunately, I need the attention of men, I *enjoy* the company of men. If I didn't, then I would be a hundred percent happy all around.

Angela agrees that a relationship with someone special would enhance an already good life:

> I would like to share my ideas and bounce them off of someone whom I respect. That's one thing I still do miss.

Even women who had painful experiences with marriages or other relationships in the past are not "soured" on men. Most would agree with Arlene, who explains that she does not view men in general as being difficult, but only the particular man to whom she was married.

Yet many single women who are not in relationships with men do nothing to seek them out, and some have turned down opportunities to marry— and to marry well, at that. Even those who are in relationships remain cautious about how much of their time and emotional resources they are willing to allocate to the maintenance of the relationship. They recognize the wonderful ways in which intimacy with a man could enhance their lives, but they also recognize that they have been able to create lives that are rich and complete on their own. They know what they want from relationships, and they know they don't have to settle for less unless they choose to do so. Moreover, they are well aware of the obstacles involved in transforming the blissful but all-too-brief state of being "in love" into a mutually satisfying long-term union.

WHAT MIDLIFE WOMEN WANT
IN A RELATIONSHIP

Single women explain that they are not concerned primarily with a man's level of income or any other material benefit, nor are they looking for a "hunk" or a "stud." While Apryl joked about wanting a man who is "single, straight, and employed," and a few women mentioned the importance of some "stud" qualities in a man such as being a good lover, these and all other talents took a back seat to the desire for companionship. The single most important attribute these women look for in a man is the *capacity to be a good friend*. They are looking for someone with whom they can share the joys of their already full lives. Audrey describes her ideal lover as "someone with a wonderful sense of humor and with the same values—a good, kind person I could have a lovely time with. Who doesn't want that?" Both Jesse and Shannon said they were looking for someone who shared their spiritual vision. Lydia stipulates that she wants someone who has "balance in his life, someone who can play, be honest, and be a friend." Morgan wants a man who can rejoice in her good fortune without feeling threatened by it—in short, the sort of reaction one would expect from a friend. She says, "I tell a friend, 'I just got a $100,000-a-year job,'" and they're excited *with* me, as opposed to thinking, "Oh damn, now she earns more than I do." Ruth wants to find "someone I could have fun with—a good playmate who loves to travel and has a sense of adventure." Sandi wants "someone with a twinkle in his eye." Arlene is emphatic: "I want love *and* respect. You can't have one without the other and I don't want a relationship unless it has both qualities."

Most importantly, the kind of companionable relationship desired by single women would preserve their independence, their life as a separate person. They want relationships with men, but not the kind their mothers had. Louise, a fifty-eight-year-old divorced African-American woman who is very happy with her life, finds it easy to be clear about what she wants and does not want from a relationship. What comes first is being true to herself:

> I enjoy male companionship, but I don't feel that I *must* have it in order to survive, in order to be myself. I'm very particular. I don't align myself with an individual just because he's a man. He has to have something to offer me, and I don't mean financial gains. First of all, he has to accept me for who I am. I don't like the phrase, "set in my ways," but I know who I am, and I know what I want. I can't be bothered with someone who wants to change me to fit into his style of living, his likes and dislikes. I'm very happy with *my* life.

Unlike younger women, many of whom crave a passion that will consume and define their lives, these are women who, as Maxine expressed it, "want to meet a nice man and fall into *like*." In short, midlife women are not looking for a man to define them and give their lives structure and meaning. They already have lives full of structure and meaning—in fact, they com-

plain of having too little time to do all the things they want to do. The issue
seems to be that, *while they are not committed to being single, they are committed to
being themselves.* Their views of "happily ever after" do not involve being
swept away, but rather finding someone who would add a particular kind of
companionship to an already rich life. Megan explains:

> For me, the ideal relationship would give me the freedom to maintain
> my contacts with my women friends and with my work associates. My
> partner would be equally invested in maintaining his own circle of
> friends and interests. We would have periods of intense togetherness
> and periods when we went our separate ways, easily and without fear
> of hurting or being hurt. There would be that kind of flexibility.

Megan is hardly alone in wanting a man who has a life of his own and is
not "hanging around her neck." We heard this same desire expressed over
and over. Marie wants a man who has "a life of his own, too." Peggy has
rejected several marriage proposals because she experienced the men who
wanted to marry her as encroaching on her freedom:

> If you were interviewing the men with whom I have had special
> relationships, they would say that I was unrelenting as far as guarding
> my time and the things I want to do. Usually, they want more of my
> time than I'm willing to give.

Shannon says, "I need an enormous amount of alone time. I want someone
who is *really* independent." Josie concurs:

> It's not clear to me that I want to live with someone, but it's also not
> clear that I don't. What is clear to me is that living with someone can't
> interfere with the way I live my life. I want someone who has a life of
> his own—that is absolutely critical. I can't think of anything more
> wonderful than a partner who would be less available than me—not
> because he didn't care about me, but because he had something else he
> loved to do.

Helen is clear about the kind of relationship she would like to have, one
which allows both freedom and intimacy. Unfortunately, she says, the men
she has met have problems with the freedom side of the equation.

I like to be able to take care of myself in lots of ways. I want a relationship in which I can come and go, and I want the other person to have the same freedom. I like a lot of space, but I also like a lot of affection. I'm a very touchy-feely person. I would like to share this side of myself with someone, but men who are willing to give women that much freedom are few and far between.

In short, if she's going to have a relationship, Helen wants a man who is willing to be the icing, not one who insists on being the whole cake. Helen's own cake is rich enough that she would rather have no relationship than one that didn't meet her basic criteria. Most midlife single women agree with her. If they are forced to choose between having no relationship and one in which their needs and desires are not considered, their choice is clear. Julia explained that she is even prepared to grow old alone, if the choice comes down to being alone or living in a relationship that doesn't provide something special in her life. She has times when she tells herself, "You're going to be one of these old ladies with plants and cats," but a moment's reflection brings her to the same conclusion: "I think that, as a trade-off to living in a relationship that doesn't make me happy, I'd rather have the cats."

The fact that these women could describe what they wanted in a relationship does not mean that they spend a great deal of time searching for it. In fact, we were astounded at how little time and effort they were willing to put into finding a suitable partner. From what they told us, we concluded there were three primary reasons for their reluctance to throw themselves into a full-scale search for their ideal relationship: gender lag, the all too predictable consequences of the urge to merge, and the depressing nature of the dating scene.

GENDER LAG: THE JET LAG OF THE SEXES

Today's women have chosen to redefine and expand their notions of what it means to be female and what it means to have a relationship with a man. These ideas often directly contradict the values of the marriage and motherhood mandate, which dictate that women should *always* and *unconditionally* desire to be in a relationship with a man—no matter what. Having adapted to the enormous cultural changes that have occurred in the short space of their own lifetime, modern women find that they are out of sync with most of the men they meet. They encounter "gender lag," a kind of cultural jet lag of the sexes, in which standing on the edge of cultural change often means standing without men. No matter what they may say they want in the personals ads, few midlife men are really ready to join their female counterparts on the cusp of cultural change. Their expectations remain anchored a couple of time zones behind the expectations of these women.

Louise, whose husband decided (once he became successful) that he no longer wished to be married, feels that the men she has met who are her age are not able to tolerate the independence she now needs. For her, there is no turning back from the freedom she has learned to cherish. She was almost indignant that we asked her if she would consider doing so:

> Why on earth would I deceive myself and put on the back burner everything that *I* stand for, everything *I* believe in, in order to fit into the mold someone else wants, or in order to fit into the mold I think I should fit into, to make that individual happy or gain his affection or love? That's selling my birthright. I can't do it.

Many of the women we interviewed reported that few men who express interest in them are attracted to their independence. This is not all that surprising. After all, most of today's midlife men have been socialized to expect the very behaviors these women are trying to eliminate from their repertoire. These men have benefited from the assumptions of the marriage and motherhood mandate and many still expect to be the center of a woman's whole existence. They assume that women will accommodate *their* schedules and *their* needs.

This phenomenon may shed some light on why midlife men tend to gravitate toward younger women. It may be not only the perky body parts of these women that attract them, but also their malleability. Younger women are less likely to have defined their personalities and established their own priorities. They are thus far more willing to defer to an older man's experience and assume he knows how things "should" be. In addition, the ability to attract younger women provides these men with reassurance that they are not old, are not going to die yet, or haven't already died in some important way. It is a comforting illusion that, for better or worse, has been rarely available to women, since it is far less acceptable for older women to mate with younger men. As it stands, the result is an ever widening gap in values and expectations between midlife women and the men who are their peers.

SABOTAGED BY THAT OLD URGE TO MERGE

The second major reason that midlife single women are reluctant to search for a relationship with a man is that, despite their current status in the forefront of cultural change, they know they are carrying a lot of "leftover baggage" from the last generation's journey. In their experience, establishing a mutually satisfying relationship with a man has always been more difficult than it appears on the surface. It isn't just the attitudes and behavior of men that some women don't trust; in fact, it isn't even *mainly* men that are the problem. Rather, *women question their own ability to stay centered.* Women worry that their own instincts, instilled by all their early training, will betray them. They worry that, in the heat of the passionate first stages of an intimate relationship, they will give up, little by little, all they have learned, all the freedoms they have fought for and achieved in their years on their own. These women fear their *own* tendencies to revert to "automatic pilot," to accommodate and defer, eventually metamorphosing into some stranger they hardly recognize and certainly don't like.

Consider the experience of Jean, a vivacious woman whom men find appealing, both as a friend and as a lover. Jean told us that when she was young, she dreamed only of freedom. She was the little girl mentioned earlier who wanted to be a doctor, who operated on worms with her mother's kitchen knives. But, she says, her family discouraged her from pursuing a career in medicine and, after college, she felt pressured to marry. "At that point I didn't care. I was so discouraged by having to give up the one thing that set me on fire. By default, I landed on other routes." Jean admits that she was not moved by love but by the pressure to conform to everyone else's dream for her:

> The message was that my success would be defined through marrying this guy. He was wild about me and there was a big rush to get married. I thought, "Oh, that's what everybody does, so should I. I should get married because all my friends are getting married, and if I'm not madly in love with him, it doesn't matter." So I married him and it was a terrible mistake—he was abusive. How about that? The guy was nuts. And I wasn't even in love with him. That's what kills me. If only I could say to myself at least that I had fallen madly in love with someone who turned out to be a jerk, but that's not the case.

After two years Jean escaped from her marriage, literally running away to another city where she knew no one. She admits she was fleeing not only the marriage but the pressure she felt from her family to make the marriage a success. To this day, she remains intensely grateful that she was able to leave before the profound depression and helplessness that so often keep women in abusive relationships took hold. "It was through the grace of God," she says, "because there was no one out there saying, 'Come here, I'll take care of you'—not a man, not a family member, no one."

Despite the bad experience of her marriage, Jean has always been attracted to men. "It's so much fun being in love," she says, quickly adding, "but that isn't always a corollary to being married." In the years since her divorce, she has been in a number of intimate relationships with men and has gained a great deal of insight into the ways in which these unions can threaten her sense of self. She reports a pattern that has occurred over and over, corroborating similar accounts from other women. Romances, Jean says, seem to push her into another world, a world in which her needs ever so subtly begin to take second place to those of her lover. And, insight alone doesn't seem to help when such a romance is in full bloom. She describes "sliding" into behaviors prescribed by the mandate, as if driven by an involuntary need to please:

> When I fall in love, I fall right back down the evolutionary ladder. Soon I'm even getting pimples again! I act like I'm just a sissy, and say things like [laughing], "Oh, you're so wonderful and it's so big." I begin to feel this tremendous meshing; the line between my personality, my life, and the other person begins to diminish; then I'll make any deal, because I get so completely engulfed.

Jean's dilemma is an example both of gender lag and of the problem of flying on the edge of cultural change, still laden with baggage from the last generation's journey. Jean, and the men with whom she has relationships, all have expectations learned in childhood that it is the woman's job to accommodate. Jean admits that early in a romance she unwittingly colludes to establish the unspoken rules of the relationship in such a way that her needs rarely come first or are considered seriously at all. Over time, she accommodates so expertly that she begins to wonder who she is, while her partner is not even aware that she is making major compromises. As long as the initial glow lasts, the relationship feels fair and balanced, even though it is far from egalitarian. But inevitably, weeks, months, or even years later, it slowly dawns on Jean that she is doing a whole lot more *giving* than *getting*:

> Its's easy to sound flip and even horrified when a woman says, "Yes, I would give up my life, my soul, my house, my toenails for this man." We were taught to do that. And I can sit here and say I would never do that, but, to be perfectly honest, I've seen myself do exactly that on a small scale. I compromised myself horribly at times.

The day Jean wakes up and realizes what she has forfeited for the relationship, her feelings go from rapture to repulsion in a nanosecond. For her, the kinds of compromises required to maintain the relationship—the losses in self-definition and self-respect that she had gained since leaving her marriage—are not worth it.

Jean is scarcely alone in fearing that her conditioned responses from childhood—that old urge to merge—will always subvert her efforts to establish a truly egalitarian relationship. She is not the only woman with a history of repeatedly losing her sense of self in a relationship. Many of the midlife women we interviewed continue to worry that they, like Jean, are highly likely to adopt, unwittingly, a position of selflessness in a serious relationship with a man. It is not surprising that they cannot trust themselves in this vulnerable area. Judith, a forty-seven-year-old divorced woman, bemusedly observes that, "You find this wonderful essence of yourself, and you want to share it—but somehow, in sharing it, you give it away and then it is *gone*." Julia, a woman who has come to understand these patterns in the fifteen years since her divorce, continues to worry that her tendency to accommodate will persist no matter what, proving once again that insight is no real defense:

> Thinking back over some of my relationships, there have been times when I have wanted to be with the other person enough to ignore some of the things I knew about myself—you know, to subvert some of the qualities I value, but thought I had to sacrifice. Fortunately, I usually got tired of sacrificing pretty soon, and I also figured out that if you spend your entire life pretending to be somebody else, you get to be real boring real fast.

If the baggage that comes with the romance of dating is perceived as threatening to a woman's sense of self, living with a man and especially

getting married are even more so. Women in long-term monogamous relationships worry about how they might change if they lived with or married
their companion. Emma, who has happily dated the same man for a number
of years, fears that if they married, the cultural values so deeply ingrained in
her would "reach up and grab her," altering her behavior against her will:

> I am afraid that I would wind up in the same situation that I got out of
> in my marriage: having dinner ready by six o'clock, washing and iron-
> ing his shirts, and things like that. It would be very difficult for me to
> say, "These are your dirty clothes, wash them yourself." You know
> what I'm saying? The "rules" are so instilled in me. I grew up learning
> a good wife cooked and washed and cleaned and had kids. You
> weren't supposed to have a brain.

Emma's fears are a testimony to the power wielded by the roles and values
prescribed by the mandate. These women are neither passive nor submissive;
indeed, in all other parts of their lives, they are assertive and straightforward.
Many even describe early romantic relationships in which they were able to
maintain positions of strength and autonomy. For example, before their
marriage, Ria and her ex-husband enjoyed a delightfully open and equal
relationship, sharing tasks that were traditionally gender specific. However,
this equality crumbled once they married. Ria explained that she married a
man whom she thought was her friend, but who quickly turned into a role,
as if transformed in the wedding ceremony by some wickedly perverse wiz-
ard:

> The first morning after we had returned from our honeymoon, while
> still lying in bed, my husband said, "What are you cooking for din-
> ner?" I said, "I have no idea." Before our marriage, he had done most
> of the cooking or we had shared the task. He got mad at me. He said,
> "You should know what you are cooking for dinner!" I can remember
> going for a walk only a week later and looking at the ocean and
> thinking, *how can I get it across to him?* I did not want to be married to his
> stepfather! That was one of the important turning points for me, be-
> cause I felt like our relationship was pretty good until we got married.

THE DATING GAME: DEPRESSING,
DEGRADING, AND DOWNRIGHT DREARY

Midlife women are not "out looking for a man" because, more often than not, they find the dating scene to be time-consuming, boring, and even humiliating. Although they know that, as Erika says, "you can't win the game without being a player," these women are not willing to put themselves through degrading experiences when they have attained the all-important feeling of being complete and capable on their own. Some told us that their experiences of playing the dating game in adolescence and young adulthood were mortifying enough to last a lifetime. Hillary explains:

> Trying to meet new men all the time would be tiring and degrading. I'd have to put myself in situations where men gather, like a bar or a club, and then stand there and wait for someone to notice me, to like me enough to say hello.

Most midlife single women have long since stopped "hanging out" in singles bars or attending singles' events. For Glenda, attempting to find a man in that way is out of the question. She says, "I think too much of myself now. Besides, easily ninety percent of the men I've met in those settings were not interesting to me." Most of the women we interviewed who were not in a relationship felt the minimal chance of meeting a desirable man wasn't worth the aggravation. Angela expressed this point well:

> I would like to have a relationship, but I won't go to bars and I won't go to singles' clubs. I'm not comfortable doing that. I meet a lot of people in my work environment, but I do not actively search for a man.

Helen says emphatically, "There is nothing I hate more than going out and looking for someone to date." Alice throws up her hands altogether, stating that, "Even if I decided I *wanted* to find a husband, I'm not sure I'd know how."

One explanation for this common, seemingly helpless attitude is that midlife women were taught to be passive, to wait patiently to be *found* rather than to *seek out* what they want. To some extent, this is probably true: It does not feel natural for them to pursue a relationship aggressively. But it is also true that the dating game can be a depressing and humiliating experience and, these days, even a dangerous one. These women have been through the blind dates, the agencies, and the personal ads, and it is largely because of these experiences that they now find it easy to turn their backs on such endeavors. Of all the women, only a few were willing to go out of their way—risk time, money, and feelings that might range from boredom to humiliation—to seek a relationship. Sandi, for instance, avoids the bar scene, but she recently joined a ski club as a way of obtaining safe exposure to available men:

> I always fantasized that a relationship would just fall into my lap. You know, here I am working in this setting with interesting, educated people and all of our contacts, our clients are interesting and educated. But it just doesn't happen. So I've got to put myself *out there,* which takes work and a commitment of time. I have to push myself past my comfort level again.

Whether it is their fear of becoming "Cheshire cat women" in relationships, smiling as they become fuzzy and eventually disappear, their reluctance to tangle with men who are likely to suffer from gender lag, or simply the depressing state of the dating scene, there is no doubt that single women would exert more effort to seek a mate if they were truly unhappy being single. While none said they would refuse a relationship were it to "fall into their laps," they all made it clear that they have no intention of putting their lives on hold to look for Mr. Right. For that matter, most believe they would probably find only a "Mr. So-So," who wouldn't be worth the compromises they would have to make. As any woman who remembers being single in her twenties can tell you, the old cliché that you have to kiss a lot of frogs before you find a prince is only too true. At midlife, most single women's lives are so full that they simply don't want to spend their spare time kissing frogs. It is not so much that these women actually expect romance to find *them* in their living rooms as it is that they feel comfortable and content as they are.

Chapter 14

Having Their Cake and Eating It Too: Encapsulated Intimacies

Sometimes I wonder if men and women really suit each other. Perhaps they should live next door and just visit now and then.

—Katharine Hepburn

If I had three wishes, I probably would wish to have a relationship in which there's love and some permanence, but it wouldn't necessarily be marriage.

—Kim

Many midlife single women are "cultural mavericks" who have broken loose from the constraints of traditional all-or-nothing approaches to relationships with men to create non-traditional relationships of their own design. They are discovering ways to experience the many joys and satisfactions of intimacy without paying the price that such relationships have extracted from them in the past. They are seeking and finding ways of protecting themselves from reverting to the old habits of accommodation, self-sacrifice, and dependency. In so doing, they are widening the parameters of possibilities in relationships between men and women.

The essential feature of these non-traditional relationships is *boundaries*: clearly defined physical, emotional, and psychological borders that protect women from losing their sense of self when they get involved with men. Women create these boundaries by living in separate residences or even different cities, and by limiting the amount of time and emotional energy they commit to the relationship. These boundaries are further reinforced by the fact that women do not strive to make these relationships into marriages;

in fact, some have ended relationships precisely because their partners wanted more of a commitment than they were willing to give. Some women even have chosen a partner who has another primary relationship, who is already married or is married to his work.

We have come to think of these relationships as "encapsulated intimacies," creative solutions to the old "urge to merge" problem many women face in their relationships with men. Whatever the limitations of these encapsulated intimacies, their advantage is that they allow women to experience love, sexuality, and companionship in a way that does not threaten their autonomy, integrity, or self-direction. These alliances give women the experience of loving *and* the time and freedom to cultivate personal interests and relationships. The boundaries that define these unions clearly protect women from "selling out" their sense of self in order to have a connection with a man. The women in these relationships have discovered that they most enjoy a relationship with a man when it is only one of many threads that make up the intricate tapestry of their lives.

TALES OF TWO CITIES

One type of relationship that provides instant, concrete boundaries is the long-distance one. Erika describes a long-term relationship she had with a man in a city about four hours away by car as the "perfect setup": "I could continue being who I am and still have an intimate relationship on weekends—it was really fun." Terry also provides an example of how well a long-distance arrangement can work, even over the long haul. She has maintained a ten-year relationship with a man even though they have never lived in the same city. Terry first met Tom while they both were working as rangers in the National Park Service in Oregon. They initiated what Terry describes as an important but "very, very loose relationship":

> It feeds the part of me that wants to play, and I think he would say the same thing. We play together better than any two human beings play together. It's absolutely wonderful and it's *always* been wonderful. There's a companionable "fit." Both of us are reduced to eleven years of age and have the capacity to close the world out for short periods of

time. Within the sort of world we make together, it's wonderful. It's a very whimsical relationship.

Tom's place in Terry's world departs significantly from tradition. Tom is a piece of the much broader and more intricately detailed pattern of Terry's life. Their relationship enhances but does not overshadow her work, her community of friends, or her relationship with herself:

> At this point in time, there is absolutely nothing missing from my life. I've got everything I could possibly want, including the right to make choices. I'm very fulfilled by my work; it provides a lot of stimulation in my life. I like the solitude of being alone and when I don't like it, I have people with whom I can spend my time, including Tom. I wouldn't trade any piece of my life.

Terry and Tom's relationship is also characterized by a striking level of equality. Terry's commitment to the other elements of her life is not only accepted but encouraged by Tom. She is able to maintain her sense of autonomy and integrity in large part because of the boundaries she and Tom have chosen to maintain in their relationship. For them, these boundaries are temporal as well as geographical: They talk on the phone about twice a month, see each other every five or six weeks for long weekends, and spend longer vacations together over the summer. We asked her what would happen if she and Tom decided to live together or make their relationship a legal one. She explained that they had considered living together when they both moved to the East Coast, but decided that it probably would not work well:

> We have always been able to carve out a time and a place that's been magical—but we've carved that out *deliberately* and under very controlled conditions. I don't know that we could sustain that level of magic and specialness on a day-to-day basis.

There are real challenges to maintaining a long-distance relationship. The "glue" that keeps people connected to one another is often the common experiences of everyday life. One woman, for whom long-distance relating didn't work, told us it was very hard for her to stay "tuned in" at such distance: "I had to work at keeping my feelings alive; sometimes they just seemed to die." There is also the risk of being replaced by someone more available, with all the jealousy and fears of rejection and loss that situation can inspire. Terry recalls such a time in her relationship with Tom:

> He was involved with this other woman. In fact, he even went to Europe to be with her for a period of time. I was not happy about the situation. Over time, I realized that I was not unhappy about his involvement with someone else; but I *was* afraid of losing my companion for vacations and summer time. It wasn't jealousy in the traditional sense. I've always believed that we would remain friends, no matter what. But it's awfully hard to maintain that kind of relationship. I sometimes wonder what would happen if either one of us got involved seriously with someone else.

Despite the challenges, long-distance encapsulated intimacies work well for many midlife single women. Although Terry recognizes that the parameters of their relationship would not work for everyone, she knows it is a perfect match for her. "I'm not trying to paint it as the perfect relationship. For most of the world, it wouldn't work—I mean, there's not very much of it. But there's enough for *us*."

Leslie, who has been involved for over two decades with a man who lives two-thirds of the way across the continent, has also discovered that, for her, the advantages of a long-distance relationship outweigh the challenges. She had been friends with Harry during medical school, lost touch with him for a number of years, and then met him again at a reunion. Sharing an interest in skiing, they started taking ski trips together as friends, writing to each other occasionally in-between. For the first four or five years, their relationship was platonic. However, when they met one autumn at a medical conference, they became sexually involved and the nature of their relationship changed forever. They began to keep in touch with greater frequency and regularity. Leslie says, "The longest we've been separated is three months. We see each other every six to eight weeks and he calls me every single day." Harry has become an important part of Leslie's life, but she also has a strong commitment to her demanding career as a physician, close family ties, and a wide circle of friends. For her, the long-distance aspect of their relationship is ideal. Periodically, Harry has pressured her to marry him, but Leslie has not wanted to change the encapsulated structure of their relationship:

> I think the relationship I have now is perfect for me because I don't have to do it all week. I couldn't sustain a full-time relationship be-

cause I'm too interested in the other parts of my life. I get a lot of satisfaction from this relationship *as it is* and I get a lot of satisfaction out of my work. If I didn't have a relationship, it would bother me—I do have a need for that connection.

Although Michelle's relationship has less distance involved than Leslie's, it works for many of the same reasons. When Michele was married, her life revolved around her husband's needs and professional dreams. Since her divorce, Michele has invested an enormous amount of time and energy in her own career. In the past few years of her obstetrics residency, she has worked countless sixty- or seventy-hour weeks. Work, however, has not been her only priority since her divorce. She also has "learned to have fun," has developed close relationships with other women as well as with her sister, and has entered a relationship with Peter, another important but distinct "slice" of her full life. Their relationship is much more open and honest, emotionally and sexually, than what she experienced with her husband:

> Peter is wonderful, especially compared to my husband! Sex is an important part of our relationship, but there are a lot of other parts, too. I mean, the fact that he's such a good friend is far more important to me. In addition to sexual intimacy, we share emotional intimacy— he *knows* who I am. He's seen me as an intern coming off thirty-six-hour calls, when there's no pretending—in your exhaustion, it's all out there. He's secure about himself, so I can tell him how I see things and he tells me how he sees things; we can *share.* It's a more intimate relationship, not only in terms of sex but in terms of talking, than I've had in the past.

Since Peter lives in the country some distance outside the city in which Michele lives and works, they commute to spend time together. Michele admits, "He's very busy, too. I mean, he's doing a million and one things. It's good that *both* of our time schedules are so packed—that we are *equally* busy." Michele laughs as she explains that, to arrange to see each other, they must each get out their appointment books to block out time. The encapsulated structure of their relationship has allowed Michele to experience all the wonderful parts of being with Peter without feeling the draining pressure to take care of him, as she did with her husband. "Both of us are satisfied with the way things are right now, partly because both of us feel okay about being by ourselves. I don't feel like he needs me to take care of him, and he doesn't feel like I need him to take care of me. What a relief."

SAME TIME NEXT WEEKEND

More common than relationships with partners in separate cities were those with men who lived in the same city. The boundaries women in these relationships maintain are usually those of having separate residences and spending restricted time together. These women often have entirely independent lives during the week, but very active relationships on weekends.

Valerie's relationship with John typifies this kind of encapsulated alliance. Valerie is a woman who thoroughly enjoys her hard-won success and independence. When she flunked out of college at the age of twenty, her parents refused to help support her, so she was forced to become responsible for herself. She moved to Los Angeles, got a job as a waitress, and roomed with women friends. She says of that time: "It taught me how to get credit, how to pay the rent, how to pay the bills. I learned all that stuff very early on and it has served me well over the years."

After a few years, she tired of the big city, moved back to the smaller city where she was raised, took a secretarial course, got a job, and got married. Her husband turned out to be an alcoholic who was never able to stand on his own. Valerie explains, "I ended up being his mother as well as his wife." On top of this caretaking "job" at home, she also continued working and went back to college in the evenings, earning her bachelor's degree. When things with her husband went from bad to worse, Valerie decided to leave him. She concentrated on her own career, worked long hours and, learning as she went, rose to a major leadership position.

Having earned success, Valerie now spends her weekday evenings developing hobbies and cultivating closer relationships with women friends. Her weekends, however, are devoted to John, with whom she has had a relationship since the end of her marriage. Along with her work and her women friends, Valerie's relationship with John is very important: "I get so much fulfillment out of it." Valerie and John spend most of their weekends at a secluded beach house John owns outside the city. The isolation of his house fosters "a lot of intimacy over the weekend—I mean, we are together constantly and we really enjoy one another." She and John have also developed a very satisfying sex life, something Valerie never had in her marriage. This aspect of their relationship is extremely important to Valerie, who explains that it contributes to her motivation to take care of herself:

> Good sex makes a difference in my outlook on life. It gives me a feeling of well-being. I've been taking really good care of myself: I work out three times a week and eat well. I like the way I look and the way I feel. I think all that is wrapped up in my sexual life with John.

Valerie has also enjoyed building relationships with John's adult children over the years. One of them recently had a child, and Valerie is now enjoying her role as a "grandmother" as well—though she adds, laughing, "If he ever calls me 'Grandma,' I'll kill him!"

Although she loves these wonderful aspects of her life with John, Valerie is clear that she does not want to change the encapsulated nature of their relationship. Early on, she struggled with the pressure of tradition, feeling that she ought to marry him. She has since decided that marriage is not right for her at this time in her life. She has worked hard to become independent, has many friends and interests separate from John, and is not willing to change this life style:

> There was that old tape playing in the back of my head that said, "If you're in a relationship and you're in love with him, you should get married." Then I realized that people get married because they want to be together *every* day, they want to have a family, to have children, to raise them. Well, we are both beyond that! The longer I am single, the more I want to stay that way. I *like* being independent; I like being responsible for just myself. For so many years I felt responsible for my mother, my brothers, and my husband. I think I do fear getting into another bad marriage, but also, I really love having my own house and my own things. I'm not sure I'm willing to mix my things with someone else's things.

Ria has also found the "same-time-next-weekend" arrangement to work well for her. Of her nine-year relationship with Mark, she states clearly, "I think it's really important that we don't live together." Although she loves Mark and, as we describe in Chapter 16, has even given birth to two children with him, at this point in her life she has no desire to become his wife:

> We both had bad marriages and we just don't want to call what we share a *marriage*. We don't want to call each other *husband* and *wife*. We

don't want to live with each other because we don't want to trigger those expectations.

Mark spends Saturday nights and Sundays at Ria's home, but they maintain separate lives during the week. Through examining her own behavior during her first marriage and the years on her own, Ria has become aware of her own internal gravitation towards the traditional roles with which she was raised—what we have called "the urge to merge." The boundaries of space and time in her relationship with Mark have allowed Ria to love him while protecting herself from these influences of her past:

> We all have our history. I grew up in a time when I learned from my grandmothers and my mother that your duty was to please your man. Even though Mark doesn't have that attitude, I rush around cooking a nice dinner and saying, "Can I get you a cup of coffee?" And then I catch myself and shake my head at how easily that pleasing behavior pops up.

The encapsulated nature of their relationship also allows Ria to determine how she wants to raise her teenage daughter, as well as the two younger children she and Mark conceived together. She acknowledges, "It's really important for me to feel like this is *my* house. I'm proud to say that I run a matriarchal home." Ria and Mark also manage their lives (and their money) in very different ways. Mark, who is an artist, earns and spends very little money and is comfortable living, day by day, on a shoestring. Although money has never been a high priority for Ria either, she believes that raising children means planning financially so that she has funds available to spend on them when it is necessary. If they tried to live with one another, Ria explains, "Our goals would put us in conflict. We would drive each other nuts!" Limiting their time together allows Ria and Mark to enjoy the aspects of life they want to share without having to hassle constantly over finances and their other differences.

Liza also has a weekend relationship that works in the context of the life she has been able to shape for herself. A thirty-nine-year-old never-married college graduate who loves her job, Liza rates her life as a nine on our ten-point satisfaction scale. She is the first to admit that growing up, she was certain she would marry and have lots of children; however, she was never so intent on marriage that she was willing to consider marrying the first man, or just any man, who came along. Because she has never been unhappy being single, she decided she would marry *only if* it would make her happier than she was on her own—a tough requirement to fill, as she has developed an active and exciting life over the years.

Six years ago Liza met Andrew and fell in love. Over the years their relationship has been through a few permutations, but finally has settled into a same-time-next-weekend arrangement that works well for both of them. Andrew and Liza are active, social people who love to travel. Liza speaks enthusiastically about some of the trips they have taken together—to Canada to backpack, to the Bahamas to sail. She and Andrew, Liza explains, "have a ball together." In large part, it is the encapsulated nature of their relationship that keeps this fun-loving side of their relationship alive. Liza is not eager to change her arrangement with Andrew, because she knows the disadvantages of their relationship would overshadow the joys if they were to make it full-time. She has some evidence for this conclusion, because at one point she did live with him. He was recovering from back surgery and couldn't manage very well, so she arrived with her bags to help him; by mutual consent, she stayed two and a half years:

> That's the only time in my entire life that I lived with a guy day in and day out. I liked it. Andrew is super and it was nice having company on Saturday morning while reading the paper. I love to have coffee and read the paper and have somebody say, "Oh, did you see . . . " in the paper. I thought the companionship was nice.

So far this arrangement sounds perfect; it would have been but for one major problem. Liza forthrightly describes why she moved back to her own residence after two and a half years:

> Andrew has a drinking problem. He works all day—he's very success-ful—but he gets completely bombed at night. I love him when he hasn't had anything to drink. I mean, he's a wonderful guy.

If Liza were married to Andrew, her only choices would be to accommo-date his drinking every day, with all the emotional insecurity that could entail, or to leave him. Living apart gives her time to pursue her work, as well as her other interests and friendships, *and* enough respite from Andrew's drinking to allow her to enjoy what is good about their relationship. Liza did not purposely structure her relationship with Andrew as a weekend-only one in order to maintain limits and cope with his drinking. It is the product of the compromise she chose to make between what is and what might be, between possibility and probability. The point is that by freeing herself from traditional expectations, Liza was able to make room for the satisfaction and pleasures her relationship with Andrew can add to her already full life.

Maintaining intertwined lives but separate homes can also be a creative solution when children, and differences about how to raise them, are involved. Separate homes would not have been Greta's initial choice, but in retrospect she recognizes that it protects her and her partner from possible conflict around the issue of how daughters should be raised. Five years ago, Greta, age forty-three, divorced and the mother of two daughters, met Joe, a widower with a daughter the same age as Greta's younger child. They were introduced by friends who thought they would be perfect together. These friends were almost right. Over the years, Greta and Joe have developed a pattern of living apart during the week but spending weekends, vacations, and holidays together. Greta says of Joe:

> We like doing a lot of the same things and we share many of the same concerns. We're very comfortable together; he's really become my best friend. I don't think I ever could have become involved with any man who wasn't a parent himself.

Ironically, the very factor that Greta feels brings them closest together, parenting, also keeps them apart:

> With the two of us, any friction in our relationship has to do with different styles of raising children. I also think that Joe is not willing to take on anyone else's children.

There was a time in their relationship when Greta felt the lure of The Dream and started talking about the two of them making more of a commitment. It was Joe who resisted, and rather than risk losing the entire relationship, Greta first came to accept and then to enjoy some of the advantages of separate homes:

> At one point, I wanted us to live together, but he didn't. Actually, I wasn't sure if I genuinely wanted to, or if I just *wanted* to *want* it. Anyway, he just didn't want to talk about it at all. For a while, that was very hurtful so I just backed off. Then I had to think about how much

he meant to me. I think now, in some ways, I'm happier doing it this way. But it's also frustrating; we would like to spend more time together, but with three kids' schedules to juggle it's difficult. It's very much up in the air at this point. I'm really very torn. Sometimes I think I have the best of both worlds—because I *do* have a stable relationship with a man as well as the freedom of living alone and a network of friends who are single.

Greta says that if she and Joe move in together after their children have moved out, her willingness to make compromises will be tempered by her experience of making it on her own during these very important years. She says, "I hope that, were we to live together, it would be as two very independent adults who were also very companionable."

THE UNAVAILABLE MAN

Boundaries of time and space are not the only ways that women can protect themselves against losing their sense of self in relationships with men. Some women establish relationships with men who come with boundaries of their own. For instance, Elaine has maintained a close relationship with Jeff, a self-described "confirmed bachelor," for eighteen years. Elaine describes him as simply "not the marrying type." His clarity about maintaining his own home and his single status has provided the boundary necessary to establish a non-traditional, encapsulated relationship.

Elaine and Jeff spend most of their free time together on weekends as well as weekday evenings. Jeff plays a distinctly non-traditional male role in the relationship: "He's protective without smothering me. He is totally committed to me and that's hard to turn down. Outside of his work, and jogging, I am his only interest." Because his schedule is more flexible than hers, he also helps out at times by picking up her dry cleaning or doing other errands. He is so committed to Elaine that, each evening before he leaves to return to his own home, he sets the breakfast table for her, putting out her bowl and favorite cereal.

This arrangement has worked well for Elaine, for whom work has always ranked as a top priority. For most of her life, she has been competitive and achievement-oriented. Although occasionally ambivalent about the boundaries imposed on their relationship by Jeff's opposition to marriage, she admits, "We don't live together—maybe that's why the relationship has lasted." She also recognizes Jeff's positive impact on her work life:

> Jeff has been very nurturing and supportive of my career. I think our relationship has helped me to achieve in a lot of ways. I've had complete independence, complete autonomy, *and* I've had support. I've had a prop the whole way.

Relationships with men who are married are another way to ensure the encapsulated nature of an intimate connection. Such relationships are often difficult to discuss neutrally without either condemning or condoning them. We wish to do neither. Undeniably, extramarital relationships are controversial. The Katharine Hepburn-Spencer Tracy liaison may have been acceptable in Hollywood but certainly was not approved in Middle America (at least, not until people had twenty or thirty years to get used to the idea). And yet, the fact remains that such relationships have always been a part of the social fabric. Although many of the women we interviewed avoided relationships with married men, others are or have been involved in them. Certainly such alliances meet our criteria of encapsulated intimacy, possessing both intensity and rather obvious boundaries. They usually also involve the potential of some stigma and some secretiveness. Women who were involved in affairs with married men were sometimes reluctant to talk about them, but when they did, their stories were more positive than one might anticipate. Far from being tales of lonely women getting only table scraps at the feast of life, cheated by all the weekends and holidays they must spend alone, many women experienced these relationships as providing the joys of romance and sex while not demanding more from them than they wanted to give.

Pamela, now fifty-four, had a relationship with a married man that started while she was still married to her second husband and helped to propel her out of a dying marriage. She did not plan to have an affair and, in fact, is not even philosophically in favor of them:

> I'm not proud of the affair I had, but it happened, and it was a very good relationship. I felt free, even though he was a married man and lived at home. The relationship worked very well for me because it allowed me to pursue my career. He was so supportive. He was my best friend, my lover. He was everything. It was not a typical affair. We

traveled together. He was at my house four or five nights a week; he was at my house on weekends. He was the best friend I ever had.

Pamela's affair lasted seven very good years. Unfortunately, just as our mothers once warned, when it ended, it didn't end well for her. Her lover chose to leave both his wife and her at the same time: "When he left me, I was devastated. Absolutely devastated. He left because he had met a younger woman who could give him a child." It took Pamela a long time to figure out why it ended the way it did, and a long time to recover. Any relationship that ends badly leaves a woman with regrets, but even with all the pain of a love lost, Pamela has little remorse about having been involved with a married man. She is certain she would never have ended the affair herself; the balance between intimacy and freedom worked well for her and, while not crucial to her well-being, the relationship added greatly to her life satisfaction.

The Question of Children

Chapter 15

Defying the Mandate: Living without Motherhood

Only when the assumption that girls must become mothers to fulfill female adulthood is challenged will a woman's destiny truly be her own.

—*Mardy S. Ireland*

Biological possibility and desire are not the same as biological need. Women have child-bearing equipment. For them to choose not to use the equipment is no more blocking what is instinctive than it is for a man who, muscles or no, chooses not to be a weight lifter.

—*Betty Rollin*

For women without children, midlife brings an awareness of the impending loss of the option to be a mother, forcing those who have not done so earlier to examine their feelings more closely. They have to decide whether or not they really want children, how important it is to give birth to their own child, how important marriage is to their notion of motherhood, and/or how willing they are to single-handedly bear the responsibilities of parenting. What is really important to women, above all else, is that they feel free to make the choices that they believe are right for them.

The stigma associated with deviating from the dictates of the marriage and motherhood mandate can complicate women's feelings and choices about becoming mothers. Women without children are usually portrayed as unhappy, unfulfilled, and incomplete. At best, they receive pity for their bad luck or misguided choices. At worst, they are condemned as selfish, unnatural, deficient. These attitudes can make it difficult for women to be honest about their feelings toward motherhood, to admit that they have anything but positive feelings about being a mother, anything but regret if they are not. Our language even lacks a satisfactory term for their experience, one that does not prejudge their status. The most frequently used term, *childless*, carries negative connotations of loss while conveying none of the empowerment and dignity of choice. Even the more positive term, *childfree*, is unsatisfactory, implying as it does that motherhood is a form of bondage from which such a woman has somehow escaped.

Women today, however, can make the choice not to have children. Effective birth control and the legalization of abortion have secured this option, while expanded professional opportunities allow women without children to develop their creative energies in other arenas. Despite the continuing pressure of the mandate, women without children are free not only to achieve but also to nurture in ways unimaginable in previous decades. They can feel good about themselves as loving and giving members of their communities, even if they find themselves living without motherhood.

VALUING THE CHOICE *NOT* TO HAVE CHILDREN

Women who want to move beyond the negative cultural attitudes toward women without children do so, in part, by separating the idea of motherhood from definitions of happiness and maturity. The two are not synonymous when applied to adult females, any more than fatherhood is synonymous with happiness and maturity when applied to adult males. Most of the women we interviewed who do not have children but feel good about their lives have been able to disengage themselves from these culturally conditioned beliefs. Jean, who greatly enjoys her life, is very clear on this subject:

> Being a mother is not an essential part of being a woman. Is it essential for a man to be a father? Of course not. Nobody would accuse a man of not being normal if he didn't want kids. But a woman is seen as a sexual organ of procreation. I think it's unfair. Your sexuality and your biological imperative have to be secondary to your identity as a human being.

Jean does not minimize the wonder of giving birth or the joy or importance of raising children; however, she strongly objects to the view that motherhood should be seen as the pinnacle of every woman's existence. In direct opposition to the messages she received in her youth, she has come to view motherhood, like marriage, as only one of the many meaningful paths open to women:

> I think all living things have the capacity to nurture. I'm not trivializing the parental bond, not at all. I think it is wonderful; it is one of the few decent feelings that we are capable of experiencing. But this silly thing of making people, men or women, victims of this imperative is a gross disservice. It makes women look like we cannot do anything except bear children and be mothers.

Women who have managed to separate their identities as women from the role of mother enjoy a sense of self which is not defined by the mandate. Often strongly committed to their work and professional pursuits, these women focus on how they can make contributions to the world in ways they feel are better suited to their needs and circumstances; at the same time, they focus on how they can develop deep relationships with others that provide alternative sources of meaning, interconnectedness, and mutual nurturance.

The reasons any woman arrives at midlife without having become a mother are a complex combination of choice and chance. The women we interviewed described a wide range of feelings and events that determined their decisions about living without motherhood and shaped the process by which they created satisfying lives without children. For some, the process was relatively easy because they never wanted to be mothers. Others wanted children, but decided not to become single mothers and accepted this as the best decision, given the circumstances of their lives. Some are still wrestling with the issue.

CLARITY OF VISION: WOMEN WHO NEVER WANTED TO BE MOTHERS

Just as some women have known from childhood that they wanted to define themselves in part by being a mother or a physician or an actress, there are some women who have always known that they did *not* want to define themselves by becoming a mother. Early in their lives, they developed the clarity of vision to recognize that they could achieve fulfillment without motherhood.

Elaine exemplifies women who have never yearned for children or traditional family life. Instead, her dreams centered more on competition. and achievement. As a young girl, she says, "I liked to play with boys more than I liked to play with dolls. I liked outdoor activities, climbing trees, all those tomboy kinds of things." Elaine never expected to have children. Thinking back on this choice, she explains:

> I always knew it was not the right option for me. I don't miss it. Sometimes, I think the Norman Rockwell family painting would be a nice thing. I mean, everybody thinks families are great. There's nothing stronger than a family. But God didn't intend it for everybody.

Elaine has devoted herself to the activities she finds the most rewarding. When we asked what she feels gives her life meaning and satisfaction, her answer was clear. "Probably my work first of all—achieving, competing." Watching other women in the workplace try to combine work and parenting has convinced Elaine that children would have made it impossible for her to achieve as much as she has. She told us about one of her closest friends, Mary, with whom she has worked for eighteen years. Mary and Elaine started out together as interior designers in the same firm and began advancing at roughly the same pace. Elaine believes Mary to be one of her brightest and most capable colleagues, yet Mary's professional progress slowed when she had children and cut back her hours. Although Mary has been able to combine having a career and a family, she has had to give up parts of her professional life that Elaine values highly. Elaine explains:

> Mary has had to give up advancement opportunities because she was not willing to work full-time. She has come as close as anybody I know to having it all—but she doesn't. She's very respected, but she's not really in the loop of what's happening here.

For Elaine, being "in the loop" is crucial; for Mary, it is not. Elaine believes that it is the sense of mastery as well as the intensity of her work that gives her the kind of pleasure she most desires.

Many of the women we interviewed discovered, like Elaine, that once they tasted success, that they did not want to give up any of the joys of working for the responsibilities of mothering. Hannah, an entertainer, realized early on that she could never give up her work to raise children. She told us that, as a child, she never fantasized about growing up to be a mother. She realized how completely she defined and expressed herself through her career when she became pregnant accidentally at the age of thirty-five. Her gynecologist suggested that she might want to take time off from her high-powered career to have the baby. Having a child was so far from her sense of what was right and possible for her that she could not believe her doctor had suggested this. "Are you crazy?" she blurted out. At that moment, she realized that she had always been committed to a vision of her life that did not include being a mother.

Women who decide that they are more suited to professional pursuits than to mothering are not devoid of the need or ability to establish close, nurturing relationships with others. Elaine has created a community of people in her life about whom she cares deeply. These friends also support her choice not to have children:

> I have surrounded myself with people who have similar values, so I don't really experience prejudice all that much. Even my friends who have traditional families think it is interesting to know somebody who doesn't have a traditional family.

Moreover, what women like Elaine experience as so satisfying about their work is the feeling of contributing to others' lives in important ways. Elaine has been a mentor as well as an employer, nurturing and supporting many younger women in the workplace. She explains:

> I very much enjoy helping women move up the ranks. I have had four secretaries whom I have carefully directed into career tracks leading to high positions. I truly love this kind of nurturing.

Myrna loves her work for similar reasons. Now a college professor, Myrna has no hesitation declaring that neither marriage nor motherhood has ever been her driving priority. At age thirteen, Myrna told her parents that she wanted to apply to a private boarding school because she wanted a better education than her local public school in rural Georgia could provide. Her parents were taken aback by her request but eventually agreed. The next fall, Myrna left the countryside for the ivy-covered halls of a New England school. Her early decision to go to boarding school was the first indication of what was to become her lifelong dedication to education. Today, she is unusually comfortable with the idea that not having children is a choice she has made freely and feels none of the stigma that women without children so often experience:

> I'm not the type of woman to say, "Oh gosh, if only I had children, I would feel that I was really a woman." I don't think that I would be a very good mother. I don't have a lot of patience for the child-rearing process. Not that I don't like children, please don't misunderstand me. I'm not anti-marriage either. Actually, I'm not anti-anything.

Myrna is comfortable with herself and can openly acknowledge that parenting would not be her strong suit. When she is around her young nieces and nephews, she enjoys herself tremendously for brief periods of time. But she gets easily frustrated when she realizes that she can't reason with them. Laughing at herself she told us, "When I'm around kids, I start to think, 'Gosh, I'm glad they're going home soon.' "

While Myrna believes it is possible to combine work and family, she has always been the kind of person who prefers to do one job well rather than spread herself more thinly:

> I have great admiration for women who can be successful wives *and* mothers *and* professionals. I think that they have the ability to juggle a lot of different roles. I'm not a person to do that. I like assuming one role and really dedicating myself to doing the best I can with that one.

On average, Myrna works about sixty hours a week and knows she would have to give something up if she were to have children. As a teacher and mentor to her students, she also knows that she has had a far-reaching impact on many people's lives. Recently, a man came to her office. When she admitted she did not remember who he was, he explained, "You were my adviser in the early seventies. I had been dismissed from school for academic reasons. You sat me down in this very chair and you preached to me about the value of an education with such passion. You actually got through to me. I just wanted to stop by and tell you that today is the first day of my doctoral program." Relating this story, Myrna glowed. "What more could a person ask for in terms of fulfillment?"

TO BE OR NOT TO BE: CAUGHT IN A WEB OF AMBIVALENCE

While the women we have just described found it relatively easy to forego motherhood, other women find that their decision about motherhood is one of the hardest they will ever have to make. Many of them are still young enough to be mothers, one way or another, and have not closed the door on the possibility. These women continue to struggle with the pros and cons, often avoiding making a final decision.

Late one December evening, we spoke with Erika at her office. Most of her staff had gone home, but Erika was tying up loose ends before leaving for Christmas vacation the following morning. We were her last appointment for the day. Looking around her office in the middle of our interview, Erika mused:

> I never thought I would be doing this. I thought by now I would have two or three kids, and they would be about six or seven years old, and I would be home trying to decorate the Christmas tree. That's how I thought my life would go. It's very different.

At the age of thirty-eight, Erika is grappling intensely with her feelings about motherhood as she anticipates the end of her childbearing years. She is still young enough to have a child if she chooses to do so, but she remains suspended by her own ambivalence. On one hand, she admits that at this point in her life she frequently thinks about having children, and that when she does she feels discouraged and unhappy about being single. Being a mother was always very closely tied to her definitions of maturity, happiness, fulfillment, and femininity. These thoughts and feelings are reinforced by her parents, who continue to pressure her to "hurry up and get married."

On the other hand, she does not want to have children outside marriage. Unlike many of the single mothers we interviewed who expected to get most of their support from other women and family members, Erika assumes that single mothers must rely on boyfriends to meet their emotional needs—a risk she is unwilling to take. Erika also believes her parents' disapproval would be inevitable if she were to have a child on her own. She is sure they would condemn such a choice vehemently: "I *know* my father would stop speaking to me. I know that he wouldn't want to see me again." Her anticipation of family rejection certainly weighs heavily against any plan of

becoming a single parent. But it isn't just her parents' disapproval that im-
pedes her; it is also her own. She believes that mothers should stay home
with children full-time for at least the first five years of their lives, and that
children should be raised in an environment with a guaranteed standard of
living. Fearing she could not fulfill both of these requirements on her own,
she believes it would be unfair to bring a child into her world.

Erika is aware that it is both necessary and important for her to acknowledge that her life has taken a different course from the one she and her
parents charted for her long ago. Although she is not ready to write off the
possibility of motherhood, she does believe that only good can come when
she makes a choice. With unusual insight about the process before her and its
potential impact on her life, she explains:

> If I don't go that route of getting married and having children, a part of
> me will feel terribly guilty, like I didn't try hard enough to find the
> right man, or whatever. But I think there also will be a part of me that
> will be much better off. I'll take my life into my own hands; I'll get
> more control of it. It's going to be a rough time for me, but once I'm
> through that time, I think I will be a different person. This latent part
> of me will explode with freedom and I will no longer be afraid to take
> risks. I will say to myself, "Geez, all along I thought it was going to be
> this way, but my little fantasy didn't come true. So what do I have to
> lose now?"

MOURNING LOST DREAMS AND CREATING
NEW ONES

Women who once dreamed of having children of their own describe going
through a grieving process in which they mourned their lost dreams of
having a child and being a mother before they were able to move on to
create satisfying lives with another focus. They confirm Erika's belief that
mourning her lost dreams will allow her to shift her focus from the negative—the lack of children in her life—to the positive—the possibilities and
opportunities a life without children can offer. Jessie, who is ten years older
than Erika, made her peace with not having children as she entered midlife
and allowed herself to mourn the loss:

Not having children was very hard for me, and as the years went by, it only became more difficult. A number of the men I became involved with had had vasectomies! When women would start to talk about their kids, I just didn't want to listen. It was too painful. But once I reached my mid-forties, it became much easier. Now I find that it isn't painful anymore. I'm actually happy I never had a child. I feel like that's not what I'm supposed to do with my life. I'm thrilled for women who are "doing" motherhood, but given my particular personality, I don't think I would have done well with a child. I feel a tremendous relief, but it was a long time coming.

Pauline also describes the pain of not having a child and the envy she felt when her brother and sister-in-law had their first child. "I'm the one who went through postpartum depression. I was overwhelmed by the feeling of 'I want her but she's not mine.'" However, after going through this depression, she began to let go of her original dreams of having a daughter of her own and forged more intimate bonds with her nieces and nephews, bonds which have softened her grief at not being a mother:

I guess I miss knowing I'll never have the experience of having a child, but I've got five nieces and nephews with whom I am very close. You might as well say they're like surrogate children. In fact, one of my nieces calls me her "other mother."

The reactions of family and friends can complicate the process of giving up the idea that motherhood is a necessary part of being complete as a woman. Susan recalls:

I was always very ambivalent about being a mother, but I never doubted that I would become one. It was a given, a defining fact of my future. But I discovered two things after I married that changed by ideas about motherhood: work was exciting and my husband really didn't want children. At first, I was very uncomfortable about not having children, but it was easy to let the years slip by without confronting the issue. Bit by bit, I just let it go, so that when I realized it was getting too late to get pregnant, I felt far less pain that I would have expected. But lots of people acted like I was committing some crime against nature. They thought there was something wrong with me for not moving heaven and earth to have a child and they weren't shy about saying so. And sometimes my mother acted as if I were deliberately cheating her by not producing a grandchild.

Once women have allowed themselves to grieve any loss they feel about not having children, they are free to enjoy the unsung advantages of life without them. The women we interviewed told us the key to finding satisfaction lay in refocusing their energies on other aspects of their lives. They are active in their careers in ways that allow them to feel good about making important contributions to their world. They have developed strong and nurturing relationships with friends and colleagues, and many have found ways to actively involve children in their lives. Liza, for instance, has established important relationships with the children of friends. They call her Aunt Liza, and considering her style, her role is no doubt a little like that of Auntie Mame, outrageous and indulgent:

> I take them to the zoo. I take them to the ballet. I buy birthday and Christmas presents. That's how I got around not having kids myself. I just sort of pick up my friends' kids. I decided that it's just as much fun to do whatever the fun things are with my friends' kids and then say "goodnight."

Many women without children also take advantage of the freedom to take off for spontaneous weekends biking in the country or hiking in the mountains. Those who can afford to—and single women who don't have children tend to have far more disposable income than those who do—pursue interests such as travel, embarking on exotic trips to Paris, the great wall of China, Macchu Pichu, or even the outback of Australia. But travel isn't the only adventure women without children are more free to pursue. Some report that they feel more free to flirt than if they had the responsibilities of motherhood, and that they enjoy the freedom to take advantage of spontaneous romantic invitations when they encounter such opportunities. Carol, who was fifty when she adopted Maria, remembers these carefree years fondly:

> I loved all the freedom and the ways I used to indulge myself, whether it was travel, reading, soaking at some Spa, or accepting some man's invitation to go to Italy for the weekend. During all those years, I didn't think much about having or not having a child. I was just living

a very different kind of life. Thinking back, I know I saw myself as a much more sexual person. Getting romantically involved was always a possibility and almost always nice. I took care of myself in all sorts of hedonistic ways, even when I was working hard. Now I rarely think about those things. Today I can't imagine life without Maria, but then I really didn't feel I was missing anything.

Elena summarizes the advantages she feels she has as a result of not having the responsibilities that motherhood entails:

I have unlimited peace and quiet. I do not have the economic burden of single parenthood. I have mobility and free time. I have the freedom to go wherever I want and do what I want. These are the reasons why I don't want to have a child.

The women we interviewed reported still other changes in their lives once they let go of the dream of being a mother. Prior to accepting the fact that she wasn't going to have children, Shannon felt frenzied to find a man she could marry before "time ran out." Now she feels more at peace and is able to commit herself to life on her own with a sense of pride and pleasure:

At the age of forty-two, I've come to terms with the fact that I probably won't have children. That has taken a lot of pressure off. Now I can just keep living my life, exploring what makes me feel fulfilled and, hopefully, along the way, find a fellow traveler. If not, I'll just keep doing what I want to do in life.

Megan agrees with Shannon. Once she allowed herself to grieve the loss of motherhood, she felt relieved of the pressure to conform to a dream that never really fit her circumstances or needs. "Somehow, by realizing that I'm not going to have children, I was able to ask myself, 'Why get married? What would be the purpose of getting married?' I never knew until then how much I connected the two."

Women who had a clarity of vision about not having children were able to capitalize on these advantages early in their lives, but even women who always cherished dreams of motherhood have come to discover the many joys of living without children. Josie, who once wanted children, now celebrates her freedom to focus on other parts of her life. She "rehearsed" the role of mother during a three-year relationship with a man who had custody of his three children. She loved them, but she was worn out by working, going to school, and parenting at the same time. Today she says, "I've had moments of grief about not having children, but they don't last as long as the sense of relief."

Chapter 16

Courageous Choices: Single Mothers by Choice

There was no question that I wanted a child. There was no question that I could raise a child. And there was definitely no question that I hadn't met Mr. Right.

—*Jane Wallace*

Making the decision to have a child—It's momentous. It's to decide forever to have your heart go walking around outside your body.

—*Elizabeth Stone*

M any women experience the coming of midlife as a time to close the door on dreams of motherhood, but for some it only strengthens their resolve to make such dreams come true. Believing that motherhood should not depend on being married, they decide that they do not want to miss the experience of raising a child. Midlife adds urgency to women's decisions about children, but it also gives them the strength and wisdom needed to make such decisions. By the time most women reach midlife, they have accumulated enough experience to know what they genuinely want and are courageous enough to go after it. In fact, the single women we interviewed who chose to become mothers in midlife wanted this experience with a *passion*—much more than they had ever wanted the experience of being a wife. Many openly declared that it was far easier to do without marriage than to do without a child. They were determined not to give up their dreams simply because they did not have a man by their side. With such inner conviction they could consider options for becoming a mother that did not have marriage as a prerequisite.

Fortunately, social and technological changes have made available options that would have been inconceivable in previous decades. New reproductive technologies, such as artificial insemination and in-vitro fertilization, are becoming increasingly accepted; also, private and international adoption agencies are gradually coming to accept single women as parents. Moreover, increasing divorce rates actually help women feel more comfortable making the choice to become an "unwed" mother, since so many children are being raised in single-parent homes.

The women we interviewed who became mothers in midlife did so by exercising one of the three options open to them, options that Ria succinctly presented to Mark when they became lovers: "It's either adoption, artificial insemination, or you." Although each option presents unique challenges to women, each also can bring tremendous joy. For most of our women who had this experience, simply making this momentous decision and summoning the courage to commit to such an adventure provided an enormous sense of excitement and well-being. The pleasure they experienced in the actual raising of their children was more than most had hoped for. They described how their children moved into the center of their already busy lives, staking a claim on their energies and their hearts, and shifting their priorities forever. Although most described the day-to-day demands as relentless, they were continually surprised by the many rewards and the depth of feeling they experienced.

THE CHOICE TO BECOME PREGNANT:
ARTIFICIAL INSEMINATION

Artificial insemination is the option of choice for an increasing number of single women who want to become mothers. Although it is far from easy, this technique gives women the greatest amount of control. It allows a woman the experience of bearing and raising her own biological child without the potential complications involved in asking a man to whom she is not married to be the father. Not all women know men whom they would want to father their child and who would agree to such a plan; even if they do, such arrangements pose a risk of complex emotional entanglements and possible future custody disputes. Choosing artificial insemination also has the advantage of bypassing all the bureaucratic obstacles single women encounter in an adoption culture that can be deeply prejudiced against them. For these reasons, many women are deciding to tolerate all of the very real problems posed by artificial insemination in order to become mothers.

Consider Jamie, now forty-two and the mother of four-year-old Josh, whom she conceived by artificial insemination. Jamie's decision to have a child, like so many of life's highly significant turning points, was the result of serendipity. Jamie loved her freedom and had spent her twenties and thirties on her own. She divided her time between work and play, building a career and exploring the world in her many adventures. She backpacked throughout Europe on her own and spent time working on a fishing boat in Alaska.

Then, when she was thirty-six, she had a ski accident that forced her off her feet and into her head. She found herself reflecting on her life and evaluating her goals:

> I remember sitting there and thinking, "What am I going to do next? Do I want to go on for my Ph.D.? Do I want another degree? Do I want to move someplace else?" And then I realized that what I really wanted more than anything else was a child.

Jamie had always wanted to be a mother, but had never paid attention to that particular voice within. She suddenly understood that she could live happily without marriage but not without motherhood:

> I have known my whole life that I wanted a child. At times I felt real pressure to meet someone because I wanted a child. Having a child was much more important than getting married.

Once Jamie became aware of the intensity of her feelings about having a child, her decision was clear. She explains, "It was probably one of the easiest decisions of my life because it was the one thing I wanted more than anything else."

As she sat housebound, reading magazines, Jamie was seized with a sense of urgency: "I was suddenly aware that time was running out and that, if I were going to have a child, it had to be *soon*." At the same time, she felt frustratingly thwarted because there was no serious contender for the role of husband/father waiting to rescue her from midlife gridlock. In the midst of her panic, she happened upon an article in *Newsweek* magazine that described the process and advantages of artificial insemination. Although she had never considered this option before, the more she read, the more excited she became. The notion of becoming artificially inseminated gave her hope and a sense of possibility. As she researched this option further, she learned of a woman in her area who was starting a group for single women considering having children on their own. With the help of the other women in the group who were also weighing their options, Jamie decided to become inseminated.

Once she began the process, Jamie quickly learned that turning this "perfect solution" into the reality of a baby was going to take time, patience, luck, commitment, and courage. Jamie explained to us that, although sperm can be ordered and received through the mail, and theoretically injected with a turkey baster, the process of becoming inseminated can nonetheless be very difficult. It is expensive, and frequently an insemination does not result in fertilization. For Jamie, the effort to become impregnated dragged on for sixteen emotionally draining months. She attempted insemination through three different agencies before she became pregnant. All the hassles, however, were more than justified by the birth of her son, Josh. Jamie now gets enormous pleasure in watching Josh grow up in a healthy and happy way, and loves being able to reexperience parts of childhood with him. When we asked her what in her life contributed most to her sense of satisfaction, she answered without hesitation, "My child." In addition, having a child has allowed her the freedom to relate to men without the desperation that she felt so strongly in earlier years to find a man to father a child.

Jamie carries burdens that her married sisters do not share, such as being alone when Josh gets sick. Jamie recalls, "I remember one night when he was really sick with a high fever. I was *scared*. I thought, 'I wish somebody were here.' " Money has been a real problem, too. Jamie insists upon excellent child-care and consequently struggles to meet all of her expenses. She recently sold her home and moved to an apartment closer to Josh's child-care center to decrease expenses and simplify their lives.

Another challenge is answering the questions Josh is beginning to ask about not having a father. With few role models to emulate, Jamie can only depend on herself to find ways to meet this particular challenge of raising Josh on her own. She tries to determine what Josh is really asking for and how much information is developmentally appropriate to share. At this point, she has emphasized that he doesn't have a father because she wasn't married when she had him. She has also tried to explain to Josh that there are different kinds of families, some that include a father and some that do not:

So far, we've discussed how there are different kinds of families and some families have a mom and a dad, some families have a mom, some families have a dad and a grandmother. I don't think that he feels there is anything wrong or unusual about our family, but I also think he is looking for a male role model.

Jamie has brought men into Josh's life as surrogate fathers. She has relied on programs for single mothers such as Parents without Partners and Big Brothers and has made an effort to help Josh develop relationships with some of her male friends. Recently, as he was falling asleep, he announced he had a great idea. He proposed that he and Jamie go out West to see if they could find two cowboy dads, one for him and one for her. Thoughtfully he added that it would be terrific if they could also pick up some horses while they were there.

Jamie faced a lot of resistance from her family when she decided to become inseminated. Her parents, she says, "were shocked, horrified. My mother's biggest fear was what would people say!" Jamie worried about the potential reactions of people in her workplace and even whether she might be fired. In her earlier years, she would not have been sufficiently sure of herself to risk these potentially negative reactions. But since she possessed the inner direction that is a gift of midlife, the opinions of others were not enough to stop her from doing something that mattered as much to her as having a child. Before she made the decision, Jamie consulted lawyers to verify for herself that she couldn't lose her job, and then asked herself:

> If I were rejected by my family, friends, and co-workers, would that be enough to make me want to live my life in a different way? To give up my dream and then choose to live in a way that pleased them? It was clear that my need or desire to have a child was much stronger than even these big issues.

Fortunately, Jamie was pleasantly surprised by the reactions of her colleagues. She answered everybody's questions very openly and, in return, received their enthusiastic support.

Jamie is fully aware of the difficulties of artificial insemination and the challenges of single parenting, but there is no question that, if she had it to do all over again, she would make the same choice. "I have no regrets," she told us unequivocally. She feels fortunate to live in a time that offers so many options to single women and recognizes that she would have been very unhappy without Josh:

> I know with certainty that, if I had not been able to have a child of my own or adopt (and I think I would have been as happy with that), I would be a very, very bitter person. The rest of my life would have been clouded by sadness if I hadn't been able to do this.

Like other women who have children at midlife, Jamie experienced great freedom and independence in her earlier years and was fully conscious of the choice she made to give it up. The fact that she (and women like her) had had freedom seemed to make it easier, not harder, to accept the ties that bind. Having gone to great lengths to become a mother, Jamie wants to enjoy every minute of it, even those minutes most parents would gladly give up (like the ones when they are exhausted and still have ten things to do before their child can be put to bed). Indeed, Jamie told us it was fortunate that she had not become a mother earlier, before she was ready to face the unrelenting responsibilities of single motherhood. Her forties turned out to be a wonderful time to have a child:

> Timing wise, my decision was perfect. I think earlier I would have resented getting pregnant. But by midlife, I really *wanted* a child. I think that's why mothering has been more of a joy than anything else. I didn't have to deal with resenting anything, with giving up time or freedom or whatever. I didn't see parenthood as a sacrifice involving loss; I saw it as a choice involving gain.

Kelly, whose five-year-old son Alex also was conceived by artificial insemination, speaks of her experience with an enthusiasm akin to Jamie's. She says with certainty, "There isn't anybody out there whose life I would rather be living." In fact, Kelly was so pleased by the experience of giving birth to and raising Alex that she wanted to become pregnant again. However, after three years of trying, she has begun to accept that she will not be able to have another child.

Kelly is unequivocally in love with being a mother for many reasons. She loves the opportunity to do "kid things" like going to the zoo or to amusement parks, camping, canoeing, and having cook-outs:

I like the constant change. He grows so fast and his cycles change so quickly that I just never know if he's going to be the same person when he wakes up as when he went to bed!

She also enjoys the unique perspective on life that Alex has to offer. "It's just great to see the world through a child's eye," she says. "His perspective is so different, it's amazing!" Finally, Kelly values the greater sense of connection she feels with her community since having Alex. Far from resulting in the social sanctions that single parenthood brought with it a generation or so ago, becoming a single mother has brought Kelly acceptance in her community and a sense of belonging. Prior to having Alex, Kelly had little in common with the women in her conservative, suburban community. Now, her neighbors seem to feel more comfortable with her. She explains, "Being a parent gives you a common denominator with most people."

THE CHOICE TO BECOME PREGNANT:
NATURAL INSEMINATION

Artificial insemination offers many advantages and has brought great joy to women like Jamie and Kelly, but it also has disadvantages. Some women want to have a child of their own but are uncomfortable with the impersonal nature of being artificially inseminated. Others are troubled by the lack of information they would have about their child's father. These women prefer the more traditional method of natural insemination, but they do not necessarily feel they have to honor the tradition of marriage as a prerequisite. For them, asking a man they know to father a child seems the best solution.

Ria, for instance, always wanted to be a mother. She fantasized about having children in a traditional marriage with the full participation of a husband whom she was sure she would adore. Before she actually married she secured her prospective husband's commitment to having a family. However, once married, he balked. First he claimed he was too young; then, as years passed, too old. Ria felt enraged and betrayed by his refusal to commit to being a parent. Marital therapy failed to resolve this difference and Ria eventually left him. Rattled, her husband reconsidered and asked for a reconciliation. Their reunion resulted in the birth of a daughter. Later, he again reneged on his promise that they could try to have another child. By this time their marriage had been mortally wounded and Ria and her husband divorced.

Being divorced did not change Ria's mind about having more children. She warned her very proper mother that if there was no husband in sight by the time her age forced her to make a decision, she was going to have children out of wedlock. She tells the story:

> I said, "Mom, you know, maybe I'm not going to find a man to father another child. But I'm going to have another child whether or not I get married." She looked at me and said [imitating an uppity sort of English accent], "Pardon me, but are you planning to have a bastard?"—with a kind smile. Within a few days she called to say, "In the Igbo tribe, all babies are welcome. It's a matriarchal system."

Ria was reassured and delighted by her mother's acceptance and, even more, by her willingness to research other traditions that would affirm her unorthodox approach to motherhood. She was even happier to have her mother's support nine years ago when she said, "It's time. That's it. I have my own home. I have my profession. I want another child." In fact, her mother even offered to help Ria financially by providing a year of "grandparent support."

Ria investigated adoption first, and had collected a file full of information when she began a romance with an old friend, Mark. She made it clear to him when they became lovers that her non-negotiable life plan was to have at least one more child. She simply wasn't willing to allow another man to break her heart by saying he wouldn't have a child with her. Ria knew that Mark was not interested in full-time parenting (he already had one adult child from his first marriage). Since she also was not eager to give matrimony another try, she did not ask for marriage, financial support, or even live-in companionship and help with child-care. She only asked Mark to father a child. He agreed and they had a daughter, Sally. Their experience was so positive that three years later they had another child, Becky.

Today, although they have never lived together, Ria and Mark have a relationship that seems more stable than many marriages. Mark has stayed at her home every Saturday night and Sunday since Sally was born. During the past winter, Ria began feeling overwhelmed and asked Mark if he would help by getting the kids ready for bed one night each week. Since then, he has come on Wednesdays to help with dinner and putting them to bed. His visits are brief but intense, full of love and play. Ria says:

That's Daddy and they love him. Sally says, "He's my best player." Mark gets down on the floor and builds blocks. They tell stories to each other, they do drawings together, and then he goes away. It's short and it's intense, but it's good. Somehow I don't seem to mind that he's not here every day because I need the relief myself, I need the space myself. I want it. I want to run my own life.

Ria likes having a house to herself and uninterrupted time with her children without having to try to meet everyone's needs simultaneously and worry that Mark is feeling neglected. She knows the power of her history, saying, "My response when the 'husband' is around is that I'm supposed to pay more attention to him than the kids." Their unusual arrangement allows Ria to enjoy her relationship with Mark without having to compromise on being the kind of mother she wants to be.

One might ask how Ria could truly be happy raising three children without the help of a husband. Surely her workload must be relentless, confining, and draining. Ria is the first to admit that there are real challenges. She explains, "I never stop—not for a minute. What's overwhelming is that there is never any time for myself now." Money has also been a problem as Ria supports herself and her children in a large and expensive city on an annual budget of $25,000. When she first had Sally, she was working as an art professor at a university. She soon realized that work was consuming most of her time and child-care was consuming most of her money. Although Ria was ambitious and had great passion for her career in earlier years, mothering was now more important to her, so she took a leave of absence from the university and started a day-care center in her own home. For extra income, she rents out her top floor to a student, and after Becky was born, Mark started contributing a small amount each month to help with expenses.

Despite the challenges, Ria wouldn't trade her life for anyone else's. When she feels particularly overwhelmed, she reminds herself of how much she longed to be a mother. She also receives a tremendous amount of support from her network of women friends who nurture and sustain each other. Ria is closest to three women, two of whom are also single mothers. They talk as much as three times a day, touching base and consulting about the kids. She explains, "I don't call Mark as much as I call Rosie, my best friend." These women are her "mother friends." One even helped to deliver Sally and Becky, and they all share a hand-me-down system to defray the cost of their children's clothing. She and Rosie, who is also a single

mother, have purchased headphone telephones that allow them to talk during the evenings while they tackle the mounds of dirty dishes that pile up
each day. One of Ria's friends commented that Ria probably has more help
in parenting than do many women in traditional marriages.

Ria believes that relying on her female friends works better for her than
expecting a husband to share equally in family life and child-care. She muses
that perhaps a female-headed family supported by a network of women is a
more natural and realistic way to raise children than our traditional nuclear
family. In any case, as a woman who always wanted to have a lot of children,
Ria has finally fulfilled her wish. Her life is so oriented around children that
it is hard to find a place to sit in her house. When we arrived to interview her
in the middle of the afternoon, her kitchen was overflowing with the remains of "snack time," the dining room held two napping boys, and a small
girl was quietly playing on the floor. In the living room, Ria had to rouse the
cat sleeping on the couch and take Becky, who was also sleeping there, onto
her lap to make a place for us to sit. In the midst of this seeming disarray, and
while nursing Becky (who had begun to cry) and petting the cat (who had
jumped back up to claim a place for herself on Ria's lap), Ria stated, "Basically, I'm happier than I've ever been in my entire life." She is well aware
that her life style would not work for everyone, but she says without reserva-
tion, "I love it and I wouldn't do it differently. The older I get, the more I
see that we all have our own life stories. I don't think my way is right for
everybody, but it is certainly satisfying for me."

THE CHOICE TO ADOPT:
A BLIND DATE FOR LIFE

Anyone who listens to the stories of single women who have decided to
adopt a child at midlife comes away impressed by their strong determination
to become mothers. They confront many obstacles, not the least of which
are the negative attitudes of adoption agencies toward single women. Helen,
for example, who eventually adopted a child from Romania, discovered that
in the United States her age and marital status meant she was eligible only for
a "special needs" child. It is ironic, she commented, that single women, who
are likely to have fewer economic resources to manage a child, are paired
with children who have the most problems. Like other single women who
choose alternative means of becoming mothers, women who adopt at mid-

life must also deal with the pessimistic attitudes of well-meaning family members and friends, who warn them somberly of the arduousness of the task they are setting out to undertake. Finally, they have to deal with their own ambivalence—that chilling fear that perhaps they are not "up" to the task after all; maybe the child they receive will have unforeseen problems they can't handle; or if they adopt an older child, maybe they won't be able to love a child who is different or maybe the child won't adjust to them. After all, adoption is a bit like going on a blind date for life; you make a lifelong commitment before you have even met. And yet, the women we interviewed who had adopted children in midlife were as unabashedly happy about becoming mothers as were Jamie, Kelly, and Ria. The following stories illustrate both the patience and perseverance needed to pursue the option of adoption, as well as the joy that can result.

Apryl's original life plan had been to get married, work for a period of time, and then get pregnant, but her marriage ended before she had children. Five years after her divorce, she realized that she really wanted a child and time was running out. Even though she was still in her early thirties, she recalls thinking, "Wow, I'm not married. I'd better have a baby quick!" At first, she wanted to pursue a plan like Ria's. She was dating a man whom she liked a great deal, but didn't want to marry. She considered getting pregnant secretly without telling him, but eventually decided to be honest and direct. She asked him if he would be willing to father her child, and he flatly refused. He had fathered a child in high school and had no desire to bring another child whom he would never really know into the world.

Apryl refused to be discouraged. She was determined to find a way to become a mother because, as she says, "Deep inside, I knew that I did not want to live my life without having that experience." After considering her options, she realized that she didn't feel the need to bear her own child. Thinking about all the children in the world who needed families, she began to pursue the idea of adoption. The hostile attitudes towards single parents she encountered at American agencies ruled out a domestic adoption. She eventually turned to the option of international adoption, which came with its own set of problems. Navigating her way through the bureaucracy of India, the country where she finally adopted her daughter, was a complicated and painful process that dragged on for over four years.

The first time Apryl was offered a child, she was told that she had been chosen to become the mother of a six-year-old girl who had just entered an orphanage. She was thrilled. The paperwork dragged on at a snail's pace, during which time the child responded to her first reasonable diet by growing dramatically. Soon it was clear that her small size was a result of severe malnutrition, not of a young age. She was actually thirteen or fourteen years old rather than six or seven. In the meantime, Apryl had been corresponding with her, had decorated a room, and had arranged schooling for her. When the agency decided the assignment was inappropriate, Apryl was devastated. She felt she had lost both a child and a dream.

A few months later the same agency called with an offer of an eighteen-month-old girl. Although she was still mourning the loss of the first child, Apryl saw the offer as a twist of fate she should embrace. She traveled to India to meet her new daughter, Minda:

> For me, bringing her back from India was very, very important. I really wanted to be the one person who accompanied her the entire way so that we could share the journey together from beginning to end. All of that was very, very important to me, and I'm glad that I did it.

Apryl admits that caring for a child is the hardest job she has ever done. She is very aware of the freedom she has sacrificed. "I don't fly solo anymore," she laughed during our interview:

> It is such a change to go from being completely free. I found my freedom to be very satisfying. I came and went as I pleased, I didn't have to answer to anybody, I didn't have to leave early, I didn't have to go home if I didn't want to, I could stay overnight at a friend's whenever I felt like it.

Even with the dramatic restrictions in her lifestyle now, Apryl is clear that adopting Minda was absolutely the right decision for her. She had always believed that the experience of being a mother would be wonderful and important to her. She now says, "Raising a child is more satisfying than I ever imagined. There are so many responsibilities, but there are also fun and sweetness and that incomparable mother–child bond. Our life together is a delight." For women like Apryl, who are unable or do not wish to have a child who is biologically their own, international adoption offers a chance to fulfill their dreams of motherhood. Apryl persevered and she now has exactly what she wanted, a bright and beautiful little girl.

Carol also persevered. After eighteen months of paperwork, classes, and screening interviews, she too was rewarded with a little girl. She tells the story of how her life changed forever from the moment they met:

I can remember the first time I saw Maria. I had traveled for two days to arrive in Punta Arenas, the very southern tip of Chile, and was picked up at the airport by the social worker who immediately took me to the children's home. While I waited in a cold little room by the front door, they went to fetch her. All I knew about her was that she was seven years old and had been in this Catholic home for children for two years. I was scared to death. What if we didn't click? She spoke no English and my Spanish was not great. What would I say? I had agreed to this blind date for life and now I wondered what on earth I had gotten myself into.

Then the nun brought her into the room and my heart melted. She was so little, so pretty, so sweet and shy. She had the most wonderful smile on her face, which the sister pointed out matched the smile in her eyes. With no further fanfare, twenty minutes later we walked out together—two people scared to death of each other. We went to court the next day to finalize the adoption, and we still needed the approval of the American Embassy in Santiago, but these were just formalities. Everyone had said how hard the process would be, but everything worked like clockwork. We emerged from just a week's worth of bureaucratic paperwork to board a plane back to Pittsburgh, forever bound into lives transformed and intertwined.

Life with Maria has gotten steadily better over the three years we have been together. I work less, travel less, read less, think and worry more. In fact, I worry more than I ever thought was possible; I worry about every decision I make for her, whether I am pushing her too hard or not hard enough. I worry about someone hurting her, and about how to keep her from harm. I even worry about staying healthy enough to take care of her for as long as she needs it.

I used to drive a sports car, own a cat, eat out, spend my weekends zipping to New York to see a play or combing antique stores for forgotten treasures. Now I eat in, and if I travel at all, I go to Disney World. I own a dog named Lady and drive a station wagon that can handle a car pool of seven giggling girls. I only need to move to the suburbs to complete my transformation to a world-class cliché.

But now I can't imagine life without her. She fills the house with noise and laughter. She challenges my priorities and my beliefs, and forces me to ask myself why I do the things I do. Life isn't as comfortable as it once was, but the trade-offs are more than worth the troubles. A famous poet once said that children hold you hostage to life, a statement which seems to capture the sense of responsibility that I feel for her, and for making the world a better and safer place for her to live in.

Adoption is probably not for everyone. Some people wonder why I would take on someone else's child. It doesn't feel that way. Someone else gave her life, but her life is now mine to protect; her needs are mine to watch over. Another woman will always be her first mother, but I'm her mother now, and we are making a wonderful life together.

Chapter 17

Flying Not Quite Solo

I think my son has received the best I could give him. If I can lay my head down at night and know that I did the best I could, today, for him, then I have no reason to feel guilty.

—Lydia

I get so angry when I hear people talk about broken homes. I wasn't married but there was nothing broken about the home I created for my children. It was strong, it was loving, it was supportive, it was secure. It had all of the things children need in a home.

—Julia

I think a lot of women are going to learn that they don't have to have a man to nurture a child.

—Grace

The women we interviewed who had children told us they wouldn't have missed the experience of motherhood for the world. Looking back at single motherhood from the perspective of midlife, they believe they have been able to give their children many gifts, strengths, and resources. They admit the job of single parenting is one of the toughest they have ever had, but they also speak of the many rewards and joys that motherhood has brought to them. They take deep pride in having been able to provide all the things their children needed to grow up healthy and strong.

Like most single mothers, the women we interviewed have flourished in the face of many obstacles. Even under the best of circumstances, parenting requires enormous energy, patience, and most of all, a good sense of humor. To sustain their morale and their continuing capacity to love and nurture, parents need to feel good about what they are giving to their children, and they need to feel supported and affirmed by their communities. Unfortunately, many single mothers do not receive this much needed support. Instead, subtle and not-so-subtle insinuations that their children are living a second-class childhood permeate our culture. Even mothers who were catapulted into the world of single parenthood by their husbands' decisions to divorce are not immune to such criticism. Countless studies and reports have focused on the deficits of single-parent families and the terrible consequences of women raising children on their own. A single-parent home, we are told, will inevitably damage children by hindering their ability to succeed at school and later at work, and by contaminating their chances of forming meaningful adult relationships of their own.

Women who have made an active choice to raise children on their own are particularly vulnerable to such criticism. Whether by leaving their marriages, or by becoming mothers through artificial insemination, adoption, or intended conception outside of marriage, they often are viewed as selfish by the world around them. Carol says of her experience:

> When I first started talking about adoption, many of my friends were against the idea. They told me that it wouldn't be fair to a child to choose to become a single mother and that I would never be able to take care of a child on my own, particularly with my work schedule. They suggested that I was thinking of my own needs more than the needs of the boy or girl who would become my responsibility. It only made it slightly more acceptable that I wanted an older child and wouldn't be depriving some young couple of a baby.

These beliefs and attitudes can leave single women feeling exasperated and undermined, even causing them to underestimate the importance of what they give to their children. At least occasionally, most feel as if they are flying into a strong headwind that prevents them from gaining credibility and respect for themselves and their children as a viable p   of their community.

The single mothers whose stories are told in this book demonstrate clearly that women on their own are able to give their children all the required ingredients of a healthy childhood. They do not feel tormented by guilt or regrets about how they could have raised their children better. They have found ways to meet their children's needs, giving them the same love, support, and guidance found in many two-parent families. And when their children have needs a mother alone cannot meet, these mothers have sought out and included a wide variety of people in their lives to help them do so. Their experiences clearly reveal that there is nothing inherently deficient or destructive about raising a child on one's own. Julia, who raised her two daughters after her divorce, summed up the matter well when she said, "I think children need to be taught values; they need to be shown how to live well and responsibly. But beyond that, I think there are lots of good ways to parent."

GIFTS SINGLE MOTHERS GIVE
THEIR CHILDREN

Whatever Dan Quayle may say, single women are able to offer their children unique gifts, some of which are not as easily available in two-parent families. For instance, single mothers can provide a flexible model of gender-role behaviors that can help their children feel less constrained by increasingly problematic traditional definitions of what it means to be male or female. Because single mothers manage the responsibilities traditionally assigned to both parents, their children may be less likely to assume that certain paths are closed to them because of their gender. This flexibility should give them an advantage in coping with the rapidly changing world they will no doubt continue to face throughout their lives. Apryl says that she feels good about the role model she is providing for her daughter:

> When you are a single parent, there is a lot more versatility and flexibility than in a family in which there are clear role divisions. In the family in which I grew up, it was very old-fashioned. My father didn't really relate to us emotionally. He earned the money, shoveled the walk, and fixed the car.

Arlene, whose community ostracized her for her decision to leave her marriage, believes she is offering her children a model of a woman who believes it is legitimate to be a mother *and* to search for self-fulfillment. By refusing to passively accept her husband's decisions and by actively making choices for herself, she is bequeathing an important legacy:

> I'm a role model for my children. I'm saying, "I know that you're important, but I need this other thing in my life, too." And I'm not

just talking—I'm *doing* it. I hope they'll realize that they can't put all their dreams into one basket. I still want my kids, and I want a career that's rewarding—and I'm going to have both.

Single mothers who raise children on their own instead of remaining part of unhappy and conflict-ridden marriages offer their children another important, but little recognized, gift: a model of a strong, independent parent who faces life squarely and addresses what is wrong. We were gratified to see this important contribution of single mothers publicly portrayed in the new sitcom, "Grace Under Fire." As her son's teacher was lecturing her on the possible impact of her "broken home" on her son's school performance, newly divorced Grace responded adamantly, "My home is *not* broken. It *was* broken, but I fixed it!" Grace's point is the same as that made by many of the real-life single mothers we interviewed: While two-parent families have distinct advantages, in some situations raising children on one's own can be the *solution*, not the problem.

Whenever there are two adults in a household, even if they are happily married, there are bound to be differences of opinion. When the marriage is troubled, children can become the battlefield on which differences of opinion explode like cannon shots fired between the warring parties. Such warfare is unhealthy for anyone in a family; but for children, it can be particularly devastating. Julia's two daughters were five and eight years old when she decided to leave her marriage fifteen years ago. She raised them on her own in such a way that today she can look at them with pride and admiration: "They are both confident women—I don't see how they could have turned out any better." She is clear, however, that their self-confidence began to develop only *after* she and her husband had separated. Divorce did not break their spirits; it *allowed* them to develop into healthy adults:

> Had I stayed in the marriage, I doubt if my daughters would have had the self-confidence they have today. When the marriage was intact, they lived in an environment of unhappiness, dissatisfaction, and dissension. We were all in pain and it showed in my children. They were crying in school; they were confused about what they wanted and who they were. Their state-of-being did not improve until the marriage ended and they had an alternative view of what it was like to be an adult. So, rather than doing irreparable harm to my children, I think my divorce probably saved them.

Although many women resist leaving bad marriages for fear that their children will be damaged in some way by divorce, bringing children along on a solo flight can turn out to be a much better choice than keeping them for years in a plane caught in severe turbulence. Peggy remarked:

I probably would have become a single woman sooner if I had known how easily my children would have adjusted to it. I stayed in a very unhappy marriage because of what I thought divorce would do to the children. Ironically, their adjustment was the easiest part.

Once out on their own, these women often discover that they are able to focus on the needs of their children in less interrupted and conflicted ways than when they were married. Greta explained that after her divorce she was able to give her children the clarity they needed: "It's easier to make decisions sometimes because you don't have to consult with somebody else and the kids don't get mixed messages." Anita told us that when she and her husband divorced, she no longer felt the tension of being torn between paying attention to her children or to him. Since she and her husband had an extremely active social life, she rarely was able to go to her teenage son's wrestling matches or to sit around talking with his friends as they watched football. After the divorce, she found she had more time and energy to get to know her son and the friends that were a part of his life. She is very grateful for the years that allowed her to become closer to him before he left for college—something she is certain would not have happened had the marriage continued.

THE REWARDS OF SINGLE PARENTING:
BETTER LIVING THROUGH LOVING

Our society's negative view of single parenting has obscured not only what single mothers give to their children, but also what the experience of parenting can give to single women. While the single mothers we interviewed did not minimize the exhaustion, stress, and heartaches inherent in raising children alone, especially if they didn't have much money, they also emphasized how incredibly gratifying the experience can be. They pointed out how mothering brought out qualities in them they never knew they had and how it gave to them at least as much as they gave to it. Many women spoke of how surprised they were at the depth of feeling they had for their children, whether they were biological or adopted.

The women we interviewed told us that their children "expanded" them, made them stretch to be more than they thought they were. Their children tested the fiber of their being, and at crucial turning points, pushed them just a bit further than they thought they could go. The rewards, they all agreed, were immense. Apryl says:

> My daughter has stirred a loving, tender part of me that I had shut away after my divorce. None of the men with whom I've had relationships have seen this side of me. I am far more open and willing to share.

Julia also emphasized the experience of becoming a more caring person by loving her children. She has a hard time imagining what kind of person she would have been had she not been a mother:

> I learned how to love better. I probably never would have realized that I had the potential to be loving and supportive and to help another person grow. And I would have missed out on such a rich experience. It is truly awful for me to think about who I would be today if I had not been a mother.

In addition to bringing out the best in a woman, being a single mother can provide her with a sense of direction during tumultuous times. Quite a few women told us that when they were divorced, their commitment to raising their children was the gyroscope that helped to steady their wings while they were getting used to flying on their own. Greta says of her experience, "I knew that I was taking on the responsibility for raising these two kids, and that gave my life purpose at all times, even when other things were going terribly."

For some women, the job of parenting provided a better balance to a life too centered on a career. Carol reports:

> I loved my career so much that, for close to thirty years, I made it my number-one priority. And still, I wouldn't want to give it up altogether. I love what I do. But being a mother is rewarding in a very different way, a way that nurtures my soul and gives me a sense of

purpose that I need at this point in my life. My daughter Maria is amazing to me. She is a never-ending series of surprises and delights, worries and challenges. She commands my attention as nothing else can, and she is never boring! I know I'm not the only woman who knows the secret that being with our children can be more interesting than the alternatives of going to a fund-raising cocktail party, or to dinner with friends committed to resolving the problems of health-care reform or foreign policy. I sometimes find myself making excuses for staying home that sound lame, even to me. Even if the alternative is a genuine no-strings-attached date, the man would have to be pretty special to take precedence over my child, who is my responsibility, my priority, *and* a proven, interesting companion. I program in "adult time," but only the adult time I really enjoy.

Having a child can even save a woman from a path headed toward destruction. Recall how Lydia was unable to extricate herself from an abusive marriage, unable to save herself from her husband's blows, until she realized that her son was at risk. This realization alone gave her the courage to flee and begin a new life on her own. She gained the strength to make a change because she did not want her son to grow up seeing his mother as a woman who could not stand up for herself. She also did not want him to be exposed to a role model of a man who was violent. She could do for her son what she could not do for herself.

These rewards of mothering for single women are unfortunately often pathologized in our society. Pop psychology books accuse single mothers of being "over-involved" with their children, causing many to wonder anxiously whether their best instincts are suspect. While over-involvement may be a particular risk in single-parent families, we found little if any evidence of this problem in the lives of the women in this book. The connections they have with their children are often intense, but rarely exclusive or confining. Though it was painful and sometimes difficult, they all had found healthy ways to let their children "try their own wings" when they reached the appropriate age. None of these mothers gave us any reason to think they avoided the task of facilitating their child's independence, nor did we hear any evidence that their children tried to cling to the nest or refused to strike out on their own. Audrey, for instance, told us that helping her daughters go off to college and establish independent lives was the most difficult *and* best task she did as a parent:

The hardest and the most successful thing I ever did as a parent was to let go of them. It was awful, but it paid off. Allowing them the independence to make mistakes, to screw up, is excruciating. I mean, you want to prevent them from ever failing or ever getting hurt. But, if you let them go through their own experiences, they *do* grow and learn, and they thank you in the end.

Glenda went so far as to insist that her boys go away for at least one of their college years because the struggles they survived together as a family left her sons closer to her than she thought they should be as adults. "We had come through so much. I mean, we were kind of like the three musketeers," she explained. Glenda has a deep sense of satisfaction about how her sons are turning out as adults:

Now that they're older, there are so many rewards. I sit back and watch. I see how so many things they do, they have learned from me. I taught them to think for themselves and to see them actually functioning in that manner is thrilling.

MANAGING THE CHALLENGES
OF "MOTHER TIME"

While raising a child on one's own may bring many gifts to both mothers and children, we did not meet any woman who said it was an easy job. The only word to describe the demands of the role of mother is *relentless*. Tillie Olsen captured the essence of the job in the following lines:

Motherhood means being constantly interruptable, responsive, responsible. Children need one *now*. . . . The very fact that these are the needs of love, not duty, that one feels them as one's self; that there is no one else to be responsible for these needs, gives them primacy. It is distraction, not meditation, that becomes habitual; interruption, not continuity; spasmodic, not constant, toil.

The general relentlessness of mothering is even *more* relentless for single mothers. One of the greatest challenges they face is the feeling that there is never enough time to take care of all of the responsibilities they must handle.

Jamie, who became a mother at age forty, spoke for many of the women when she said, "I have no regrets at all about becoming a mother, but I don't think anyone is *ever* prepared for the constancy of it. It's impossible to imagine."

Kelly often feels overwhelmed by the incessant experience of being pulled in a hundred directions at once. Kelly feels as if she's "just barely keeping all the balls in the air," even though she has scaled down her once high-powered and all-consuming career and spends less time with friends. She laments her plight:

> I'm not talking about taking vacations or going to bed-and-breakfast inns around the country or even reading the latest book. The only movies I ever see are on the VCR. I have never seen Kevin Costner in anything—but I can tell you anything you ever wanted to know about Ninja Turtles.

Carol resonates with Kelly's point:

> During the first two years I had with Maria, I sometimes wondered if I would ever see an adult movie again. Even now, I haven't seen anything with an "R" rating for months, but I can recite from memory every lyric of every song from *Aladdin, Annie,* and *Beauty and the Beast.*

Conflicting demands between work and children also present a major challenge for most single mothers, as few work environments are responsive to the demands of parenting, much less single parenting. Mothers in the workplace, especially those in professional positions, find themselves under constant pressure to maintain their credibility when they cannot be as flexible and available as their colleagues. Carol could list at least ten times over the last few weeks when it has been close to impossible to meet scheduling demands everyone else at work accepted with ease. With little notice, two meetings were called for 7:30 A.M., which she was expected to attend even though her daughter doesn't leave for school until 7:45. Three meetings were scheduled for 6:30 P.M., which most single mothers will tell you is prime time for dinner and homework. Worse, she was notified of two retreats and one out-of-town meeting, all of which would require an overnight stay. What makes all of these scheduling problems worse is that they are often changed at the last minute, after women have gone to great lengths to arrange child-care.

These demands put the single working mother in the frustrating position of having to swallow her irritation or set herself apart as different or more difficult than the rest of the team. Does she love her job? Yes. Do her children come first? Yes. Are these priorities incompatible? No, but it certainly feels that way sometimes, and there is *always* tension. A woman who has children finds they are always on her mind. As American writer Margaret Culkin Banning said, "She never quite leaves her children at home, even when she doesn't take them along." Eventually many women executives find that they are not taken as seriously as their colleagues who are always prepared to put the company or the organization first. As former Israeli Prime Minister Golda Meir summarized this dilemma:

> At work, you think of the children you have left at home. At home, you think of the work you've left unfinished. Such a struggle is unleashed within yourself. Your heart is rent.

Time is not the only challenge of single parenting, nor even the most significant one. Most single mothers will tell you that their main challenge is money. While money can't buy happiness, it can go a long way toward buying sanity in the department of single parenting. Having the resources to hire a cleaning service, buy treats, take kids to movies, or hire tutors to help with homework can make a tremendous difference. Also, it is painful to always have to say no to children when they want something that is quite reasonable. Unfortunately, most single mothers struggle to keep themselves and their children in groceries and other essentials of survival such as rent, utilities, clothes, and school supplies, not to mention the priority of most children—video rentals. Moreover, each year the average amount fathers pay in child support to women and children struggling to make it on their own *decreases*. The women in our project were no strangers to the challenges of these circumstances. Even so, few of the divorced women said they would choose to return to the "safe" havens of their marriages, and none of them would give up the experience of being a mother simply to have an easier time.

In addition to the daunting logistical and financial problems of being a single parent, the women we interviewed reported all the inevitable worries and heartaches experienced by any parent, but stressed the fact that they have no partner with whom to share either of these burdens. While most don't want their ex-husbands back, they sometimes wish they had another in-house adult to rely on when their children are sick or in trouble. Many were also aware that there was no one to share the joyful times or the pleasure of watching their children grow. As Audrey explained:

> There isn't another human being on the face of the earth who thinks my kids are as wonderful as I do. And I'm sorry about that. I would love to have a partner who thought they were as neat as I do.

But most of the single mothers we interviewed did not spend much time or energy focusing on what they didn't have. They found ways to cope with the challenges of single parenting. Many emphasized the importance of making time for *themselves*. As any expert on families will tell you, time spent alone or with other adults is critical for parent survival. Parents in healthy two-parent families do not allow their children to consume their lives; they get their adult needs met in adult relationships—and so must single women. Without this sort of refueling, at least occasionally, it gets increasingly difficult to manage the unrelenting tasks of child-care. When asked what advice she would give women just getting a divorce, Peggy said flatly, "I would say, if you've got children, don't devote your entire life to them."

Any single woman who works and has children can tell you that maintaining a social life is easier said than done. Many obstacles stand in the way of single mothers taking the breaks they need. When single mothers come home exhausted after a day's work, still having to cook dinner for their children, most do not feel like going out, even if a baby sitter is available. When Glenda was working full-time and going to school, rest was her first priority when she had any free time. Although her sons would try to convince her to go out and have fun with her friends on a Friday night, all she wanted to do after a very long week was to collapse on her living-room couch. Most single mothers can relate to Glenda's experience, but those women who make the effort to have social lives are adamant that these activities are crucial to their mental health. Greta thinks baby sitters are vital: "I've hired baby sitters even when I had very, very little money. To keep my own sanity, I had to make this a priority."

When women don't have extra money for child-care, it is particularly important to cultivate friends or family members who are willing to help provide some of the breaks they need. Julia, for instance, was blessed with an ex-husband who stayed involved with the children after their divorce. She believes she was able to successfully manage single parenting because, no matter how stressful life got, she knew she would have a break when their father took them two nights a week. "It allowed me to be an attentive mother and still not lose myself in the process," she says. Tina was not as lucky as Julia; her ex-husband took little responsibility for raising their daughter after their divorce. But she *did* get help from other family members. Making ends meet often required that she work two jobs. At one point, she had a second job in a weekend after-hours bar. She would go directly from her day-job to night waitressing, not coming home until six the following morning. This schedule almost broke her. "Try doing that for about six years," she says. "By the time Sunday arrived, I was a zombie. My day was ruined because I couldn't get out of the chair." Part of what kept her going during those difficult years was knowing that she could trust her sister or brother to take care of her daughter during the night.

Sustaining a long-term perspective can also make the job of single parenting easier. When the demands of mothering get particularly overwhelming for Ria, for instance, she reminds herself that she is having the "mother time" she always wanted. She says, "The hardest part is that there isn't much time for myself and that I feel like I'm on the constant clean-up crew. But it helps if I compare that to how I felt on the other side, when I didn't know when or if I was going to be able to have my two youngest daughters." Taking a step back to be able to see the "big picture" helps Ria appreciate that, as she says, "Basically, I'm happier than I've ever been in my entire life."

Challenges and Triumphs of Flying Solo

Chapter 18

Grit and the Art of Airplane Maintenance: Managing the Mechanics of Flying Solo

The hardest part about being single is having to do everything for yourself; knowing that no one is going to take the garbage out but you. The little things are the hardest. I'm the person who *always* has to do the shopping, who *always* has to go to work, who *always* has to pay the bills every month. It's tiring knowing that I can never share any of those responsibilities with anybody.

—*Tina*

The biggest problems for me were really very practical. I had never taken care of my car, I had never done any survival kind of things—but I learned!

—*Apryl*

You gain strength, courage, and confidence by every experience in which you must stop and look fear in the face . . . you must do the thing you think you cannot do.

—*Eleanor Roosevelt*

Our interview with Lydia took place in her living room while she was in the process of remodeling. Amidst spattered dropcloths and empty paint cans, we asked question after question about her life. Finally, we asked her what question she would most like to ask if she were interviewing other single women for this book. She paused for a moment, looking around the room thoughtfully. She started and then dismissed questions about loneliness

and relationships with men, and then exclaimed, "Okay, this is a big one.
How do you get the ceiling plastered?"

Single women may love many things about *flying solo*, but most, like
Lydia, struggle with the hassles of routine "airplane maintenance." It is these
daily challenges of single living that undermine their morale more than any
others—certainly more than the loneliness everyone seems to think they
endure. Cooking for one, balancing the checkbook, finding a plumber or a
mechanic who won't "rob" them, moving heavy furniture, or getting to
work when their car isn't running—these are the problems that drive single
women to the edge. To this list of seemingly trivial but genuinely aggravat-
ing chores, add the inconvenience of not having someone handy with
whom to go to a movie at the last minute or take a walk at night. Perhaps
worst of all, single women have no one in-house to bring them chicken soup
or walk the dog when they are too sick to get out of bed.

At particularly stressful times, when the nuisance factor of living singly is
especially acute, women sometimes fantasize that things would be so much
easier if only they had a husband. They envision themselves whipping up a
delicious soufflé for a romantic dinner for two, while *he* deals with the
plumber, the auto mechanic, and the IRS. Such fantasies persevere, no
matter how much their happily married sisters raise their eyebrows or roll
their eyes in response, pointing out that all too often, it is *they* who call the
plumber, take the car to be fixed, balance the family checkbook, and get
their tax records prepared for the accountant. Some add that they *also* move
the heavy furniture, make the chicken soup for the rest of the family even
when they too are sick, and half the time end up walking the dog as well.

For most of us, married or single, the fantasy that as women we would not
have to cope with many of these mundane tasks is one of the most cherished
beliefs associated with the marriage and motherhood mandate. It is part of
what we thought went into "happily ever after." Our parents fed us this
fantasy. Like people who put off writing a will because of a superstitious
belief that it will hasten their demise, our parents' generation seemed to fear
that teaching their daughters the skills to master the mechanics of daily life
would somehow jinx their chances of marriage by making them less attractive and appealing to men.

As a result, whole categories of life-maintenance tasks were "staked out"
as the province of the American husband. We were raised to believe that we
were *not supposed to have to know these things*. We were not supposed to know
how to deal with surly auto mechanics or even, for that matter, how to
check the oil level in our cars or the air pressure in our tires. We were not

supposed to have to balance our checkbooks or do our own taxes. We were not supposed to have to figure out how to save enough money to live comfortably in retirement. We were raised to expect that we would be taken care of, that our husbands would willingly manage all these unsavory little details in return for those delicious soufflés, clean shirts, and readily available sex. Jean reports that her family always admonished her to keep in mind the same list of do's and don't's:

> Jean, just remember, let your husband handle the money. The man is going to take care of all the important matters in life. Your job is to be at home, making sure that the linens are clean and the silver is polished so that you can entertain beautifully when need be. It is crucial that you know how to do all these things the right way.

Many women thus make it into adulthood secretly believing that, by divine decree, it is men who fix cars, toilets, and lawn mowers; it is men who deal with mechanics, plumbers, contractors, the bank, and the IRS. This deeply ingrained resistance to mastering these maintenance skills blinds women to the fact that they have as much capacity to get a grip on these skills as any male partner they might find. After all, the high-tech world of the nineties has been a great equalizer of this gender-determined imbalance by rendering men and women similarly inept. Many areas of life maintenance have become so specialized that the average person, male or female, doesn't know enough to fix a car or even get the VCR to cooperate with the cable TV box. Once single women have *decided* to master these skills, they can learn to do so as well as any man, and certainly well enough to enjoy the freedom of flying solo.

BEING TAKEN SERIOUSLY
VERSUS BEING TAKEN

In addition to learning the skills to make basic repairs on their cars and homes, single women find they must learn how to hire people who will take their wishes seriously and who will not take advantage of them. The most competent women, even in midlife, can find this to be an uphill battle. Women continually receive the patronizing message that they are not quite capable of understanding, much less making decisions about, these manly tasks, no matter how knowledgeable they have become in other parts of their lives. For example, Julia, who is forty-four years old and manages both a large staff and a large budget at work, complains that she continues to be told that she doesn't know what she's doing when it comes to "guy things":

> Plumbers and other repairmen don't take you seriously. It is so hard to get them to do what I want them to do. When somebody comes to my house to repair something, I tell him exactly how I want it done. And then he says, "Oh honey, you don't really want that—let me show you what I'm going to do."

Pauline expresses a similar view:

> Quite frankly, getting a man to take me seriously in terms of what's wrong or what's not wrong seems impossible. We're still living in a man's world, that's for sure.

Repairmen are not the only ones who don't take single women seriously. Often, women don't take *themselves* seriously. Many single women still believe it is risky to own houses without also having a man with a well-equipped tool belt. Erika, for example, knew it made financial sense to buy a home, but she postponed doing so for a long time because she doubted whether she could handle all the practical tasks on her own. She kept discouraging herself by saying, "When you buy a house, you take on all these responsibilities that you never thought about before: the water, the gas, mowing the lawn, shoveling the walk." She finally took the plunge and bought a house at age thirty-eight. She had been living in it for a total of four days when we met her. Erika knows that she will encounter some of the problems she used to worry about, but she is very pleased with herself for facing the challenge:

> The fact that I just bought a house is very significant to me. It's a step that I've been putting off for a long time. Now I regard it as a positive challenge. I know there will be times when I burst into tears—like when water is spurting all over the place or the roof is leaking during a storm. I will probably think it's the end of the world, but it's not going to be the end of the world!

Erika is right; it won't be the end of the world. In fact, such challenges can help women develop a sense of mastery. Sandi too was plagued with questions about how she would manage after her husband left:

> What would become of me and my children? Would I manage to keep up a car? Would I be able to fix my hot-water heater when it broke or change the washer of a dripping faucet? It all seemed scary and dismal.

With two young children and little money, Sandi had little choice but to force herself to learn how to handle the duties that her husband had always performed. She has since discovered that the very tasks which inspire dread and fear *also* have the potential to make her feel empowered. When we asked Sandi what was satisfying about being single, she spoke with confidence about the effect of learning to manage the mechanics of life on her own:

> I feel *complete* on my own. I can manage my responsibilities on my own. I can meet my emotional and physical needs. I can provide for my children. I can go out and buy a car on my own. I can change insurance companies so that I get what I want. I can transform a porch into a room because I need extra space. I can do it all on my own.

Helen also radiated a sense of pride and self-assurance as she described her recent experience buying a new car:

> People laughed at me when I bought my last car. A friend said her husband would help me, but instead, I took a copy of *Consumer Reports* to a dealer I've used before and he said, "Since you traded your other car here, we'll sell you a car for cost plus $100." I thought to myself, "Well, no man could have done better than that."

Women are thrilled and exhilarated when they realize they can master these "male" skills themselves and/or insist that the people they hire do them properly. There is a palpable sense of self-respect and achievement as women describe how they have used tools to fix something in their homes or cars, or how they directed contractors or repairmen to honor their requests. Mastering these skills is not necessarily easy, however. Single women almost always have a number of "good learning experiences" before they acquire them.

Susan, who comes from a family in which doing everything yourself is a moral imperative, likes to tell about the first time she tried to solve a pipe blockage. First, she sallied forth to the plumbing supply house to ask about proper tools and procedures and was told to purchase a large pipe snake and a huge wrench. She began by trying to wrestle this large snake down the very small pipe in her bathroom sink and was feeling quite proud of herself, until she realized that she had inadvertently wrapped the shower curtain around the other end of the snake, covering it and her clothing with grease. She then noticed that the bathroom rug was also smeared with shiny black stuff, which she had failed to note was covering the snake when she took it out of its package. The whole chore turned out to be much ado about nothing, since the pipe remained clogged even after her considerable struggle to disentangle the snake from the shower curtain and out of the sink pipe! She then tried to use the wrench to remove and check the elbow part of the sink pipe, but the wrench was so heavy, she poked a hole in the pipe trying to remove the elbow. Fortunately, she had learned from her ex-husband how to use the Yellow Pages (a practice not condoned in her diehard family-of-origin), so she was able to call a plumber. At least, she says, she learned what her limits were, plumbing-wise. She denies that this experience had any influence on her subsequent decision to move close to family members who know how to fix everything, including her brother's children who were born knowing how to program VCRs.

THE FATIGUE OF "LOGISTICS OVERLOAD"

Regardless of their success in managing the specific tasks at hand, the sheer *number* of household and/or child-care responsibilities to be managed each and every day can be overwhelming for a single woman. The responsibility of handling every single chore, making every decision, large and small, on one's own, can spoil women's ability to feel like carefree pilots soaring above the clouds. Instead, they end up feeling like frantic air-traffic controllers trying to avoid the collision of several jumbo jets.

Women who are managing a high-powered job and a household often wish they had a wife, even more than a husband. Wives are woefully underappreciated. Everyone who works full-time, male or female, needs one. Having a career is much easier when there is someone at home handling all those essential life tasks and details wives traditionally manage for their husbands. Even today, when many wives also have careers, they still tend to do the majority of the chores that keep a home and family aloft: grocery shopping, car pool duty, school conferences, and errands to the cleaners and post office. Their efforts create a wonderful safety net that removes anxieties about what to do if you have to work late on an unexpected deadline or need to create an intimate little dinner party with just the right ambiance to impress the boss or an out-of-town customer. By handling all the nagging little details of daily living, wives free their spouses to concentrate on more important activities such as advancement, power, and glory. As family therapist Monica McGoldrick says:

> A wife, of course, is a very good thing to have. She takes care of your home, your kids, your meals, and anticipates your needs even before you realize you have them. She packs your bags for your trips and gives you extra hugs when you return because of all the stress and strain you've had. She explains to the kids anything you've forgotten to say, especially all your good intentions.

Single women don't have wives. Not only must they support themselves and their dependents, but they must do so without help from anyone, let alone a person whose mission in life is to look out for their welfare and promote their careers. Paid housekeepers, cleaning services, babysitters, or caterers simply don't fulfill this function, however competent they may be in their circumscribed area. Single women really are *flying solo* in the job support department.

In part, what makes these multitudinous tasks so overwhelming is the fact that, in order to manage them successfully, especially when there are children in the household, everything must be coordinated and planned in advance. Spontaneity is a paradise lost; "going with the flow," a laughable concept. Organization, precision, and endless forethought are the necessary staples. Consider one single car repair. How do you get your child to school without a car? Even if your child rides the bus, how will you arrange to get to the garage and to work on time, when the school bus doesn't arrive until long after the time you are supposed to leave? And car repair problems are only one example. How do you arrange for child-care on a school "snow day" with an hour's notice and ten people waiting for you to lead an important meeting at the office? What do you do when the baby sitter gives you three days' notice before she leaves for Afghanistan?

Whether or not a single woman has a child, she has no one with whom to share the responsibilities for making the everyday decisions in life, such as whether or not to have a new roof put on, and if so, by whom. As Elena remarked, "I sometimes wish I could share the decision-making. A part of me still longs to be able to be in strong collaboration with another person." It is very convenient to have a partner to share the blame for any decision which turns out to be a bad one, whether it be the choice of a workman or a place to invest money. After all, misery loves company in no small part because you then can get mad at someone else and not yourself. Peggy insists that it is the solitary aspect of this logistics overload, not loneliness, that has the power to depress her:

> I get depressed at times, but it's not from loneliness. It is the crazy things, like when the car breaks down and I don't know the best way to get it fixed; or something in the house breaks. These kinds of things that are an annoyance and a financial burden will trigger me into depression more than anything else.

Jean agrees:

> Every time the car breaks down or something goes wrong, I just want to say, "Oh, sweetie, you take care of it. This is your job." I have to do *everything*. I don't mind it as much now as I did when I was younger because I'm used to doing it, but at first it seemed monumental. Still, once in a while it would be nice to take a breather from feeling that the whole burden for my survival is on my own shoulders alone. I know, of course, realistically it is anyway, married or not.

Being responsible for all of life's onerous daily tasks and decisions is unquestionably overwhelming, but women explain that there is also much to be gained. Terry makes the important point that taking responsibility for her decisions has reinforced her commitment to take charge of her own life. She recalls how difficult this was for her in the early days after she moved to Philadelphia:

> It once took me forty-five minutes to get across the Walt Whitman Bridge. Sitting in my car at a dead stop, I was convinced I'd really made a bad choice. What was I doing in this Godforsaken city where it snowed in the winter? But I also knew that I could leave if I decided to and that nobody had forced me to move to Pennsylvania. There was something important about owning the decisions I had made.

Taking a step back to gain a perspective on the merits of being in charge of one's life is crucial for women at the height of overload. As Kelly explained:

> I know I'm in a bad way when I start thinking to myself, "I want someone to rescue me from all this!" That's when I realize it's time to regroup and turn the situation around. It's easy to get overwhelmed.

Many single women maintain their sanity in part by accepting the fact that some of the things they have always thought they *had* to do are not really essential after all. Trying to keep the house clean, for instance, is a goal that can be given up for years, if not decades. Dust balls can be given names and kept as pets. Clothes, makeup, and hair don't have to require a lot of time, unless taking that time is pleasurable. Children can learn to fend for themselves in some areas and even help around the house. And sometimes, it is just easier to pay someone to do a hated chore, even if it means giving up some other little treat.

FINANCIAL VULNERABILITY: THE MORBID FEAR OF BECOMING A BAG LADY

Dealing with car mechanics and repairmen is hard, but dealing with the bank, retirement accounts, and the IRS is even harder. The tasks women now in midlife have been least prepared to master are those related to money. Among the women we interviewed, a large percentage reported that managing money was one of the most formidable challenges they had encountered in their single lives. Money is power and teaching women anything about power was, and in many households still *is*, seen as irrelevant. The basic training women now in midlife received in the boot camp of family life simply did not prepare them for financial independence. They were not taught to manage money any more than they were taught the basics of automobile maintenance. For many women, dealing responsibly with money, especially in relation to long-term planning, is the final frontier of their independence. Even when single women are soaring freely above the clouds of life's routine tasks, dealing with their own financial issues can feel like flying into the heart of a treacherous storm. They rarely crash, but the ride can be rough and frightening.

Most single women *have had*, currently *have*, or are afraid that they *will have* financial problems. The threats of being alone and poor generate an atmosphere of insecurity and a context of vulnerability that extends far beyond the actual issue of having enough money. As Megan says, "It isn't just not having enough money to buy the material things in life. It's the feeling of vulnerability that accompanies that." Even single women with ample incomes and steady jobs, some of whom competently administer multimillion dollar businesses, can be affected by the threat of financial vulnerability. Although these women's fears are based less on real-life circumstances or experiences, they continue to worry that they are not equipped to manage their own money just because they are women, and that they are at risk of becoming impoverished because they don't have a man to depend on, should disaster strike. Apryl, a woman with several advanced degrees and an excellent income, speaks for many women when she says, "I never believed that I would have to support myself financially, so money continues to be an issue for me."

Jean told us about an article she read called "The Bag Lady in All of Us," which struck a chord in her by stating that, no matter how well a single woman does financially, she is always afraid that she will end up a bag lady, mumbling to herself in a subway station. A surprising number of financially secure women explicitly identified this same fear, often using the same dreaded image of the bag lady. Nell talks about her irrational fear of poverty, despite her six-figure income:

> For a number of years after my divorce, I was absolutely terrified to spend money. I can remember two years after my husband left, I was rolling my cart down the market aisle one day. I wanted lettuce but the lettuce was one dollar a head, and I was *afraid* to buy it. I thought to myself, "What in the world is wrong with me? I have a great job, I'm earning a good salary. *What* is wrong with me that I'm afraid to buy a head of lettuce?"

Why do women have such a hard time feeling competent to manage their money and prepare for a secure financial future? After all, as Jane Bryant Quinn pointed out on the television program "Women Aloud," there are as many men as women who are inept at managing money. Part of the struggle for women stems from the fact that, as mentioned earlier, they were never encouraged to think in terms of supporting themselves. In addition, the financial "deck" continues to be stacked against them. Women still earn less than men for the same work and are chronically relegated to less stable and lower-status employment. Moreover, they also have to pay more than men for the very same products and services. In her book, *Why Women Pay More,* Frances Cerra Whittelsey states that white women pay $150 more for the same new car than do white men and black women pay $800 more. Compared to men, she asserts, women also pay more for the same dry cleaning services and clothing items.

A few of the women we interviewed are currently living on very little money and many of them have done so in the past. Those who married young, raised children on their own, and did not have the opportunity to pursue an advanced education have wrestled with the difficulty of making ends meet on a limited income. They experienced the well-known fate of most divorced women, whose standard of living, as compared to their ex-husbands', plummets after divorce. These women talked openly about their early days on their own, when they literally didn't know how they were going to provide the next meal for their children. Remember how Sandi had to watch her grocery bills like a hawk and how Glenda limited herself to eating every other day. Julia, who now earns a respectable salary, recalls a similar situation:

> I was very poor when I first got divorced. I hadn't finished college and I didn't have a job of any kind at that point. It was *hard* worrying about money all of the time and struggling with having to wonder: Can I buy shoes for the kids? Will I be able to pay the heating bill?

As these struggling single mothers reached midlife and their children left home, they usually experienced relief from the demands of being the sole provider. Only then were they able to begin saving money for their retirement and, often for the first time in their adult lives, spend a little on luxuries for themselves. But for those women who had to stay too long in whatever low-paying jobs they could get, simply to keep their children in clothes and tuition, saving for retirement still seems only a distant and possibly unattainable dream. Emma, for example, had a high-school education and worked as a school secretary in order to be home when her children were. With a smile she admits, "I cannot think about retirement because I will probably be working at whatever job I can get with blue hair. And I will probably die at my desk."

Financial instability is not limited to the experience of single mothers. Megan never thought about the need to save money during her twenties and thirties because she always assumed she would eventually find a husband.

She explains, "More than I would like to admit, I always thought that, one day, I would marry some man who would pay the bulk of our living expenses. I was never raised to support myself." Jessie is just starting to think seriously about her financial state, one marked by worrisome instability:

> There have been times when I haven't been able to pay my rent or buy food. This is not unusual. Am I going to be on the streets? For many years I have lived hand-to-mouth and still, in large measure, do. I wasn't able to pay my taxes this year. So, it's an ongoing challenge.

Although we found that women don't need great wealth to enjoy life on their own, it is difficult to feel good about being single if life feels too financially precarious. Most women on their own will agree that achieving some degree of financial security is essential, because, as Aleta explains, "The quality of your life depends on having enough money to be free to do what you want." Audrey also stresses that financial competence is part of what enables women to feel truly independent. "Over the years, I've known several single women who have propelled themselves into a second marriage, not because they met the man of their dreams, but because of stark financial fear." Jean agreed, explaining, "The more financial security women create for themselves, the more they can make reasonable and informed choices." Each of these women has come to realize what Elizabeth Cady Stanton expressed long ago when she said, "Woman will always be dependent until she holds a purse of her own."

The pervasive state of vulnerability created by real or perceived financial difficulties is usually not insurmountable, although women like Emma, who have sacrificed their long-term goals to meet the immediate needs of their children, have fewer options than those who were able to start saving money earlier. Women who have decent earning capacities can learn to deal with money matters with competence and confidence, once they decide to make finances a priority. Many women admitted that one reason for their financial insecurity and incompetence was the simple fact that they had not wanted to pay attention to it—in short, their own *resistance*. Balancing checkbooks each month and keeping track of credit-card purchases takes time and patience if not much skill, while learning about options for investing money takes not only time and energy but also a commitment to face one's insecurities about flying in unfamiliar skies.

With a little determination—often born of the very fear of becoming a bag lady—financial stability is attainable. In the same way they were able to learn to deal with car problems and household repairs, women can learn to manage their money by forcing themselves to make it a priority. For instance, when Megan was in her mid-thirties, she suddenly realized that she needed more financial stability in her life and that she could no longer afford to wait for marriage to provide it. Admonishing herself, "I can't live this artistic life style of hand-to-mouth forever—I don't like living this way," she decided to acquire a profession with more reliable earning power. She has since built a successful career with a significantly better income. Although she has not yet been able to save for a home or for her retirement, she knows she is at last headed in the right direction.

Many women said that, once they actually began to think about money matters, it wasn't as complicated as they were led to believe. Ruth found that, once she resigned herself to learning something about money management, she was able to do very well for herself. She happily reports, "I've made several sound investments, and I think that if I cared enough about money, I could invest full-time and make *a lot* of money." Shawna was also pleasantly surprised when she sat down to do her own taxes the first time and discovered she wouldn't need to get a master's degree in business to complete them successfully. While she doesn't earn a lot of money in her work as a computer programmer, she manages her finances well and takes pleasure in having learned to do so. Julia thought she would never be able to compose a simple household budget after many years of watching her husband design complicated tables and graphs to track their monthly bills:

> I figured, oh my God, when I get out there on my own, I'm going to be a disaster. I'll be arrested. It turned out, it's really easy to manage money. There is one simple rule: Don't spend as much as you make. I was really surprised to discover how well I could manage money.

Over the years, Julia has bought her own home and a couple of rental properties for investment, and now that her children are out of college, she has increased her retirement funds considerably.

When women encounter difficulty learning money management skills on their own, they can turn to their social networks for help. Susan had always relied on her husband for financial advice, figuring that if he could multiply three figures by three figures in his head, surely he must know something about money. Sometime after her divorce, she stopped working for the large institution which had offered her structured opportunities to invest for retirement. She was totally baffled about how to safely put money aside. She didn't even know who to contact to talk to about investing without some-how committing herself to something she didn't understand. At first, she felt embarrassed to ask even her close friends basic questions such as the differ-ence between stocks and bonds, but once she learned how much her pride was costing her, she started pestering her friends, married and single, about what they did to save money. She finally found a friend who actually made a living giving financial advice and started asking her what she would do if she were in her shoes. Susan is still far from sophisticated on the subject, but she has some basic knowledge of what she can expect from different forms of investments, as well as how to go about making them. Like Susan, Elaine had difficulty managing her money until she turned to a number of women in her network who have careers in financial management. They gave her advice and information and helped her to think more seriously about what she calls "those Keogh things." Valerie also turned to her network of single women to find a financial planner when she first got divorced. Since then, she has been putting aside more and more money each year and is confident that she will always be able to take care of herself.

Those women who don't have knowledgeable friends willing to tutor them can hire qualified help. Grace admits that she is terrible at managing her money, yet she owns her car, her home, a couple of rental properties, and has accrued an impressive retirement account. How? By hiring an ac-countant and a financial adviser, both of whom have made it possible for her to bypass her shortcomings and create a stable financial future.

Not all of the women we interviewed, however, had to rely on their networks or struggle through the lessons of trial and error to learn to handle their finances. A few women were introduced to money management in their youth. Audrey was blessed with the example of her great-aunt Jane, who taught her early on that women are perfectly capable of managing their own money with wisdom and competence. Aunt Jane, who never married, lived next door to Audrey's paternal grandparents. Every Sunday Audrey and her family would pay their regular weekly visit, only to behold Aunt Jane, sitting at a round table in her parlor, squinting through her green eye shade at stock market reports. She invested money so wisely that she became wealthy, a particularly laudable achievement for a woman of her era. Audrey learned from her aunt to invest her own finances wisely as well. Today, she is able to work at a job she loves, even though the pay is not outstanding, and still indulge her love of travel and her secret passion for shoes. Audrey also has been fortunate to have had a safety net of family funds left to her by her aunt and her parents. Unlike most single women, she admits that, although there were hard times, she had the "comfort of knowing that financial desperation was not really going to be a factor for me."

BECOMING COMPETENT

Women certainly do not claim that it is easy to master the many challenges of flying solo. But they do say that it is possible, and that learning how to manage the mechanics of single living can offer tremendous rewards. For example, Marie has never forgotten the exhilaration of mastering the first challenge she faced on her own after her husband ran off with his graduate student. Since he had managed all the details of their car, finances, and home, Marie doubted that she could make it without him. When she discovered that mice were living in her house, she was filled with horror. Unable to afford a professional exterminator, she was forced to overcome her distaste and set traps. When she caught the first mouse, she was convinced she would never be able to stomach taking it out of the trap. Eventually, faced with the inevitability of its mortal decay in her kitchen, she gritted her teeth and did it. By some people's estimation, this would be, at most, a small victory. For Marie, it was Bastille Day and the Fourth of July rolled into one. She knew she had taken her first step towards confronting her fear that she was incapable of surviving without her husband. For the first time in her life, she exclaimed, "I felt like I could do anything!"

Although most women probably would not have chosen to do some of the things being single has forced them to do, once they have done it (whatever *it* might be), they feel proud, competent, and strong. Managing even the most trivial and mundane tasks, such as changing the oil in the car or fixing a leaky faucet, becomes a symbol of the deeper changes that have occurred. Small tasks are a concrete reminder of progress made, of no longer waiting for a man to manage all of life's little problems. These many small successes prove to women that they are capable of flying solo, and in many cases, help them to see that they are already doing so with grace.

Chapter 19

One at a Table for Two: The Personal Challenges of Flying Solo

> You're wondering if I'm lonely:
> OK then, yes, I'm lonely
> as a plane rides lonely and level
> on its radio beam, aiming
> across the Rockies
> for the blue-strung aisles
> of an airfield on the ocean
> —*Adrienne Rich*, "Song" from *Diving into the Wreck*

Practical problems are not the only obstacles that women face as they learn to fly solo. They also must learn to become comfortable with doing things alone in public, find ways to manage their sexual needs, and deal with times of loneliness. The women we interviewed discovered that they had to confront these social and psychological challenges before they were able to feel good about lives on their own. Fortunately, they also found that mastering these challenges was possible and, in some cases, much easier than they ever expected. Their experiences demonstrate that women can learn to do things alone, that the problem of loneliness frequently turns out to be very small indeed, and that while there is not a perfect solution to the problem of sex, women can find acceptable, if partial, ways to deal with their sexual desires.

AN EAMES CHAIR AMID LOUIS XIV ANTIQUES

Much of the world is organized around the notion of couples, as if the Great Flood were coming again and we all might be asked to board the ark at any moment. Anyone who is single for an extended period of time must deal with the reality of *not* being part of a pair, of going out in public as a "party of one." Being single presents a special problem in those areas of life in which one is expected to have an escort, such as formal dinner parties, and even in those in which having a companion can make an activity more fun, such as going to a museum. The issue is more acute for women than men because being one at a table for two is still socially less acceptable for women, and for many, psychologically less comfortable as well. Some women who are otherwise content on their own worry about how their being alone in public will look to other people.

There are good reasons for women to worry about how they will be treated when they venture out alone. Part of the problem with living on the cutting edge of cultural change is that there is no universal list of things to do or places to go where you know being a single woman will be seen as acceptable. The common assumption that a woman alone is on the prowl can create some awkward moments when she goes places or does things unaccompanied. Men think she is fair game and women assume she is after their man. Even if she becomes an expert at sending "go hither" signals, the very fact that she is alone in public makes her the subject of speculation and suspicion.

To cope with these challenges of being one at a table for two, some women draw a relatively small circle around themselves, limiting their excursions into the world to places they know will include a friendly face. Marie, for instance, feels comfortable traveling to see someone she knows, but not traveling to an unfamiliar place where she will be on her own. Within the city, she also knows her limits; she has no problem going solo to the symphony, but she doesn't like to eat out alone. "I feel like someone stood me up, or like people *think* someone stood me up," she says. Julia, on the other hand, is comfortable going to dinner or the movies alone, but feels particularly awkward at business-related social events that are dotted with duos, such as formal balls and dinner parties. Unfortunately, these events may be unavoidable for single women, whose success in the workplace can be affected by their attendance. Their level of discomfort in these environments is often exacerbated when other people don't seem to know how to treat them. They feel starkly out of place, like a modern Eames chair in a room full of Louis XIV antiques. Julia, who has learned to manage these situations better than most, describes the difficulties for single women inherent in most workplaces:

> Even in my work, it is something of a handicap not to have a spouse or a date with whom to take clients out to dinner. I mean, the wife is always uncomfortable. I just know she is thinking, "Who is this single woman my husband is spending all of his time with?" The guy is uncomfortable because he is alone with his wife and another woman. Office parties, office functions are also hard. I'm an officer in the department and there are a lot of parties given. Everybody is part of a couple except me. But, you know, it doesn't bother me anymore. I would rather go by myself than drag along some guy I just met. But, all the same, people don't know what to do with me. There aren't many comfortable social contexts for single women in the world.

Single women report that being viewed with such suspicion is far more painful than simply feeling out of place. They have seen the distrustful looks that pass across the faces of their office pals' wives when they are introduced. They have experienced their colleagues' going out of their way to avoid them at social events because they are afraid their wives will become jealous. The same men who treat them in a reasonably friendly fashion at the office suddenly shun them, with little apparent awareness of their own insensitivity and even cruelty. One of Susan's friends, who married for the first time at age forty, told her, "Getting married changed everything for me. Everyone in the office looked at me differently. It was only after I married Dave that I—well, *we* really—got invited to the homes of people I had worked with for years."

Doing things on one's own requires an ability to protect oneself from feeling the stigma of being one where everyone expects two. Some single women develop such an immunity early in life. These are often women who are unusually secure and self-directed, women who are unconcerned with how they appear to others. They are single because they choose to be single and are not defensive about it. Peggy, for example, easily disregards the negative stereotypes about single women: "I don't think those stereotypes have affected me. I've done pretty much what I've wanted to do. Most people who know me well know that if I wanted to be married, I would be married." Karen, who thinks nothing of trekking around the outback in

Australia by herself, dismisses the issue out of hand: "I'm comfortable with myself. I know that I can walk into a room by myself. I don't need an escort."

Most single women do not come by the comfort Karen speaks of easily or early in life. They learn to venture out on their own by first deciding that they do not want to miss out on life's experiences simply because they are single. Not wanting to become prisoners in their own homes or communities, or confined to a small circle of protective friends, they learn to overcome this particular challenge of flying solo by starting with small steps. Even Peggy and Karen, with all their confidence, would agree that going out to dinner alone or vacationing alone for the first time takes courage. After all, Karen took her first trip alone to the civilized cities of Europe years before she hazarded the Australian outback. Women told us that, to their surprise, they found that going places alone was usually easy and fun once they tried it. Women who have traveled alone explain, for instance, that other tourists go out of their way to include them in their plans, and the residents of the places they are visiting make a special effort to make them comfortable and welcome, often telling them about the local attractions and inviting their participation. As a result, they seem to meet more people and get more exposure to the local culture when they travel alone.

Fortunately, becoming comfortable doing things on one's own is another challenge of being single that just gets easier and easier with time. As women reach midlife, they are increasingly able to make decisions about their social life based on their own desires, not out of fear that they will be seen by others as man-hunting or as pathetically unable to find another living soul willing to accompany them. They are no longer willing to take responsibility for the reactions of others to their behavior. Shawna explains that practice and the confidence that comes with midlife has helped her tremendously to feel free to do things alone:

> Learning to do things alone took a little doing. Going to the movies and eating out alone seemed weird at first. But, when you're over forty, you don't care anymore what other people think, you know? There is a certain stage in your life when you *finally* can say, "Who cares?" If I want to sit at a bar and have a beer, I will, and I don't care. That's the way it is.

Arlene takes great pleasure in listing the range of her adventures:

I go to the movies alone; I go to dinner by myself; I travel by myself. I was just abroad and had a wonderful time. One day, on this trip, I realized I always had the ability to do things alone, but had never bothered to try as long as somebody was at my side. What a feeling to do things alone!

SEX: A PROBLEM FOR SOME
BUT NOT FOR OTHERS

Bette Davis once said, "The act of sex, gratifying as it may be, is God's joke on humanity." Presumably she was referring to the distinctly undignified physical contortions intrinsic to its enjoyment, but she might well have been alluding to the social and psychological contortions single people go through to satisfy this basic human drive. Finding ways to manage the intertwining needs for sexual gratification and physical affection is one of the most difficult challenges faced by single people of either gender.

The attitudes and sexual practices of the women we interviewed were a testament to the enormous range of human diversity in adapting to changing life circumstances. Some women, as Michele explains, "can be single and enjoy their lives and be satisfied without sex. It just depends on the woman." Others acutely miss sex and intimate physical affection and certainly are not willing to give up their active sexuality this early in their lives. As singer Lena Horne says, "Honey, sex doesn't stop until you're in the grave." Peggy points out that only since her divorce has she been able to give full expression to this part of herself. She was surprised and delighted to find that sex with men other than her ex-husband could be wonderful:

> I discovered I liked sex. If I had never had another sexual partner other than my husband, I would have gone to my grave thinking sex was terrible. I'm glad that didn't happen!

In general, there was surprisingly little weeping and wailing over the lack of an active sex life among these women. Whatever their felt needs, those women who did not have a committed sexual relationship had found three primary approaches to the management of their sexual desires. These approaches frequently overlap in the same individuals at different times, but we have divided them for the sake of discussion: acceptance of celibacy with an abatement of felt need, casual sex, and sublimation or substitution. Some women report great success with these solutions, while others are still searching for the best way to deal with their sexual appetites and longings.

CELIBACY, SEX, AND THE PROBLEM WITH PEANUTS

Sex is not crucial to the life satisfaction of every woman. Although enjoying sex and acknowledging the ways in which a good sexual relationship can enrich their lives, many of the women we interviewed separate their sense of satisfaction *in life* from the experience of being *sexually active*. As Glenda explained, "I just don't see any relationship between happiness and having an active sex life. I could be extremely sexually active and *that* could make me as miserable as could be!" These women do not experience their sexual needs as so intense that periodic denial of them would cause severe repercussions. Pamela, for whom sex was an important part of her seven-year relationship with her lover, says sex in and of itself has never been a very central factor in her life: "Sex, even though I like it, is not a priority at all—even when I am in a relationship. I think it can be wonderful, but it was never the driving force in me."

Most of these women report that after a period of celibacy, whether voluntary or involuntary, their libido seems to go into hibernation. Some told us they seldom even feel the desire to masturbate. They simply don't miss sex the way they did when they were in a relationship and their lover was absent. Jean compares her attitude toward sex to that well-known phenomenon of eating peanuts: "If you eat one peanut, you're sunk—you want a whole bunch of them. For me, the same is true with sex. But, if I'm celibate, my libido goes underground; it doesn't haunt me with cravings." Elsie is another woman who is not troubled by the lack of sex in her life. She does not deny her sexuality or the importance of her desires, but neither is she tormented by them. Once she accepted the absence of sex in her life, she was able to move on:

I have sexual needs and urges, but I just go on about my business, because I know, for now, that's how things are. I've accepted that. I guess that's the bottom line: you have to accept it.

Hillary also is gradually moving toward a position of accepting the lack of sexuality in her life and is less bothered by it as time goes by:

> Whenever I make it through a certain stretch of time without sex and still feel okay, it's a new growth experience and I think, "I can do it." I guess I would be okay without sex. I can see myself still living a good life without it.

Claire, a lively, energetic, successful woman, told us that because she has never been married and her religious faith forbids sex without marriage, she has never had a sexual relationship in her life. Far from being distressed about what others might regard as an enormous loss, she chooses to take a positive attitude:

> Maybe I'm asexual, I don't know. It's never been an issue for me. I laugh about the fact that, you know, I'm the last of a dying breed of virgins. Celibacy is exceedingly rare today, and I joke about that, but it's never been a problem for me.

CASUAL SEX: A HANDFUL OF PEANUTS

Calm acceptance of the lack of sexual activity in their lives is simply not possible for all women. Some experience their sexual needs and desires intensely in ways that are difficult to ignore. For these women, life satisfaction and sexuality are more intimately intertwined. They could not feel good about being single, if being single meant they had to eliminate sex with men from their lives. Often, these women have traditionally "male" attitudes towards sex: wanting it *without* emotional involvement. They want to feel flesh-on-flesh contact with a live body, even if it is just a "temporary fix." They agree with Elena, who flatly stated, "I'm not much for long stretches of celibacy." They try to separate their sexual needs from issues of love and romance, with mixed results. For them, casual sex represents an acceptable solution, although keeping it casual can be difficult.

Megan, for whom both sex and the single life are important, acknowledges that, over the years, "My sexuality has changed to be more like a man's: I just want some physical contact." Erika considers casual sex one viable way for her to meet her needs as a single woman, but she is frustrated by the drawbacks of this option. These, she explains, are getting unintentionally emotionally involved with partners in whom she has no real interest and the fact that our society generally does not approve of casual sex for women. However, she is simply not willing to give up sex as a part of her life. She hasn't found the perfect solution, but she knows she needs to find some way to deal with her sexual needs and energy if she is going to continue to feel good about being single:

> If I am going to live my life as a single person, then I need to figure out how to incorporate sex in a positive way that does not offend anybody around me and does not make me want to be connected to this person. For me, the sexual act is not this sacred encounter in which "you can't have my body unless you love me." I wish there were a way that I could have sex with men and it would be okay on all levels, you know, morally, physically, emotionally. Maybe somebody will come up with something eventually!

Erika fantasizes about having a relationship with a man that is episodic and focused primarily on the need to experience sexual pleasure and release sexual energy. She imagines creating a kind of "pleasure ritual" with a man that does not entail sharing or intertwining the rest of their lives. She admits she hasn't had much luck establishing such a relationship:

> A lot of times I find having sex ruins friendships because it makes it too hard to deal with one another after you've done "IT," even though that's really all you wanted from him and that's all he wanted from you. You just needed to get some sort of sexual energy used up.

Hannah also likes the pleasures of casual sex—sex uncontaminated by the pressures of relationship ties and promises. She prefers her sexual relationships *al dente*, brief and without obligation. In fact, sexual encounters work best for her if there are pre-existing boundaries that prevent her partners from demanding too much from her. She decries the death of purely recreational sex and the casual relationships of the seventies. She would prefer an uncomplicated sexual relationship, but like Erika, is aware of the obstacles:

> Unfortunately, you can't be involved in a sexual relationship very easily without being involved emotionally. Sex for the sake of sex is greatly enjoyable. Sex as this mystical union is made up. I'm not saying

that it doesn't happen, that it isn't a metaphor for union on some deep level. But to always approach sex with that expectation is insane to me.

Unfortunately, clean get-aways are not her lot in life. She complains that these days she can never go to bed with a man without him calling the next day to ask her to pick him up from the airport or some such thing—as if having slept with him now obligates her to go out of her way to please him. She tells us that she most enjoys having sex with men who are friends, but not really good friends, adding that she has found it best not to complicate her really good friendships with sexuality. Historically, her favorite sexual encounters occurred when she was traveling or with a man who was living with or married to someone else. Today, Hannah feels cheated by the fear of AIDS, which has forced her to curtail some of her casual sexual trysts. She now tries to substitute other ways to take pleasure in her body, made possible for her in no small part by her considerable financial success. She has a personal yoga teacher and a masseur, and she fantasizes about being able to contract for sexual gratification in the same way she contracts for these other personal services. Then, she explains, you could find someone with good references you liked and respected, and pay him a fair wage. No guilt, no complications.

While Carla might frown on Hannah's desire to contract for sex in such a businesslike manner, she also seeks the pleasure and simplicity of casual sex. She has a relationship with a man who lives in a distant city, whom she sees several times a year. During these visits they have an active sex life, but the rest of the time they expect nothing from each other. This arrangement works well for her:

I have one friend whom I see every three or four months. I like the relationship because he doesn't put demands on me. And our contact is enough for me. I mean, I don't walk around in a state of sexual frustration. I think I use my energy for other things. So if sex is available, that's great, but if it's not, I don't sit around and cry and wring my hands about it.

SUBLIMATION: "SWIMMING UNTIL THE COWS COME HOME"

Many of the women we interviewed experience their sexual needs as intensely as women like Megan, Erika, Hannah, and Carla, but they do not see casual sex as a viable option. They insist that only sex in the context of a loving relationship is satisfying for them. For these women, sexual intimacy cannot be separated from affection and emotional connection. They may have experimented with casual sex in their youth, but it now holds little appeal for them. As Elena expressed, "I'm much more prone to monogamous relationships. When I was younger, I was more likely to act impulsively." Hillary, who is among the younger women we interviewed, does not want to accept life without sex, but she too is learning that casual sex is not an answer for her:

> Sex—or the lack of it—is not one of the easier aspects of being single. I'll tell you, right now, I'm very worried about it. I'm nervous about AIDS and all the terrible things you hear. As I have gotten older, I'm not sure I've gotten wiser, but I think that having sex with somebody just for the sake of sex is no good anymore. Now, I need more feeling. When I have sex with somebody with whom I am not totally in love, I find myself feeling very repulsed. I don't enjoy it and look forward to getting him out of my house.

If the unsatisfying experiences of casual sex weren't enough to discourage some women, clearly the threat of AIDS is. Helen echoes Hillary's feelings and concerns:

> I don't want to have sex with just anybody. I've done that in the past, but I'm not interested in it anymore. In the first place, it's dangerous, and in the second place, it's not even fun. So why do it?

Lydia summed up the feelings of many of the women we interviewed:

> I want a friend more than I want sex. I mean, sex is important, but what I really want out of the relationship is friendship. I've had short-term relationships in which sex was the main focus, and they go nowhere. I've also had wonderful friendships in which sex is great because we were friends first.

Although few of these women would say they have found the perfect solution, they are finding alternative ways to satisfy some of their needs and to use their sexual energy that rely neither on calm acceptance nor on casual sex. For example, although Aleta would never choose to return to her marriage, she often misses the sex and physical intimacy that were an ongoing part of it. For her, the lack of sex and physical closeness are the greatest disadvantages of her single life. Exploring different ways to manage this challenge, Aleta has discovered that she can meet her sexual needs to some degree through masturbation, but that she continues to yearn for physical intimacy and touching. Aleta is not alone in these feelings. Often women explain that it is not so much intercourse that they miss as much as it is being held and caressed. Aleta has tried to meet these needs, at least in a partial way, by finding non-sexual sources of physical contact such as massage and affectionate embraces with close friends.

Other women describe how they have learned to sublimate, by throwing their sexual energies into their work. Josie and Lydia both spoke of the ways in which they use work to discharge sexual feelings when they are not in relationships, a common partial solution that produces a lot of secondary gains for single women who are ambitious. Josie says:

> I don't tend to have sex unless I'm really involved with a man. I mean, I'm not into casual sex. I also think I probably sublimate so much through my intellectual life. I know I miss it less than some women do. I only start to think about it when I get involved with somebody. But when I'm not, I work it off!

Lydia feels her sexual urges powerfully and is aware of needing to find outlets for that energy. She sublimates her sexual energy both into work and physical exercise: "I run and hike and do aerobics—I find *outlets*. In the summer, I swim outdoors; I swim until the cows come home!" Lydia is particularly vulnerable to feeling the loss of sex and intimacy when she is feeling overwhelmed by other things:

> Lack of sex becomes an issue for me when I'm feeling sorry for myself, feeling tired, wondering what to do with this ceiling that needs to be plastered, wishing somebody else would come over and take care of it. When I don't want to deal with one more thing, I just want someone to hold me.

During these intense times, her two steady sources of sublimation, exercise and work, provide little relief. She admits, "I know that work brings me a certain amount of fulfillment and happiness, but I don't want to be taking legal journals to bed when I need to be held instead." Although Lydia has felt the absence of sexual contact sharply, over the years she, like most single women, has learned that these moments of longing eventually come less and less often and pass more quickly.

THE TRANSFORMATION OF LONELINESS

The most frightening myth about single life—the one that haunts women in the darkest hours of the night—is that being single inevitably means being lonely. The threat of loneliness, with its looming shadows of despair, has driven countless women into hasty marriages and kept them prisoners in dead-end relationships. So insidiously has the notion of loneliness been tied to being single that few even question this correlation. The inevitability of overwhelming loneliness, in and of itself, becomes *the* compelling reason to avoid single life at all costs. As one woman explained, "I actually think a lot of people, both men and women, are not single for the sole reason that they are afraid of being alone. They literally don't know how to be alone."

The threat of loneliness has little power over the women we interviewed. While they continue to search for satisfying resolutions to the challenge of including sex in their single lives, they have come much further in dealing with loneliness. They told us that the anticipation of loneliness is far more powerful and terrifying than the reality of being alone. Even those who experienced "forced liberation"—who *never* would have volunteered to be alone—did not complain about problems with loneliness. Several women, in fact, told us that their loneliest moments occurred while they were still in unsatisfying marriages or relationships, even though they were surrounded by the very things they believed were essential to their happiness. As Liv Ullmann has observed, "Sometimes it is less hard to wake up feeling lonely when you are alone than to wake up feeling lonely when you are with someone."

To our surprise, we found that loneliness was such a minor concern for the women we interviewed that few even raised the topic. We had to ask specific questions about loneliness to get any reactions whatsoever. We were

impressed by the relative ease with which they dismissed loneliness as a
threat to their sense of contentment. Consider this exchange with Angela:

Are there ever times when you feel lonely?

[Chuckling] I think yesterday afternoon, about four o'clock, I felt
lonely. It was the first time I had felt even a pang of loneliness in
months.

Do you feel the need to do anything about it?

No. [Laughing]

Angela has a lot of company in the way she feels about loneliness. Other
women were surprised to discover that they were not devastated to find
themselves alone at the end of their workday. Michele talks about her experience of being alone for the first time in her life:

I went from a protected family to life in a very restricted religious
college, to a very protective marriage. I was terrified of what would
happen to me without having someone there to take care of me.
When my husband left, I had a sinking feeling of, "Oh, this house is so
big," and coming home to it after work was kind of weird. Then I
began to really like it. You know, I could eat when I wanted to, I
could plan what I wanted to, I could come and go. I began to feel very
liberated. I really liked putting my feet up and reading *People* magazine
and saying to myself, "I don't care, I don't think I'll fix anything for
dinner" and calling out for pizza. I loved just having quiet, relaxing
time. To my complete surprise, I found that I was very comfortable
being by myself. In fact, it was enjoyable! If I wanted to eat a big bag of
cookies, I could. If I wanted to leave the house all messed up, that was
okay, too. So, I wasn't lonely. And I was surprised by that. Happily
surprised.

This is not to say that single women never get lonely. They do, as do most
married women, from time to time; however, the single women we interviewed have found ways to cope with these brief episodes. Their methods of
coping range from calling friends, to diving into a project, to "riding
through the emotions." They find to their relief that being alone is less
frightening when they know they can control how much time alone they

want. But more important than their specific coping styles is the fact that these women have found reasons to value their time alone. Jamie, for example, describes how she has grown to accept time alone as a natural part of life, not something to be feared or avoided:

> Another part of my learning process was realizing that there was something to gain from those times of feeling lonely. I've learned to live with it and not run from it. I've learned that feeling lonely doesn't have to be overwhelming or something that becomes pervasive. I've learned to see it for what it is—as an experience that is part of life at different times.

For many single women, time alone actually becomes a resource, one more benefit of being on their own. It is as if the alchemist's dream of turning lead into gold comes true for single women: The fear of loneliness is transformed into an appreciation of solitude. Many women directly linked their time alone to their feelings of satisfaction in their lives. Their words endorsed what Anne Morrow Lindbergh expressed when she said:

> Certain springs are tapped only when we are alone. . . . women need solitude in order to find again the true essence of themselves; that firm strand which will be the indispensable center of a whole web of human relationships.

As Audrey says, "Being alone goes with liking yourself. I can't fathom not having quality time to yourself." Elena agrees:

> My sense of satisfaction has a lot to do with being at peace with having time alone. When a relationship dissolves and you're suddenly on your own, you are confronted by loneliness and you learn to make friends with it, really. I didn't expect to enjoy my solitude as much as I do.

Women can gain an enormous sense of mastery and self-esteem by surviving and even flourishing on their own. Taking control of their lives, loneliness and all, allows them to value themselves in unprecedented ways. Their comfort with time alone is far greater than anyone immersed in the marriage and motherhood mandate, and the cultural myths it spawns, could predict. Those women still hanging onto the myth of the prince, those still caught in the web of waiting, may continue to experience loneliness as an acute problem. But these women have accepted being alone as a natural part of life, one which holds as much potential for reward as it does for pain. As one woman we interviewed commented, "It's just how you look at it. Do you look at it as loneliness or do you look at it as *freedom*?"

Chapter 20

Flying on the Wings of Change

In youth, it was a way I had
To do my best to please
And change, with every passing lad,
To suit his theories.
But now I know the things I know,
And do the things I do;
And if you do not like me so,
To hell, my love, with you!
—*Dorothy Parker*, "Indian Summer"

The women whose stories we have told in this book have lives that work, but not because they have been blessed with fewer adversities than the rest of us. Some may have come from Ozzie and Harriet families, but others were abused or neglected as children. Most came from the same sort of families we all came from, families who did the best they could to cope with depressions, wars, and social changes they did not always understand. Few were raised with any kind of positive role models they could use for the lives they are now living in these times of profound social change. All face enormous challenges. And yet, the women in this book explain that the burdens of living as single women, without models or maps to guide the future, can be more than balanced by the exhilarating joy of realizing that they can choose for themselves which flight path they will take.

Women like Grace, Sandi, Jean, Ria, Terry, and the others in this book make it clear that women can celebrate flying solo. Like Dorothy Parker, they have freed themselves from trying to please everyone else and can, as a result, have lives defined in their own terms. They have struggled to hold onto who they are and what they want in the face of great opposition from those who assume that they should always place the needs of others above their own priorities. They tell us that they have decided not to passively wait for the good things in life to be given to them by someone else. They have refused to resign themselves to second-class lives weighed down by joyless relationships or consumed by a constant search for someone to fill them up. Instead, they are living singly with a passion for love, freedom, and adventure, showing us new definitions of "happily ever after."

Flying solo successfully, they say, is very much a question of attitude. Of course, women do need resources and opportunities, but securing these begins with realizing that they deserve to fly. And, while all this is possible earlier in life, it is easier at midlife, as our middle years bring us the confidence and courage many of us need to give our souls the gift of flight. How the women in this book got to this place of confidence and belief in their own worth boils down to three deceptively simple points:

ACCEPT WHO YOU ARE

> True emancipation begins neither at the polls nor in the courts. It begins in a woman's soul.
>
> —*Emma Goldman*

The first step towards successfully flying on the wings of change is accepting who you are enough to stop worrying about how you look and how you can impress others. You must, as Jean says, stop "primping":

> When you stop primping, it doesn't mean that everything about you has changed—it's just that you've stopped fibbing about it. You're not trying to put the best face on things for everybody. You're not trying to anticipate what they'd like you to be saying or how they want you to look. How you deal with people in your life is little bit different.

Maxine, who is small, dark, and slim, achieved a major change in her life when she stopped saying, "If only I were five-feet-six-inches tall and blond with big breasts, I could have been Marilyn Monroe." Like most of us, Maxine once measured herself against the images of women spawned by the mandate. But, she explained, when she decided that she was good enough as is, she felt the power and confidence to move forward in pursuit of her dreams. This is a crucial attitude for all of us to embrace when we begin anew. Lydia tells us that self-acceptance is the key to her current happiness:

> You don't have to be anything else; just be who you are. That's okay. The feeling that who we are isn't enough is so undermining. I *never* felt good enough. Good enough for *what*, I don't know.

Part of accepting who we are is coming to terms with the past, getting rid of as much excess baggage, as much unfinished business, as possible. The past cannot be changed, but we can change how we think about it. One of the most powerful and self-affirming steps we can take is to forgive ourselves for what we have and haven't done, for all the times our courage failed, or when we "sold our souls" too cheaply. Some of us may have made choices that we now see as poor ones, embracing men who failed to meet our needs, men who were unavailable or even physically or psychologically abusive. Some of us may have married out of sheer fear of the stigma of *not* marrying, or because we didn't have a clue as to what else we could do with our lives. Looking back on past relationships and marriages, we may think we tried too hard, stayed too long, or did not try hard or long enough. We may think we should have gotten an education, or given ourselves time for a career before we had babies. We may wish we had never given up the last man we turned away, who in the rosy afterglow of hindsight now resembles Harrison Ford, Kevin Costner, or Robert Redford. But, instead of living with bitterness and regret, we can tell ourselves we did the best we could with what we knew at the time and move on to emphasize our strengths and resources for creating a satisfying future.

Once we forgive ourselves, we can let go of past relationships, experiences, and choices that have caused us hurt or disappointment. We can learn to look back with a perspective that, while not denying the bad, also acknowledges the good. Such a balanced view goes a long way toward eliminating bitterness and regret. Maxine sets an example:

> In some ways my marriage was like serving a sentence in a maximum security prison for a crime I never committed. But no picture is *all* black or *all* white. There were certainly material advantages; we were prosperous, we were safe, we had good health.

Some experiences, such as physical or sexual abuse, cannot and perhaps should not be forgiven. However, even this pain can be eased, and it is possible to take strength from the knowledge that as adults, we are no longer as helpless as we were when such events occurred. We now have the power to protect ourselves from harm and the ability to create lives that are less vulnerable. We may even recognize ways in which we have grown stronger from these experiences. Jamie, who was sexually abused by her father, explains:

> My life growing up was so repressed and restricted that once I got out of there, I started to realize that there was so much to experience, and so much to do and see that I really wanted to be free to do that. My childhood was a negative experience, but I think out of that negative experience, I have gained some strengths. One of those strengths is learning that my happiness and satisfaction has to come from inside.

Once a woman has made peace with her past, she is free not only to accept herself as she is but also to become truly attuned to her own needs and what gives her pleasure. Aleta is clear that she has arrived at this spot:

> I'm at a point where I am not striving to become something else. I'm just conscious of what gives me pleasure, when I am excited, when I am interested, when I am enriched. I'm conscious right now of the wind coming through that door, I'm conscious of the quality of light and of the loveliness of this house. This is such an obvious thing for me but it's so different from how it used to be. Now, just that *I am* is sufficient.

DARE TO DREAM OF A NEW DESTINATION

It is for each of us to find a course that is valid by our own reckoning.
—*Gail Sheehy*

While The Dream may no longer work, having *a* dream is crucial. Having a dream allows us to chart our future along a new course; it provides the inspiration that keeps us moving. The choice we face at midlife is not whether to change. Change is both inevitable and necessary. The only question is which changes to pursue and which to resist. For that, we need to know what we want.

Ria told us earlier that she found happiness only when she started paying attention to her dream:

> I have finally learned to listen to myself and I did something that I really wanted to do. I think I'm happy because I was able to say, "This is what I really want."

Every woman's dream is different. There is no right way of flying solo. There are no standards for a woman to meet except her own. Since most of us were trained to wait passively for others to set our course, the first thing we have to recognize is that we have a choice. Maxine, who received no encouragement from her parents or her husband, describes the constriction of her earlier life and the dawning of choice:

> With both my parents and my husband, if I showed any spark, it was quickly squelched. I had to accept that as a way of being. But in the last few years, I've started to understand choice. *I have choice!* I can give in to feeling powerless and wallow around in it blindly or I can make a choice. And the choice could be anything! It could be a walk on the beach, getting into the hot tub, going for a drive, drawing a picture.

Once we recognize our freedom, we need to realize that, regardless of whether we choose excitement or a quiet discovery of our inner selves, what matters most is that we choose dreams of our own, dreams based on our needs, personalities, and circumstances. Some of us may have a thirst for risk and adventure, while others, who have had more than their share of turmoil and drama, may want and deserve a time of quiet stability. Elena points out:

> It's important not to make choices in life because you think you should be making certain choices. It's important to be clear about who you are and what makes you happy, and then try to set your life up in such a way that you are more often happy than not.

Jamie also advises women to take risks to explore many choices as they strive to define their own dreams:

> Try lots of different things and don't be afraid to fail. Explore your interests and discover what really makes you happy. I want all of us as women to follow our dreams, our goals, the stirrings that are in our

hearts. Women too readily fall into doing things we *think* we should do or that we think we need to do to feel secure. We need to have these experiences of choice and self-exploration to feel powerful, to feel like we can make a difference in our own lives.

TAKE ACTION

Is there anything as horrible as starting on a trip? Once you're off, that's all right, but the last moments are earthquake and convulsion, and the feeling that you are a snail being pulled off your rock.
> —*Anne Morrow Lindbergh*

Passivity is the enemy of a woman's heart and soul. Our dreams will get us nowhere unless we can put them into action. But many of us are not used to going after what we want and need. Taking responsibility for our lives can seem overwhelming. But life is made up of small moments. We can translate our dreams into realities by breaking them down into a series of small steps that, in time, take us where we want to go. Our prime directive becomes one of staying attuned to our inner radar and looking for updrafts to buoy up our flights. Our accomplishments contribute to our growing sense of competence, providing the momentum we need to reach for more.

Two factors must be addressed by women in their plans to make their dreams more attainable—money and time. Whether women intend to marry eventually or remain on their own, they need to start viewing themselves, as Aleta says, as "independent economic entities." Flying solo is a whole lot easier if you can afford a good plane, and the impact of unexpected landings in unfamiliar territory can be cushioned significantly by sound finances. Jean is unequivocal on the subject:

> The smartest move women can make is to get on their feet financially. This is a hard world. The worst thing we can do to our daughters and to other women is to say, "Don't worry about money. You won't have to get a job, because you'll be married." We should be educating our daughters about their options from the get-go.

Second only to creating a financial safety net, investing time in herself will provide a woman with the best flight insurance she can have. In particular, women advise against making a commitment to a new relationship on the way out of an old one. Instead, they suggest that women should take the time to get the education or training they need so they can achieve the financial independence necessary to pursue their dreams.

THE GIFT OF FLIGHT

Megan told us that although she got the message from her mother that following the mandate might not give her what she wanted, she could find no clues as to what to do with her life instead. That situation is changing. While some of our cultural icons, such as Elizabeth Taylor, keep marrying and remarrying, our popular culture is finally beginning to provide us with some public role models of midlife women on their own. Single women are no longer ashamed of their lives. Actress Diana Rigg, divorced and a single mother at fifty-five, has a thriving career and refuses to play the role of a grieving divorcée. She says, "It's not a particularly good part; it has lousy lines and absolutely no laughs." She flies solo with courage and conviction, adding, "I'm not some sad or lonely woman. Life for me is wonderful and I wouldn't want it any other way." Lauren Hutton, the never-married super model of the sixties, became invisible around the age of thirty. Now fifty and still single, she is suddenly finding herself courted by top modeling agencies—twenty years after she thought her career was over! At forty-five, Diane Keaton has had wonderful affairs but relishes her solitude and freedom. Cybill Shepherd, twice-divorced at forty-one, says, "I don't view being single as some sort of waiting period between marriages. For me, it is a genuine alternative to marriage. I am quite happily single." Tina Turner has emerged from the shadow of her marriage to a dominating and abusive man to strike out on her own. At fifty-three, she is not only successful, but sexier than ever. Jana Snyder, forty-one, a former cheerleader turned actress who divorced after eleven years of marriage, is now a news photographer exposing the horrors of "ethnic cleansing" in Sarajevo. Having covered eighteen world conflicts in the last five years, she continues to overcome tremendous adversities to live on the edge and pursue the story. Janet Reno, fifty-four, has earned a reputation for being both tough and fair as Attorney General of the United States. A never-married self-confessed workaholic, Reno has pursued her own dream relentlessly and is now one of the most respected members of the President's cabinet. Her success sends a clear message to all of us about what is now possible for single women.

While famous women such as these provide marvelous midlife role models for all of us, we do not need to be unusually rich, beautiful, or talented to relish the joys of flying solo. The women in this book are ordinary women like ourselves who are flying solo and thriving. The paths they have taken can inspire us, keep us on course when things look bleak, and offer alternatives to outdated behaviors. They stand as models of authentic selfhood— proof that, despite the difficulties and uncertainties of living on the edge of cultural change, we can all fashion satisfying lives for ourselves. We want for you what we want for ourselves, to be able to respond as Angela does:

What would the ideal happy life be for you?

I'm living it.

Do you have any regrets, looking back?

No [surprised]! Isn't that interesting? I have no regrets.

Notes

Introduction

13   "Whether you're married or not": Gilda Radner, quoted in *Sounds Like a New Woman* (New York: Penguin, 1993), p. 4.

28   ". . . the sign of a good marriage": Carolyn G. Heilbrun, *Writing a Woman's Life* (New York, Norton, 1988), p. 95.

Chapter 2. "Fish Got to Swim and Birds Got to Fly"

42   "A man and wife": Barbara Leigh Smith Bodichon (1854), *Married Women and the Law,* quoted in *Strong-minded Women and Other Lost Voices from Nineteenth-century England,* Janet Murray (New York: Pantheon, 1982), p. 118.

43   As one nineteenth-century: quoted in *Strong-minded Women and Other Lost Voices from Nineteenth-century England,* Janet Murray (New York: Pantheon, 1982), p. 49.

43   "Early on the morning": Elizabeth Parson Ware Packard, quoted in "Women's Accounts of Psychiatric Illness and Institutionalization," J.L. Geller, *Hospital and Community Psychiatry,* 1985, *36* (10), 1056–1062.

Chapter 3. The Marriage and Motherhood Mandate

50   ". . . all that [a woman]": Charlotte Perkins Gilman, *Women and Economics,* Carl Degler (Ed.) (New York: Harper & Row, 1966), p. 71.

50   "In those days, it didn't matter": Billie Jean King, *Billie Jean* (New York: Harper & Row, 1974).

51   During the 1600s and 1700s: Carol F. Karlsen, *The Devil in the Shape of a Woman: Witchcraft in Colonial New England* (New York: Vintage, 1987).

51   When England's 1851 census: Janet Murray, *Strong-minded Women and Other Lost Voices from Nineteenth-century England* (New York: Pantheon, 1982), p. 48.

51   "[The Spinster], unobtrusive, meek, soft-footed": Sheila Jeffreys, *The Spinster and Her Enemies: Feminism and Sexuality: 1880–1930* (Boston: Pandora Press, 1985), p. 95.

52   "The woman who doesn't want": Mrs. Thomas Edison, quoted in *American Chronicle: Six Decades in American Life*, Lois Gordon (New York: Atheneum, 1987).

52   "Biologically and temperamentally": Benjamin Spock, quoted in *The Women's Movement: Political, Socioeconomic and Psychological Issues*, Barbara S. Deckard (New York: Harper & Row, 1975).

58   "I wanted us to work": Gloria Naylor, *Mama Day* (New York: Vintage Contemporaries, 1989), p. 146.

59   "Above all other prohibitions": Carolyn G. Heilbrun, *Writing a Woman's Life* (New York: Norton, 1988), p. 13.

60   "Women who openly express": Harriet Goldhor Lerner, *The Dance of Anger* (New York: Harper & Row, 1985), p. 2.

61   "Most women today have grown": Mary Catherine Bateson, *Composing a Life* (New York: Penguin, 1990), p. 39.

Chapter 4. The Mandate Goes Underground

65   ". . . where the nights are chilly": Barbara Creaturo, "Sketches from Single Life," *Cosmopolitan*, 196(3), March 1984, p. 221.

65   ". . . will discover that": Jane Campbell, "Have You Lost the Will to Date?" *Cosmopolitan*, 212 (1), January 1992, p. 50.

67   "The best single woman": Susan Faludi, *Backlash* (New York: Crown, 1991), p. 123.

68   "In films like": Susan Faludi, *Backlash* (New York: Crown, 1991), p. 123.

70   Although a more complete examination: see Susan Faludi, *Backlash* (New York: Crown, 1991), pp. 9–19.

70   *Newsweek* magazine went so far: Eloise Salholz et al., "Too Late for Prince Charming," *Newsweek*, June 2, 1986, pp. 54–61.

71   Other media published reports: Charles Westoff and Noreen Goldman, "Figuring the Odds in the Marriage Market," *Money Magazine*, December 1984, pp. 32–42.

72   As Janet Harris said: Janet Harris, *The Prime of Ms. America: The American Woman at Forty* (New York: G.P. Putnam's, 1975).

73   "The habits of a lifetime": Tillie Olsen, "One Out of Twelve: Women Who Are Writers in Our Century" in Sara Ruddick and Pamela Daniels (Eds.), *Working It Out: 23 Women Writers, Artists, Scientists, and Scholars Talk about Their Lives and Work* (New York: Pantheon, 1977), p. 335.

74   "Many single women are upset": Grace Baruch, Rosalind Barnett, and Caryl Rivers, *Lifeprints: New Patterns of Love and Work for Today's Women* (New York: Signet, 1985), p. 273.

74   Helen Gurley Brown advises single women: Jamie Laughridge, "The Elusive American Man," *Harper's Bazaar,* August 1983, pp. 34–40.

75   "[Men] want to see legs": "25 ways to find a good man," *Ebony,* March 1987, pp. 146–150.

76   "A woman who believes": Dana Crowley Jack, *Silencing the Self: Women and Depression* (Cambridge, MA: Harvard University Press, 1991), p. 139.

Chapter 5. Giving Up the Dream

81   "The need for change": Maya Angelou, *I Know Why the Caged Bird Sings* (New York: Random House, 1969).

87   As Adrienne Rich has observed: Adrienne Rich, "When We Dead Awaken: Writing as Re-Vision" in *On Lies, Secrets, and Silence: Selected Prose 1966–1978* (New York: Norton, 1979).

Chapter 6. No More Waiting for the Prince: Tales of the Never Married

89   "When people ask me": Sarah and A. Elizabeth Delaney with Amy Hill Hearth, *Having Our Say: The Delaney Sisters' First 100 Years* (New York: Kodansha International, 1993).

89   "Some luck lies in": Garrison Keillor quoted in *1,911 Best Things Anybody Ever Said,* Robert Byrne (Ed.) (New York: Fawcett, Columbine, 1988), p. 378.

89   "Of all the old maid's": Florence King, "Staunch Spinsters Give Women a Good Name," *Los Angeles Times,* August 10, 1986, p. 3.

Chapter 8: Leaving Normal: Women Who Have Chosen to Leave Their Marriages

126   "I had marriage and a child": Adrienne Rich, "When We Dead Awaken: Writing as Re-Vision" in *On Lies, Secrets, and Silence: Selected Prose 1966–1978* (New York: Norton, 1979), p. 42.

Chapter 9. Midlife's Gifts to Single Women

141   As Lillian Rubin suggested: Lillian Rubin, *Women of a Certain Age: The Midlife Search for Self* (New York: Harper & Row, 1990), p. 28.

Chapter 10. Accidental Careers: Circuitous Paths, Recovered Dreams, and Midcourse Corrections

144   "Our lives are littered": Ellen Goodman, "Reunion of the Ungeneration," *Washington Post,* June 1988.

144   "It is now time to explore": Mary Catherine Bateson, *Composing a Life* (New York: Penguin, 1990), p. 9.

155   "the ultimate joy": Carolyn Heilbrun, "Middle-aged Women in Literature" in
      Grace Baruch and Jeanne Brooks-Gunn (Eds.), *Women in Midlife* (New York:
      Plenum, 1984), p. 72.

Chapter 11. Turbulence and Tailwinds: The Challenges of Flying Solo at Work

156   "To improve the lot": Dierdre English, "She's Her Weakness Now," *New York
      Times Book Review*, February 2, 1992, p. 7.

156   "It's as if we women": Naomi Weisstein, " 'How can a little girl like you teach a
      great big class of men?' the Chairman Said, and Other Adventures of a Woman in
      Science" in Sara Ruddick and Pamela Daniels (Eds.), *Working It Out: 23 Women
      Writers, Artists, Scientists, and Scholars Talk about Their Lives and Work* (New York:
      Pantheon, 1977), p. 248.

157   "Are you now": Barbara Ehrenreich, *The Worst Years of Our Lives: Irreverent Notes
      from a Decade of Greed* (New York: Harper Perennial, 1991), p. 172.

157   A *New York Times* poll in 1989: cited in Susan Faludi, *Backlash* (New York:
      Crown, 1991), p. xvi.

165   "There may be a poor fit": Barbara Ehrenreich, *The Worst Years of Our Lives:
      Irreverent Notes from a Decade of Greed* (New York: Harper Perennial, 1991), p. 167.

169   "What is going to happen": Charles Westoff, quoted in Susan Faludi, *Backlash*
      (New York: Crown, 1991), p. 16.

*Chapter 12. A Good Ground Crew: Intimacy, Friendship, and Community in
the Lives of Single Women*

171   Women not only: Carol Gilligan, *In a Different Voice* (Cambridge, MA: Harvard
      University Press, 1982), p. 17.

171   "The loneliest woman": Toni Morrison, speech at Sarah Lawrence College,
      Bronxville, New York, 1978.

183   "You need to put": quoted in Robert Bellah, *Habits of the Heart: Individualism and
      Commitment in American Life* (Berkeley: University of California Press, 1985).

Chapter 13. Men: The Icing, Not the Cake

189   "Why is it men": Barbra Streisand, quoted in *Sounds Like a New Woman* (New
      York, Penguin, 1993).

Chapter 15. Defying the Mandate: Living without Motherhood

217   "Only when the assumption": Mardy S. Ireland, *Reconceiving Women: Separating
      Motherhood from Female Identity* (New York: Guilford, 1993), p. 1.

217   "Biological possibility and desire": Betty Rollin, "Motherhood: Who Needs It?"
      Look, May 16, 1971.

Chapter 16. Courageous Choices: Single Mothers by Choice

229 "There was no question": Jane Wallace, quoted in *Sounds Like a New Woman* (New York, Penguin, 1993), p. 46.

Chapter 17. Flying Not Quite Solo

250 "Motherhood means being": Tillie Olsen, "One Out of Twelve: Women Who Are Writers in our Century" in Sara Ruddick and Pamela Daniels (Eds.), *Working It Out: 23 Women Writers, Artists, Scientists, and Scholars Talk about Their Lives and Work* (New York: Pantheon, 1977), p. 331.

Chapter 18. Grit and the Art of Airplane Maintenance: Managing the Mechanics of Flying Solo

263 As family therapist Monica McGoldrick says: *The Family Therapy Networker*, May–June, 1987, p. 33.

267 White women pay $150 more: Frances Cerra Whittelsey, *Why Women Pay More: How to Avoid Marketplace Perils* (Center for Study of Responsive Law, 1993).

Chapter 19. One at a Table for Two: The Personal Challenges of Flying Solo

276 "Honey, sex doesn't stop": Lena Horne, quoted in *Sounds Like a New Woman* (New York, Penguin, 1993), p. 44.

Chapter 20. Flying on the Wings of Change

293 "I don't view being single": Cybill Shepherd quoted in *Sounds Like a New Woman* (New York: Penguin, 1993), p. 18.

Index